John Brown

John Brown

John Brown

by W. E. Burghardt
Du Bois

International Publishers
New York

ISBN 0–7178–0375–9

This Printing, 1996

To
the memory of
Elizabeth

PUBLISHER'S NOTE
This edition follows the first edition
published in September 1909
by George W. Jacobs & Company of Philadelphia.
Dr. W. E. B. Du Bois has provided a Preface
for this edition, some new comment in the text, and
has added new conclusions. The old text has
not been changed. New material is printed
in italics.

Contents

Maps

Books by W.E.B. Du Bois

Suppression of the African Slave Trade to America
(Harvard PhD thesis, published as Vol. I of Harvard
University Historical Series, 1896)
The Philadelphia Negro (1899)
Atlanta University's Studies of the Negro Problem
(1897-1910)
Souls of Black Folk (1903)
John Brown (1909). New edition, 1962
Quest of the Silver Fleece (1911)
The Negro (1915)
Darkwater (1920)
The Gift of Black Folk (1924)
Dark Princess (1924)
Black Reconstruction (1935)
Black Folk, Then and Now (1939)
Dusk of Dawn (1940)
Color and Democracy (1945)
In Battle for Peace (1952)
The Black Flame (A Trilogy)
    I. *Ordeal of Mansart* (1957)
    II. *Mansart Builds a School* (1959)
    III. *Worlds of Color* (1961)
Editor: *The Crisis*, 1910-1934
    The Encyclopedia of the Negro
    *An Appeal to the World, On the Status of the Negro in
the U.S.A.* (Presented to the United Nations, 1947)
The World and Africa (New Edition, 1965)
The Autobiography of W.E.B. Du Bois (1968)

Preface
For the New Edition

A full century has passed since John Brown started in America the Civil War which abolished legal slavery in the United States and began the emancipation of the Negro race from the domination of white Europe and North America. John Brown in Kansas met murder with murder and tried in Virginia to arm slaves so that they might resist and escape slavery. Ever since his violent murder of the border ruffians who were trying to force slavery on Kansas and his attempt to seize the armory at Harper's Ferry so as to arm the slaves, there had been bitter debate as to how far force and violence can bring peace and good will. This is a question that can never be completely answered for all circumstances and for all time. It is quite possible that time and searching conscience could have brought the emancipation of the slaves of the South without the catastrophe of war, murder and destruction, but that is by no means certain. It is quite possible that in time public opinion of an Abolitionist North could have forced the whole nation to embrace freedom for all men. But that certainly was not true before the American Civil War.

On the other hand it was true that the violence which John Brown led made Kansas a free state; that the flight of the fugitive slaves was the beginning of abolition, and the plan of John Brown to put arms in their hands could have hastened it. Although John Brown's plan failed at the time, it was actually arms and tools in the hands of a half-million Negroes that won the Civil War.

W. E. BURGHARDT DU BOIS

Preface

After the work of Sanborn, Hinton, Connelley, and Red-path, the only excuse for another life of John Brown is an opportunity to lay new emphasis upon the material which they have so carefully collected, and to treat these facts from a different point of view. The view-point adopted in this book is that of the little known but vastly important inner development of the Negro American. John Brown worked not simply for Black Men — he worked with them; and he was a companion of their daily life, knew their faults and virtues, and felt, as few white Americans have felt, the bitter tragedy of their lot. The story of John Brown, then, cannot be complete unless due emphasis is given this phase of his activity. Unfortunately, however, few written records of these friendships and this long continued intimacy exist, so that little new material along these lines can be adduced. For the most part one must be content with quoting the authors mentioned (and I have quoted them freely), and other writers like Anderson, Featherstonhaugh, Barry, Hunter, Boteler, Douglass and Hamilton. But even in the absence of special material the great broad truths are clear, and this book is at once a record of and a tribute to the man who of all Americans has perhaps come nearest to touching the real souls of black folk.

W. E. BURGHARDT DU BOIS

Chronology

BOYHOOD AND YOUTH

1800 — John Brown is born in Torrington, Conn., May 9th. Attempted insurrection of slaves under Gabriel in Virginia, in September.

1805 — The family migrates to Ohio.

1812 — John Brown meets a slave boy.

1816 — He joins the church.

1819 — He attends school at Plainfield, Mass.

THE TANNER

1819–1825 — John Brown works as a tanner at Hudson, O.

1821 — He marries Dianthe Lusk, June 21st.

1822 — Attempted slave insurrection in South Carolina in June.

1825–1835 — He works as a tanner at Randolph, Pa., and is postmaster.

1831 — Nat Turner's insurrection in Virginia, August 21st.

1832 — His first wife dies, August 10th.

1833 — He marries Mary Ann Day, July 11th.

1834 — He outlines his plan for Negro education, November 21st.

1835–1840 — He lives in and near Hudson, O., and speculates in land.

1837 — He loses heavily in the panic.

1839 — He and his family swear blood-feud with slavery.

1840 — He surveys Virginia lands for Oberlin College, and proposes buying 1,000 acres.

THE SHEPHERD

1841 — John Brown begins sheep-farming.

1842 — He goes into bankruptcy.

1843 — He loses four children in September.

1844 — He forms the firm of "Perkins and Brown, wool-merchants."

1845–51 — He is in charge of the Perkins and Brown warehouse, Springfield, O.

1846 — Gerrit Smith offers Adirondack farms to Negroes, August 1st.

1847 — Frederick Douglass visits Brown and hears his plan for a slave raid.

1849 — He goes to Europe to sell wool, and visits France and Germany, August and September.

1849 — First removal of his family to North Elba, N. Y.

1850 — The new Fugitive Slave Law is passed.

1851–1854 — Winding up of the wool business.

1851 — He founds the League of Gileadites, January 15th.

IN KANSAS

1854 — Kansas and Nebraska Bill becomes a law, May 30th. Five sons start for Kansas in October.

1855 — John Brown at the Syracuse convention of Abolitionists in June. He starts for Kansas with a sixth son and his son-in-law in September. Two sons take part in Big Springs convention in September. John Brown arrives in Kansas, October 6th. He helps to defend Lawrence in December.

1856 — He attends a mass meeting at Osawatomie in April. He visits Buford's camp in May. The sacking of Lawrence, May 21st. The Pottawatomie murders, May 23–26th. Arrest of two sons, May 28th. Battle of Black Jack, June 2d. Goes to Iowa with his wounded son-in-law and joins Lane's army, July and August. Joins in attacks to rid Lawrence of surrounding forts, August. Battle of Osawatomie, August 30th, Missouri's last invasion of Kansas, September 15th. Geary arrives and induces Brown to leave Kansas, September. Brown starts for the East with his sons, September 20th.

THE ABOLITIONIST

1857 — John Brown is in Boston in January. He attends the New York meeting of the National Kansas Committee in January. Before the Massachusetts legislature in February. Tours New England to raise money, March and April. Contracts for 1,000 pikes in Connecticut.

1857 — He starts West, May. He is at Tabor, I., August and September. He founds a military school in Iowa, December.

1858 — John Brown returns to the East, January. He is at Frederick Douglass's house, February. He reveals his plan to Sanborn in February. He is in Canada, April. Forbes' disclosures, May.

Chatham convention, May 8–10th. Hamilton's massacre in Kansas, May 19th. Plans postponed, May 20th. John Brown starts West, June 3d. He arrives in Kansas, June 25th. He is in South Kansas, coöperating with Montgomery, July–December. The raid into Missouri for slaves, December 20th.

THE HARPER'S FERRY RAID

1859 — John Brown starts with fugitives for Canada, January 20th. He arrives in Canada, March 12th. He speaks in Cleveland, March 23d. Last visit of John Brown to the East, April and May. He starts for Harper's Ferry, June. He and three companions arrive at Harper's Ferry, July 3d. He gathers twenty-two men and munitions, June–October. He starts on the foray, Sunday, October 16th at 8 p.m. The town and arsenal are captured, Monday, October 17th at 4 a.m. Gathering of the militia, Monday, October 17th at 7 a.m. to 12 m. Brown's party is hemmed in, Monday, October 17th at 12 m. He withdraws to the engine-house, Monday, October 17th at 12 m. Kagi's party is killed and captured, Monday, October 17th at 3 p.m. Lee and 100 marines arrive, Monday, October 17th at 12 p.m. Brown is captured, Tuesday, October 18th at 8 a.m.

1859 — Preliminary examination, October 25th. Trial at Charlestown (then Virginia, now West Virginia), October 27th–November 4th. Forty days in prison, October 16th–December 2d. Execution of John Brown at Charleston, December 2d. Burial of John Brown at North Elba, N. Y., December 8th.

John Brown

I

Africa and America

"That it might be fulfilled which was spoken of the Lord by the prophet saying, Out of Egypt have I called My son."

The mystic spell of Africa is and ever was over all America. It has guided her hardest work, inspired her finest literature, and sung her sweetest songs. Her greatest destiny — unsensed and despised though it be, — is to give back to the first of continents the gifts which Africa of old gave to America's fathers' fathers.

Of all inspiration which America owes to Africa, however; the greatest by far is the score of heroic men whom the sorrows of these dark children called to unselfish devotion and heroic self-realization: Benezet, Garrison, and Harriet Stowe; Sumner, Douglass and Lincoln — these and others, but above all, John Brown.

John Brown was a stalwart, rough-hewn man, mightily yet tenderly carven. To his making went the stern justice of a Cromwellian "Ironside," the freedom-loving fire of a Welsh Celt, and the thrift of a Dutch housewife. And these very things it was — thrift, freedom, and justice — that early crossed the unknown seas to find asylum in America. Yet they came late, for before them came greed, and greed brought black slaves from Africa.

The Negroes came on the heels, if not on the very ships of Columbus. They followed De Soto to the Mississippi; saw Virginia with D'Ayllon, Mexico with Cortez, Peru with Pizarro; and led the western wanderings of Coronado in his search for the Seven Cities of Cibola. Something more than a decade after the Cavaliers, and a year before the Pilgrims, they set lasting foot on the North American continent.

These black men came not of their own willing, but because the hasty greed of new America selfishly and half-thoughtlessly sought to revive in the New World the dying but unforgotten custom of enslaving the world's workers. So with the birth of wealth and liberty west of the seas, came slavery, and a slavery all the more cruel and hideous because it gradually built itself on a caste of race and color, thus breaking the common bonds of human fellowship and weaving artificial barriers of birth and appearance.

The result was evil, as all injustice must be. At first the black men writhed and struggled and died in their bonds, and their blood reddened the paths across the Atlantic and around the beautiful isles of the Western Indies. Then as the bonds gripped them closer and closer, they succumbed to sullen indifference or happy ignorance, with only here and there flashes of wild red vengeance.

For, after all, these black men were but men, neither more nor less wonderful than other men. In build and stature, they were for the most part among the taller nations and sturdily made. In their mental equipment and moral poise, they showed themselves full brothers to all men — "intensely human"; and this too in their very modifications and peculiarities — their warm brown and bronzed color and crisp curled hair under the heat and wet of Africa; their sensuous enjoyment of the music and color of life; their instinct for barter and trade; their strong family life and government. Yet these characteristics were bruised and spoiled and misinterpreted in the rude uprooting of the slave trade and the sudden transplantation of this race to other climes, among other peoples. Their color became a badge of servitude, their tropical habit was deemed laziness, their worship was thought heathenish, their family customs and government were ruthlessly overturned and debauched; many of their virtues became vices, and much of their vice, virtue.

The price of repression is greater than the cost of liberty. The degradation of men costs something both to the degraded and those who degrade. While the Negro slaves sank to listless docility and vacant ignorance, their masters found themselves whirled in the eddies of mighty movements: their system of slavery was twisting them backwards toward darker ages of force and caste and cruelty, while forward swirled swift currents of liberty and uplift.

They still felt the impulse of the wonderful awakening of culture from its barbaric sleep of centuries which men call the Renaissance; they were own children of the mighty stirring of Europe's conscience which we call the Reformation; and they and their children were to be prime actors in laying the foundations of human liberty in a new century and a new land. Already the birth pains of the new freedom were felt in that land. Old Europe was begetting in the new continent a vast longing for spiritual space. So there was builded into America the thrift of the searchers of wealth, the freedom of the Renaissance and the stern morality of the Reformation.

Three lands typified these three things which time planted in the New World: England sent Puritanism, the last white flower of the Lutheran revolt; Holland sent the new vigor and thrift of the Renaissance; while Celtic lands and bits of lands like France and Ireland and Wales, sent the passionate desire for personal freedom. These three elements came, and came more often than not in the guise of humble men — an English carpenter on the *Mayflower*, an Amsterdam tailor seeking a new ancestral city, and a Welsh wanderer. From three such men sprang in the marriage of years, John Brown.

To the unraveling of human tangles we would gladly believe that God sends especial men — chosen vessels which come to the world's deliverance. And what could be more fitting than that the human embodiments of freedom, Puritanism and trade — the great new currents sweeping across the back eddies of slavery, should give birth to the man who in years to come pointed the way to liberty and realized that the cost of liberty was less than the price of repression? So it was. In bleak December, 1620, a carpenter and a weaver landed at Plymouth — Peter and John Brown. This carpenter Peter came of goodly stock, possibly, though not surely, from that very John Brown of the early sixteenth century whom bluff King Henry VIII of England burned for his Puritanism, and whose son was all too near the same fate. Thirty years after Peter Brown had landed, came the Welshman, John Owen, to Windsor, Conn., to help in the building of that commonwealth, and near him settled Peter Mills, the tailor of Holland. The great-grandson of Peter Brown, born in Connecticut in 1700, had for a son a Revolutionary soldier, who married one of the Welshman's grandchildren and had in turn a son, Owen Brown, the father of John Brown, in February of 1771. This Owen Brown a neighbor remembers "very distinctly, and that he was very much respected and esteemed by my father. He was an earnestly devout and religious man, of the old Connecticut fashion; and one peculiarity of his impressed his name and person indelibly upon my memory: he was an inveterate and most painful stammerer — the first specimen of that infirmity that I had ever seen, and, according to my recollection, the worst that I had ever known to this day. Consequently, though we removed from Hudson to another settlement early in the summer of 1807, and returned to Connecticut in 1812, so that I rarely saw any of that family afterward, I have never to this day seen a man struggling and half strangled with a word stuck to his throat, without remembering good Mr. Owen Brown, who could not speak without stammering, except in prayer."*

In 1800, May 9th, wrote this Owen Brown: "John was born, one hundred years after his great-grandfather. Nothing else very uncommon."**

* Redpath, *Public Life of Captain John Brown*, p. 25.
** Autobiography of Owen Brown in Sanborn, *Life and Letters of John Brown*, p. 7.

II

The Making of the Man

"There was a man called of God and his name was John."

A tall big boy of twelve or fifteen, "barefoot and bare-headed, with buckskin breeches suspended often with one leather strap over his shoulder"* roamed in the forests of northern Ohio. He remembered the days of his coming to the strange wild land — the lowing oxen, the great white wagon that wandered from Connecticut to Pennsylvania and over the swelling hills and mountains, where the wide-eyed urchin of five sat staring at the new world of wild beast and the wilder brown men. Then came life itself in its realness — the driving of cows and the killing of rattle-snakes, and swift free rides on great mornings alone with earth and tree and sky. He became "a rambler in the wild new country, finding birds and squirrels and sometimes a wild turkey's nest." At first the Indians filled him with strange fear. But his kindly old father thought of Indians as neither vermin nor property and this fear "soon wore off and he used to hang about them quite as much as was consistent with good manners."

The tragedy and comedy of this broad silent life turned on things strangely simple and primitive — the stealing of "three large brass pins"; the disappearance of the wonderful yellow marble which an Indian boy had given him; the love and losing of a little bob-tailed squirrel for which he wept and hunted the world in vain; and finally the shadow of death which is ever here — the death of a ewe-lamb and the death of the boy's own mother.

All these things happened before he was eight and they were his main education. He could dress leather and make

* The quotations in this chapter are from John Brown's Auto-biography, Sanborn, *Life and Letters of John Brown*, pp. 12–17.

whip-lashes; he could herd cattle and talk Indian; but of books and formal schooling he had little.

"John was never quarrelsome, but was excessively fond of the hardest and roughest kind of plays, and could never get enough of them. Indeed when for a short time he was sometimes sent to school, the opportunity it afforded to wrestle and snowball and run and jump and knock off old seedy wool hats, offered to him almost the only compensation for the confinements and restraints of school.

"With such a feeling and but little chance of going to school at all, he did not become much of a scholar. He would always choose to stay at home and work hard rather than be sent to school." Consequently, "he learned nothing of grammar, nor did he get at school so much knowledge of common arithmetic as the four ground rules."

Almost his only reading at the age of ten was a little history to which the open bookcase of an old friend tempted him. He knew nothing of games or sports; he had few or no companions, but, "to be sent off through the wilderness alone to very considerable distances was particularly his delight. . . . By the time he was twelve years old he was sent off more than a hundred miles with companies of cattle." So his soul grew apart and alone and yet untrammeled and unconfined, knowing all the depths of secret self-abasement, and the heights of confident self-will. With others he was painfully diffident and bashful, and little sins that smaller souls would laugh at and forget loomed large and awful to his heart-searching vision. John had "a very bad foolish habit. . . . I mean telling lies, generally to screen himself from blame or from punishment," because "he could not well endure to be reproached and I now think had he been oftener encouraged to be entirely frank . . he would not have been so often guilty of this fault, nor have been (in after life) obliged to struggle so long with so mean a habit."

Such a nature was in its very essence religious, even mystical, but never superstitious nor blindly trustful in half-known creeds and formulas. His family was not rigidly Puritan in its thought and discipline but had rather fallen into the mild heathenism of the hard-working frontier until just before John's birth. Then, his father relates in quaint Calvinistic *patois:* "I lived at home in 1782; this was a memorable year, as there was a great revival of religion in the town of Canton. My mother and my older sisters and brother John dated their hopes of salvation from that summer's revival under the ministry of the Rev. Edward Mills. I cannot say as I was a subject of the work; but this I can say that I then began to hear preaching. I can now recollect most if not all of those I heard preach, and what their texts were. The change in our family was great; family worship set up by brother John was ever afterward continued. There was a revival of singing in Canton and our family became singers. Conference meetings were kept up constantly and singing meetings — all of which brought our family into a very good association — a very great aid of restraining grace."

Thus this young freeman of the woods was born into a religious atmosphere; not that of stern, intellectual Puritanism, but of a milder and a more sensitive type. Even this, however, the naturally skeptical bent of his mind did not receive unquestioningly. The doctrines of his day and church did not wholly satisfy him and he became only "to some extent a convert to Christianity." One answer to his questionings did come, however, bearing its own wonderful credentials — and credentials all the more wonderful to the man of few books and narrow knowledge of the world of thought — the English Bible. He grew to be "a firm believer in the divine authenticity of the Bible. With this book he became very familiar." He read and reread it; he committed long passages to memory; he copied the simple vigor of its English, and wove into the very essence of his being, its history, poetry, philosophy, and truth. To him the cruel grandeur of the Old Testament was as true as the love and sacrifice of the New, and both mingled to mold his soul. "This will give you some general idea of the first fifteen years of his life, during which time he became very strong and large of his age, and ambitious to perform the full labor of a man at almost any kind of hard work."

Young John Brown's first broad contact with life and affairs came with the War of 1812, during which Hull's disastrous campaign brought the scene of fighting near his western home. His father, a simple wandering old soul, thrifty without foresight, became a beef contractor, and the boy drove his herds of cattle and hung about the camp. He met men of position, was praised for his prowess and let listen to talk that seemed far beyond his years. Yet he was not deceived. The war he felt was real war and not the war of fame and fairy tale. He saw shameful defeat, heard treason broached, and knew of cheating and chicanery. Disease and death left its slimy trail as it crept homeward through the town of Hudson from Detroit: "The effect of what he saw during the war went so far to disgust him with military affairs that he would neither train nor drill."

But in all these early years of the making of this man, one incident stands out as foretaste and prophecy — an incident of which we know only the indefinite outline, and yet one which unconsciously foretold to the boy the life deed of the man. It was during the war that a certain landlord welcomed John to his home whither the boy had ridden with cattle, a hundred miles through the wilderness. He praised the big, grave and bashful lad to his guests and made much of him. John, however, discovered something far more interesting than praise and good food in the landlord's parlor, and that was another boy in the landlord's yard. Fellow souls were scarce with this backwoodsman and his diffidence warmed to the kindly welcome of the stranger, especially because he was black, half-naked and wretched. In John's very ears the kind voices of the master and his folk turned to harsh abuse with this black boy. At night the slave lay in the bitter cold and once they beat the wretched thing before John's very eyes with an iron shovel, and again and again struck him with any weapon that chanced. In wide-eyed silence John looked on and questioned, Was the boy bad or stupid?

No, he was active, intelligent and with the great warm sympathy of his race did the stranger "numerous little acts of kindness," so that John readily, in his straightforward candor, acknowledged him "fully if not more than his equal." That the black worked and worked hard and steadily was in John's eyes no hardship — rather a pleasure. Was not the world work? But that this boy was fatherless and motherless, and that all slaves must of necessity be fatherless and motherless with none to protect them or provide for them, save at the will or caprice of the master — this was to the half-grown man a thing of fearful portent and he asked, "Is God their Father?" And what he asked, a million and a half black bondmen were asking through the land.

III
The Wanderjahre

"Where is the promise of His coming? For since the fathers fell
asleep, all things continue as they were from the beginning of the
creation."

In 1819 a tall, sedate, dignified young man named John
Brown was entered among the students of the Rev. Moses
Hallock at Plainfield, Mass., where men were prepared for
Amherst College. He was beginning his years of wandering
— spiritual searching for the way of life, physical wandering in the wilderness where he must earn his living. In after
years he wrote to a boy:
"I wish you to have some definite plan. Many seem to
have none; others never stick to any that they do form. This
was not the case with John. He followed up with great
tenacity whatever he set about as long as it answered his
general purpose; hence he rarely failed in some degree to
effect the things he undertook. This was so much the case
that he habitually expected to succeed in his undertakings."*
In this case he expected to get an education and he came to
his task equipped with that rare mixture of homely thrift
and idealism which characterized his whole life. His father
could do little to help him, for the war was followed by the
"hard times" which are the necessary fruit of fighting. As the
father wrote: "Money became scarce, property fell and that
which I thought well bought would not bring its cost. I had
made three or four large purchases, in which I was a heavy
loser."
It was therefore as a poor boy ready to work his way that
John started out at Plainfield. The son of the principal tells
how "he brought with him a piece of sole leather about a
foot square, which he had himself tanned for seven years, to

* John Brown's Autobiography, Sanborn, p. 16.

resole his boots. He had also a piece of sheepskin which he had tanned, and of which he cut some strips about an eighth of an inch wide, for other students to pull upon. Father took one string, and winding it around his finger said with a triumphant turn of the eye and mouth, 'I shall snap it.' The very marked, yet kind immovableness of the young man's face on seeing father's defeat, father's own look, and the position of the people and the things in the old kitchen somehow gave me a fixed recollection of this little incident." *

But all his thrift and planning here were doomed to disappointment. He was, one may well believe, no brilliant student, and his only chance of success lay in long and steady application. This he was prepared to make when inflammation of the eyes set in, of so grave a type that all hopes of long study must be given up. Several times before he had attempted regular study, but for the most part these excursions to New England schools had been but tentative flashes on a background of hard work in his father's Hudson tannery: "From fifteen to twenty years of age he spent most of his time working at the tanner's and currier's trade"; and yet, naturally, ever looking here and there in the world to find his place. And that place, he came gradually to decide in his quiet firm way, was to be an important one. He felt he could do things; he grew used to guiding and commanding men. He kept his own lonely home and was both foreman and cook in the tannery. His "close attention to business and success in its management, together with the way he got along with a company of men and boys, made him quite a favorite with the serious and more intelligent portion of older persons. This was so much the case and secured for him so many little notices from those he esteemed, that his vanity was very much fed by it, and he came forward to manhood quite full of self-conceit and self-confidence, notwithstand-

* Heman Hallock, in the New York *Journal of Commerce,* quoted in Sanborn, p. 32

ing his extreme bashfulness. The habit so early formed of being obeyed rendered him in after life too much disposed to speak in an imperious or dictating way."* Thus he spoke of himself, but others saw only that peculiar consciousness of strength and quiet self-confidence, which characterized him later on.

Just how far his failure to get a college training was a disappointment to John Brown one is not able to say with certainty. It looks, however, as if his attempts at higher training were rather the obedient following of the conventional path, by a spirit which would never have found in those fields congenial pasture. One suspects that the final decision that college was impossible came to this strong free spirit with a certain sense of relief — a relief marred only by the perplexity of knowing what ought to be the path for his feet, if the traditional way to accomplishment and distinction was closed.

That he meant to be not simply a tanner was disclosed in all his doing and thinking. He undertook to study by himself, mastering common arithmetic and becoming in time an expert surveyor. He "early in life began to discover a great liking to fine cattle, horses, sheep and swine." Meantime, however, the practical economic sense of his day and occupation pointed first of all to marriage, as his father, who had had three wives and sixteen or more children, was at pains to impress upon him. Nor was John Brown himself disinclined. He was as he himself quaintly says, "naturally fond of females, and withal extremely diffident." One can easily imagine the deep disappointment of this grave young man in his first unfortunate love affair, when he felt with many another unloved heart, this old world through, "a steady, strong desire to die."

But youth is stronger even than a first love, and the widow who came to keep house for him had a grown daughter, a homely, good-hearted and simple-minded country lass; the

* John Brown's Autobiography, Sanborn, p. 16.

natural result was that John Brown was married at the age of twenty to Dianthe Lusk, whom he describes as "a remarkably plain, but neat, industrious and economical girl, of excellent character, earnest piety and practical common sense."*

Then ensued a period of life which puzzles the casual onlooker with its seemingly aimless changing character, its wandering restlessness, its planless wavering. He was now a land surveyor, now a tanner and now a lumber dealer; a postmaster, a wool-grower, a stock-raiser, a shepherd, and a farmer. He lived at Hudson, at Franklin and at Richfield in Ohio; in Pennsylvania, New York, and Massachusetts. And yet in all this wavering and wandering, there were certain great currents of growth, purpose and action. First of all he became the father of a family: in the eleven years from 1821 to 1832, seven children were born — six sons and one girl. The patriarchal ideal of family life handed down by his fathers, strengthened by his own saturation in Hebrew poetry, and by his own bent, grew up in his home.

His eldest son and daughter tell many little incidents illustrating his family government: "Our house, on a lane which connects two main roads, was built under father's direction in 1824, and still stands much as he built it with the garden and orchard around it which he laid out. In the rear of the house was then a wood, now gone, on a knoll leading down to the brook which supplied the tan-pits."**

"Father used to hold all his children while they were little at night and sing his favorite songs," says the eldest daughter. "The first recollection I have of father was being carried through a piece of woods on Sunday to attend a meeting held at a neighbor's house. After we had been at the house a little while, father and mother stood up and held us, while the minister put water on our faces. After we sat down father wiped my face with a brown silk handkerchief with

* John Brown's Autobiography, Sanborn, pp. 16, 17.
** John Brown, Jr., in Sanborn, p. 34.

yellow spots on it in diamond shape. It seemed beautiful to me and I thought how good he was to wipe my face with that pretty handkerchief. He showed a great deal of tenderness in that and other ways. He sometimes seemed very stern and strict with me, yet his tenderness made me forget he was stern. . . .

"When he would come home at night tired out with labor, he would before going to bed, ask some of the family to read chapters (as was his usual course night and morning); and would almost always say: 'Read one of David's Psalms.' . . .

"Whenever he and I were alone, he never failed to give me the best of advice, just such as a true and anxious mother would give a daughter. He always seemed interested in my work, and would come around and look at it when I was sewing or knitting; and when I was learning to spin he always praised me if he saw that I was improving. He used to say: 'Try to do whatever you do in the very best possible manner.' "*

"Father had a rule not to threaten one of his children. He commanded and there was obedience," writes his eldest son. "My first apprenticeship to the tanning business consisted of a three years' course at grinding bark with a blind horse. This, after months and years, became slightly monotonous. While the other children were out at play in the sunshine, where the birds were singing, I used to be tempted to let the old horse have a rather long rest, especially when father was absent from home; and I would then join the others at their play. This subjected me to frequent admonitions and to some corrections for eye-service as father termed it. . . . He finally grew tired of these frequent slight admonitions for my laziness and other shortcomings, and concluded to adopt with me a sort of book-account something like this·

* Ruth Brown in Sanborn, pp. 37–39.

"John, Dr.,

   "For disobeying mother — 8 lashes.

   For unfaithfulness at work — 3 lashes.

   "For telling a lie — 8 lashes.

"This account he showed to me from time to time. On a certain Sunday morning he invited me to accompany him from the house to the tannery, saying that he had concluded it was time for a settlement. We went into the upper or finishing room, and after a long and tearful talk over my faults, he again showed me my account, which exhibited a fearful footing up of debits. I had no credits or offsets and was of course bankrupt. I then paid about one-third of the debt, reckoned in strokes from a nicely prepared blue-beach switch, laid on 'masterly.' Then to my utter astonishment, father stripped off his shirt and seating himself on a block gave me the whip and bade me lay it on to his bare back. I dared not refuse to obey, but at first I did not strike hard. 'Harder,' he said, 'harder, harder!' until he received the balance of the account. Small drops of blood showed on his back where the tip end of the tingling beach cut through. Thus ended the account and settlement, which was also my first practical illustration of the doctrine of the atonement."[*]

Even the girls did not escape whipping. "He used to whip me often for telling lies," says a daughter, "but I can't remember his ever punishing me but once when I thought I didn't deserve, and then he looked at me so stern that I didn't dare to tell the truth. He had such a way of saying, 'Tut, tut!' if he saw the first sign of a lie in us, that he often frightened us children.

"When I first began to go to school," she continues, "I found a piece of calico one day behind one of the benches — it was not large, but seemed quite a treasure to me, and I did not show it to any one until I got home. Father heard me then telling about it and said, 'Don't you know what

[*] John Brown, Jr., in Sanborn, pp. 91–93.

girl lost it?' I told him I did not. 'Well, when you go to school to-morrow take it with you and find out if you can who lost it. It is a trifling thing but always remember that if you should lose anything you valued, no matter how small, you would want the person who found it to give it back to you.'" He "showed a great deal of tenderness to me," continues the daughter, "and one thing I always noticed was my father's peculiar tenderness and devotion to his father. In cold weather he always tucked the bedclothes around grandfather when he went to bed, and would get up in the night to ask him if he slept warm — always seeming so kind and loving to him that his example was beautiful to see."

Especially were his sympathy and devotion evident in sickness: "When his children were ill with scarlet fever, he took care of us himself and if he saw persons coming to the house, would go to the gate and meet them, not wishing them to come in, for fear of spreading the disease.*... When any of the family were sick he did not often trust watchers to care for the sick one, but sat up himself and was like a tender mother. At one time he sat up every night for two weeks while mother was sick, for fear he would oversleep if he went to bed, and then the fire would go out and she take cold."**

The death of one little girl shows how deeply he could be moved: "He spared no pains in doing all that medical skill could do for her together with the tenderest care and nursing. The time that he could be at home was mostly spent in caring for her. He sat up nights to keep an even temperature in the room, and to relieve mother from the constant care which she had through the day. He used to walk with the child and sing to her so much that she soon learned his step. When she heard him coming up the steps to the door, she would reach out her hands and cry for him to take her. When his business at the wool store crowded

---

* Ruth Brown in Sanborn, pp. 93–94.
** *Ibid.*, p. 104.

him so much that he did not have time to take her, he would steal around through the wood-shed into the kitchen to eat his dinner, and not go into the dining-room where she could see or hear him. I used to be charmed myself with his singing to her. He noticed a change in her one morning and told us he thought she would not live through the day, and came home several times to see her. A little before noon he came home and looked at her and said, 'She is almost gone.' She heard him speak, opened her eyes and put up her little wasted hands with such a pleading look for him to take her that he lifted her up from the cradle with the pillows she was lying on, and carried her until she died. He was very calm, closed her eyes, folded her hands and laid her in her cradle. When she was buried father broke down completely and sobbed like a child."*

Dianthe Lusk, John Brown's first wife, died in childbirth, August 10, 1832, having borne him seven children, two of whom died very young. On July 11, 1833, now thirty-three years of age, he married Mary Ann Day, a girl of seventeen, only five years older than his oldest child. She bore him thirteen children, seven of whom died young. Thus seven sons and four daughters grew to maturity and his wife, Mary, survived him twenty-five years. It was, all told, a marvelous family — large and well-disciplined, yet simple almost to poverty, and hard-working. No sooner were the children grown than the wise father ceased to command and simply asked or advised. He wrote to his eldest son when first he started out in life, in characteristic style:

"I think the situation in which you have been placed by Providence at this early period of your life will afford to yourself and others some little test of the sway you may be expected to exert over minds in after life, and I am glad on the whole to have you brought in some measure to the test in your youth. If you cannot now go into a disorderly country school and gain its confidence and esteem, and reduce it to

* Ruth Brown in Sanborn, p. 44.

31

good order and waken up the energies and the very soul of every rational being in it — yes, of every mean, ill-behaved, ill-governed boy and girl that compose it, and secure the good-will of the parents, — then how are you to stimulate asses to attempt a passage of the Alps? If you run with footmen and they should weary you, how should you contend with horses? If in the land of peace they have wearied you, then how will you do in the swelling of Jordan? Shall I answer the question myself? 'If any man lack wisdom, let him ask of God, who giveth liberally and upbraideth not.'"*

Not that Brown was altogether satisfied with his method of dealing with his children; he said to his wife: "If the large boys do wrong, call them alone into your room and expostulate with them kindly, and see if you cannot reach them by a kind but powerful appeal to their honor. I do not claim that such a theory accords very well with my practice; I frankly confess it does not, but I want your face to shine even if my own should be dark and cloudy."**

The impression which he made on his own family was marvelous. A granddaughter writes me of him, saying: "The attitude of John Brown's family and descendants has always been one of exceeding reverence toward him. This speaks for something. Stern, unyielding, Puritanic, requiring his wife and daughters to dress in sober brown, disliking show and requesting that mourning colors be not worn for him — a custom which still obtains with us — laying the rod heavily upon his boys for their boyish pranks, he still was wonderfully tender — would invariably walk up hill rather than burden his horse, loved his family devotedly, and when sickness occurred, always installed himself as nurse."

In his personal habits he was austere: severely clean, sparing in his food so far as to count butter an unnecessary luxury; once a moderate user of cider and wine — then a

* Letter to John Brown, Jr., 1841, in Sanborn, p. 139.
** Letter to his wife, 1844, in Sanborn, p. 61.

strong teetotaler; a lover of horses with harassing scruples as to breeding race-horses. All this gave an air of sedateness and maturity to John Brown's earlier manhood which belied his years. Having married at twenty, he was but twenty-one years older than his eldest son; and while his many children and his varied occupations made him seem prematurely aged, he was, in fact, during this period, during the years from twenty to forty, experiencing the great formative development of his spiritual life. This development was most interesting and fruitful.

He was not a man of books: he had Rollins' *Ancient History*, Josephus and Plutarch and lives of Napoleon and Cromwell. With these went Baxter's *Saints' Rest*, Henry *On Meekness* and *Pilgrim's Progress*. "But above all others the Bible was his favorite volume and he had such perfect knowledge of it that when any person was reading he would correct the least mistake."*

Into John Brown's religious life entered two strong elements; the sense of overruling inexorable fate, and the mystery and promise of death. He pored over the Old Testament until the freer religious skepticism of his earlier youth became more formal and straight. The brother of his first wife says, "Brown was an austere fellow," and when the young man called on the sister and mother Sundays, as his only holiday, Brown said to him: "Milton, I wish you would not make your visits here on the Sabbath."

When the panic of 1837 nearly swept Brown from his feet, he saw behind it the image of the old Hebrew God and wrote his wife: "We all must try to trust in Him who is very gracious and full of compassion and of almighty power; for those that do will not be made ashamed. Ezra the prophet prayed and afflicted himself before God, when himself and the Captivity were in a strait and I have no doubt you will join with me under similar circumstances.

* Ruth Brown in Sanborn, pp. 38–39.

33

Don't get discouraged, any of you, but hope in God, and try all to serve Him with a perfect heart."*

When Napoleon III seized France and Kossuth came to America, Brown looked with lofty contempt on the "great excitement" which "seems to have taken all by surprise." "I have only to say in regard to those things, I rejoice in them from the full belief that God is carrying out His eternal purpose in them all."**

The gloom and horror of life settled early on John Brown. His childhood had had little formal pleasure, his young manhood had been serious and filled with responsibility, and almost before he himself knew the full meaning of life, he was trying to teach it to his children. The iron of bitterness entered his soul with the coming of death, and a deep religious fear and foreboding bore him down as it took away member after member of his family. In 1831 he lost a boy of four and in 1832 his first wife died insane, and her infant son was buried with her. In 1843 four children varying in ages from one to nine years were swept away. Two baby girls went in 1846 and 1859 and an infant boy in 1852. The struggle of a strong man to hold his faith is found in his words, "God has seen fit to visit us with the pestilence and four of our number sleep in the dust; four of us that are still living have been more or less unwell. . . . This has been to us all a bitter cup indeed and we have drunk deeply; but still the Lord reigneth and blessed be His holy name forever." Again three years later he writes his wife from the edge of a new-made grave: "I feel assured that notwithstanding that God has chastised us often and sore, yet He has not entirely withdrawn Himself from us nor forsaken us utterly. The sudden and dreadful manner in which He has seen fit to call our dear little Kitty to take her leave of us, is, I need not tell you how much, in my mind. But before Him I will bow my head in submission and hold my peace. . . . I have sailed

* Letter to his wife, 1839, in Sanborn, p. 69.
** Letter to his wife, 1851, in Sanborn, p. 146.

over a somewhat stormy sea for nearly half a century, and have experienced enough to teach me thoroughly that I may most reasonably buckle up and be prepared for the tempest. Mary, let us try to maintain a cheerful self-command while we are tossing up and down, and let our motto still be action, action, — as we have but one life to live." *

His soul gropes for light in the great darkness: "Sometimes my imagination follows those of my family who have passed behind the scenes; and I would almost rejoice to be permitted to make them a personal visit. I have outlived nearly half of all my numerous family, and I ought to realize that in any event a large proportion of my life is traveled over." **

Then there rose grimly, as life went on in its humdrum round of failure and trouble, the thought that in some way his own sin and shortcomings were bringing upon him the vengeful punishment of God. He laments the fact that he has done little to help others and the world: "I feel considerable regret by turns that I have lived so many years and have in reality done so little to increase the amount of human happiness. I often regret that my manner is not more kind and affectionate to those I really love and esteem. But I trust my friends will overlook my harsh rough ways, when I cease to be in their way as an occasion of pain and unhappiness." ***

The death of a friend fills him with self-reproach: "You say he expected to die, but do not say how he felt in regard to the change as it drew near. I have to confess my unfaithfulness to my friend in regard to his most important interest. ... When I think how very little influence I have even tried to use with my numerous acquaintances and friends in turning their minds toward God and heaven, I feel justly condemned as a most wicked and slothful servant; and the

* Letter to his wife, 1846, in Sanborn, p. 142.
** Letter to his daughter, 1847, in Sanborn, p. 142.
*** Letter to his wife, 1844, in Sanborn, pp. 60–61.

more so as I have very seldom had any one refuse to listen when I earnestly called him to hear. I sometimes have dreadful reflections about having fled to go down to Tarshish."*

Especially did the religious skepticism of his children, so like his own earlier wanderings, worry and dismay the growing man until it loomed before his vision as his great sin, calling for mighty atonement. He pleads with his older children continually:

"My attachments to this world have been very strong and divine Providence has been cutting me loose, one cord after another. Up to the present time notwithstanding I have so much to remind me that all ties must soon be severed, I am still clinging like those who have hardly taken a single lesson. I really hope some of my family may understand that this world is not the home of man, and act in accordance. Why may I not hope this for you? When I look forward as regards the religious prospects of my numerous family — the most of them, — I am forced to say, and feel too, that I have little — very little to cheer. That this should be so is, I perfectly well understand, the legitimate fruit of my own planting; and that only increases my punishment. Some ten or twelve years ago I was cheered with the belief that my elder children had chosen the Lord to be their God and I relied much on their influence and example in atoning for my deficiency and bad example with the younger children. But where are we now? Several have gone where neither a good nor a bad example from me will better their condition or prospects or make them worse. I will not dwell longer on this distressing subject but only say that so far as I have gone it is from no disposition to reflect on any one but myself. I think I can clearly discover where I wandered from the road. How now to get on it with my family is beyond my ability to *see* or my courage to *hope*. God grant you thorough conversion from sin, and full purpose of heart to continue steadfast in

* Letter to his father, 1846, in Sanborn, pp. 21, 22.

His way through the very short season you will have to pass." *

And again he writes: "One word in regard to the religious belief of yourself and the ideas of several of my children. My affections are too deep-rooted to be alienated from them, but 'my gray hairs must go down in sorrow to the grave' unless the true God forgive their denial and rejection of Him and open their eyes."

And again: "I would fain hope that the spirit of God has not done striving in our hard hearts. I sometimes feel encouraged to hope that my sons will give up their miserable delusions and believe in God and in His Son, our Saviour."**

All this is evidence of a striving soul, of a man to whom the world was a terribly earnest thing. Here was neither the smug content of the man beyond religious doubt, nor the carelessness of the unharassed conscience. To him the world was a mighty drama. God was an actor in the play and so was John Brown. But just what his part was to be his soul in the long agony of years tried to know, and ever and again the chilling doubt assailed him lest he be unworthy of his place or had missed the call. Often the brooding masculine mind which demanded "Action! Action!" sought to pierce the mystic veil. His brother-in-law became a spiritualist, and he himself hearkened for voices from the Other Land. Once or twice he thought he heard them. Did not the spirit of Dianthe Lusk guide him again and again in his perplexity? He once said it did.

And so this saturation in Hebrew prophecy, the chastisement of death, the sense of personal sin and shortcoming and the voices from nowhere, deepened, darkened and broadened his religious life. Yet with all this there went a peculiar common sense, a spirit of thrift and stickling for detail, a

* Letter to his daughter, 1852, in Sanborn, p. 45.
** Letter to John Brown, Jr., 1852, and to his children, 1853, in Sanborn, pp. 151 and 155.

homely shrewd attention to all the little facts of daily existence. Sometimes this prosaic tinkering with things burdened, buried and submerged the spiritual life and striving. There was nothing left except the commonplace, unstable tanner, but ever as one is tempted thus to fix his place in the world, there wells up surging spiritual life out of great unfathomed depths — the intellectual longing to see, the moral wistfulness of the hesitating groping doer. This was the deeper, truer man, although it was not the whole man. "Certainly I never felt myself in the presence of a stronger religious influence than while in this man's house," said Frederick Douglass in 1847.

IV
The Shepherd of the Sheep

"And there were in the same country shepherds abiding in the field, keeping watch over their flock by night.

"And, lo, the angel of the Lord came upon them, and the glory of the Lord shone round about them; and they were sore afraid."

The vastest physical fact in the life of John Brown was the Alleghany Mountains — that beautiful mass of hill and crag which guards the sombre majesty of the Maine coast, crumples the rivers on the rocky soil of New England, and rolls and leaps down through busy Pennsylvania to the misty peaks of Carolina and the red foothills of Georgia. In the Alleghanies John Brown was all but born; their forests were his boyhood wonderland; in their villages he married his wives and begot his clan. On the sides of the Alleghanies he tended his sheep and dreamed his terrible dream. It was the mystic, awful voice of the mountains that lured him to liberty, death and martyrdom within their wildest fastness, and in their bosom he sleeps his last sleep.

So, too, in the development of the United States from the War of 1812 to the Civil War, it was the Alleghanies that formed the industrial centre of the land and lured young men to their waters and mines, valleys and factories, as they lured John Brown. His life from 1805 to 1854 was almost wholly spent on the western slope of the Alleghanies in a small area of Ohio and Pennsylvania, beginning eighty miles north of Pittsburg and ending twenty-five miles southeast of Cleveland. Here in a half-dozen small towns, but chiefly in Hudson, O., he worked in his young manhood to support his growing family. From 1819 to 1825, he was a tanner at Hudson. Then he moved seventy miles westward toward the crests of the Alleghanies in Pennsylvania, where he set up his tannery again and became a man of importance in the town. John Quincy Adams made him post-master, the village school was held at his log-house and the

39

new feverish prosperity of the post-bellum period began to stir him as it stirred this whole western world. Indeed, the economic history of the land from the War of 1812 to the Civil War covers a period of extraordinary developments — so much so that no man's life which fell in these years may be written without knowledge of and allowance for the battling of gigantic social forces and welding of material, out of which the present United States was designed.

Three phases roughly mark these days: First, the slough of despond following the war, when England forced her goods upon us at nominal prices to kill the new-sprung infant industries; secondly, the new protection from the competition of foreign goods from 1816 to 1857, rising high in the prohibitory schedules of 1828, and falling to the lower duties of the forties and the free trade of the fifties, and stimulating irregularly and spasmodically but tremendously the cotton, woolen and iron manufactories; and finally, the three whirlwinds of 1819, 1837-1839, and 1857, marking frightful maladjustments in the mushroom growth of our industrial life.

John Brown, coming to full industrial manhood in the buoyant prosperity of 1825, soon began to sense the new spirit. After ten years' work in Pennsylvania, he again removed westward, nearer the projected transportation lines between East and West. He began to invest his surplus in land along the new canal routes, became a director in one of the rapidly multiplying banks and was currently rated to be worth $20,000 in 1835. But his prosperity, like that of his neighbors, and indeed, of the whole country, was partly fictitious, and built on a fast expanding credit which was far outstretching the rapid industrial development. Jackson's blind tinkering with banking precipitated the crisis. The storm broke in 1837. Over six hundred banks failed, ten thousand employees were thrown out of work, money disappeared and prices went down to a specie level. John Brown, his tannery and his land speculations, were sucked into the maelstrom.

The overthrow was no ordinary blow to a man of thirty-

seven with eight children, who had already trod the ways of spiritual doubt and unrest. For three or four years he seemed to flounder almost hopelessly, certainly with no settled plan or outlook. He bred race-horses till his conscience troubled him; he farmed and did some surveying; he inquired into the commission business in various lines, and still did some tanning. Then gradually he began to find himself. He was a lover of animals. In 1839 he took a drove of cattle to Connecticut and wrote to his wife: "I have felt distressed to get my business done and return ever since I left home, but know of no way consistent with duty but to make thorough work of it while there is any hope. Things now look more favorable than they have but I may still be disappointed."*
His diary shows that he priced certain farms for sale, but especially did he inquire carefully into sheep-raising and its details, and eventually bought a flock of sheep, which he drove home to Ohio. This marked the beginning of a new occupation, that of shepherd, "being a calling for which in early life he had a kind of enthusiastic longing." He began sheep-farming near Hudson, keeping his own and a rich merchant's sheep and also buying wool on commission.

This industry in the United States had at that time passed through many vicissitudes. The change from household to factory economy and the introduction of effective machinery had been slow, and one of the chief drawbacks was ever the small quantity of good wool. Consequently our chief supply came from England until the embargo and war cut off that supply and stimulated domestic manufacture. Between 1810 and 1815 the value of the manufacture increased five-fold, but after the war, when England sent goods over here below price, Americans rightly clamored for tariff protection. This they got, but their advantage was nearly upset by the wool farmers who also got protection on the commodity, although less on low than on better qualities; and it was the low grades that America produced. From 1816 to 1832 the tariff

* Letter to his wife, 1839, in Sanborn, p. 68.

wall against wool and woolens rose steadily until it reached almost prohibitive figures, save on the cheapest kind. In this way the wool manufacture had by 1828 recovered its wartime prosperity; by 1840 the mills were sending out twenty and a half million dollars' worth of goods yearly, and nearly fifty millions by 1860 despite the fact that meanwhile the tariff wall was weakening. Thus by 1841 when John Brown turned his attention to sheep-farming, there was a large and growing demand for wool, especially of the better grades, and by the abolition of the English tariff in 1824, there was even a chance of invading England.

Because, then, of his natural liking for the work, and the growing prosperity of the wool trade, John Brown chose this line of employment. But not for this alone. His spirit was longing for air and space. He wanted to think and read; time was flying and his life as yet had been little but a mean struggle for bread and that, too, only partially successful. Already he had had a vision of vast service. Already he had broached the matter to friends and family, and at the age of thirty-nine he entered his new life distinctly and clearly with "the idea that as a business it bid fair to afford him the means of carrying out his greatest or principal object."*

His first idea was to save enough from the wreck of his fortune to buy and stock a large sheep farm, and in accordance with his already forming plans as to Negro emancipation, he wanted this farm in or near the South. A chance seemed opening when through his father, a trustee of Oberlin College, he learned of the Virginia lands lately given that institution by Gerrit Smith, whom Brown came to know better. Oberlin College was dear to John Brown's heart, for it had almost from the beginning taken a strong anti-slavery stand. The titles to the Virginia land, however, were clouded by the fact of many squatters being in possession, which gave ample prospects of costly lawsuits. Brown wrote the trustees early in 1840, proposing to survey the lands for a

* Sanborn, p. 58.

42

nominal price, provided he could be allowed to buy on reasonable terms and establish his family there. He also spoke of school facilities which he proposed for Negroes as well as whites, according to a long cherished plan. The college records in April, 1840, say: "Communication from Brother John Brown of Hudson was presented and read by the secretary, containing a proposition to visit, survey and make the necessary investigation respecting boundaries, etc., of those lands, for one dollar per day and a moderate allowance for necessary expenses; said paper frankly expressing also his design of viewing the lands as a preliminary step to locating his family upon them, should the opening prove a favorable one; whereupon, *voted* that said proposition be acceded to, and that a commission and needful outfit be furnished by the secretary and treasurer."* The treasurer sent John Brown fifty dollars and wrote his father, as a trustee of Oberlin, commending the son's purpose and hoping "for a favorable issue both for him and the institution." He added, "Should he succeed in clearing up titles without difficulty or lawsuits, it would be easy, as it appears to me, to make provision for religious and school privileges and by proper efforts with the blessing of God, soon see that wilderness bud and blossom as the rose."**

Thus John Brown first saw Virginia and looked upon the rich and heavy land which rolls westward to the misty Blue Ridge. That he visited Harper's Ferry on this trip is doubtful but possible. The lands of Oberlin, however, lay two hundred miles westward in the foothills and along the valley of the Ohio. He wrote home from Ripley, Va., in April (for he had gone immediately): "I like the country as well as I expected, and its inhabitants rather better; and I have seen the spot where if it be the will of Providence, I hope one day to live with my family. ... Were the inhabitants as resolute and industrious as the Northern people and did

* Records of Oberlin College, quoted in Sanborn, pp. 134–135.
** Levi Burnell to Owen Brown, 1840, in Sanborn, p. 135.

they understand how to manage as well, they would become rich."*

By the summer of 1840 his work was accomplished with apparent success. He had about selected his dwelling-place, having "found on the right branch of Big Battle a valuable spring, good stone-coal, and excellent bottoms, good timber, sugar orchard, good hill land and beautiful situation for dwelling — all right. Course of this branch at the forks is south twenty-one degrees west from a beautiful white oak on which I marked my initials, 23d April."**

The Oberlin trustees in August, "voted, that the Prudential Committee be authorized to perfect negotiations and convey by deed to Brother John Brown of Hudson, one thousand acres of our Virginia land on the conditions suggested in the correspondence which has already transpired between him and the committee."***

Here, however, negotiations stopped, for the renewal of the panic in 1839 overthrew all business calculations until 1842 and later, and forced John Brown to take refuge in formal bankruptcy in 1842. This step, his son says, was wholly "owing to his purchase of land on credit — including the Haymaker farm at Franklin, which he bought in connection with Seth Thompson, of Hartford, Trumbull County, Ohio, and his individual purchase of three rather large adjoining farms in Hudson. When he bought those farms, the rise in value of his place in Franklin was such that good judges estimated his property worth fully twenty thousand dollars. He was then thought to be a man of excellent business judgment and was chosen one of the directors of a bank at Cayahoga Falls."**** Probably after the crash of 1837, Brown hoped to extricate enough to buy land in Virginia

* Letter to his family, 1840, in Sanborn, p. 134.
** MS. Diary, Boston Public Library. Vol. I, p. 65.
*** Records of the Board of Trustees, Oberlin College, Aug. 28, 1840, quoted in Sanborn, p. 135.
**** John Brown, Jr., in Sanborn, p. 87.

44

and move there, but things went from bad to worse. Through endorsing a note for a friend, one of his best pieces of farm property was attached, put up at auction and bought by a neighbor. Brown, on legal advice, sought to retain possession, but was arrested and placed in the Akron jail. The property was lost. Legal bankruptcy followed in October, 1842, but Brown would not take the full advantage of it. He gave the New England Woolen Company of Rockville, Conn., a note declaring that "whereas I, John Brown, on or about the 15th day of June, a. d. 1839, received of the New England Company (through their agent, George Kellogg, Esq.) the sum of twenty-eight hundred dollars for the purchase of wool for said company, and imprudently pledged the same for my own benefit and could not redeem it; and whereas I have been legally discharged from my obligations by the laws of the United States — I hereby agree (in consideration of the great kindness and tenderness of said company toward me in my calamity, and more particularly of the moral obligation I am under to render to all their due) to pay the same and the interest thereon from time to time as divine Providence shall enable me to do."*

He wrote Mr. Kellogg at the same time: "I am sorry to say that in consequence of the unforeseen expense of getting the discharge, the loss of an ox, and the destitute condition in which a new surrender of my effects has placed me, with my numerous family, I fear this year must pass without my effecting in the way of payment what I have encouraged you to expect."** He was still paying this debt when he died and left fifty dollars toward it in his will.

It was a labyrinth of disaster in which the soul of John Brown was well-nigh choked and lost. We hear him now and then gasping for breath: "I have been careful and troubled with so much serving that I have in a great measure neglected the one thing needful, and pretty much stopped all

* Agreement quoted in Sanborn, pp. 55–56.
** Letter to George Kellogg, 1844, in Sanborn, p. 56.

45

correspondence with heaven."* He goes on to tell his son: "My worldly business has borne heavily and still does; but we progress some, have our sheep sheared, and have done something at our haying. Have our tanning business going on in about the same proportion — that is, we are pretty fairly behind in business and feel that I must nearly or quite give up one or the other of the branches for want of regular troops on whom to depend."** He again tells his son: "I would send you some money, but I have not yet received a dollar from any source since you left. I should not be so dry of funds, could I but overtake my work;"*** and then follows the teeth-gritting word of a man whose grip is slipping: "But all is well; all is well."****

Gradually matters began to mend. His tannery, perhaps never wholly abandoned, was started again and his wool interests increased. Early in 1844 "we seem to be overtaking our business in the tannery," he says, and "I have lately entered into a co-partnership with Simon Perkins, Jr., of Akron, with a view of carrying on the sheep business extensively. He is to furnish all the feed and shelter for wintering, as a set-off against our taking all the care of the flock. All other expenses we are to share equally, and to divide the property equally." John Brown and his family were to move to Akron and he says: "I think that is the most comfortable and the most favorable arrangement of my worldly concerns that I ever had and calculated to afford us more leisure for improvement by day and by night than any other. I do hope that God has enabled us to make it in mercy to us, and not that He should send leanness into our souls. Our time will all be at our own command, except the care of the flock. We have nothing to do with providing for them in the winter, excepting harvesting rutabagas and potatoes. This I think

* Letter to John Brown, Jr., 1843, in Sanborn, p. 58.
** *Ibid.*, pp. 58–59.
*** *Ibid.*, p. 59.
**** *Ibid.*, p. 59.

will be considered no mean alliance for our family and I most earnestly hope they will have wisdom given to make the most of it. It is certainly endorsing the poor bankrupt and his family, three of whom were but recently in Akron jail in a manner quite unexpected, and proves that notwithstanding we have been a company of 'belted knights,' our industrious and steady endeavors to maintain our integrity and our character have not been wholly overlooked."*

Indeed, the offer seemed to John Brown a flood of light: a beloved occupation with space and time to think, to study and to dream, to get acquainted with himself and the world after the long struggle for bread and butter and the deep disappointment of failure almost in sight of success. By July, 1844, Brown was reporting 560 lambs raised and 2,700 pounds of wool, for which he had been offered fifty-six cents a pound, showing it to be of high grade. He began closing up his tanning business. "The general aspect of our worldly affairs is favorable. Hope we do not entirely forget God,"** he writes.

His daughter says: "As a shepherd, he showed the same watchful care over his sheep. I remember one spring a great many of his sheep had a disease called 'grub in the head,' and when the lambs came, the ewes would not own them. For two weeks he did not go to bed, but sat up or slept an hour or two at a time in his chair, and then would take a lantern, go out and catch the ewes, and hold them while the lambs sucked. He would very often bring in a little dead-looking lamb, and put it in warm water and rub it until it showed signs of life, and then wrap it in a warm blanket, feed it warm milk with a teaspoon, and work over it with such tenderness that in a few hours it would be capering around the room. One Monday morning I had just got my white clothes in a nice warm suds in the wash-tub, when he came in bringing a little dead-looking lamb. There seemed

* Letter to John Brown, Jr., 1844, in Sanborn, pp. 59–60.
** *Ibid.*, p. 61.

to be no sign of life about it. Said he, 'Take out your clothes quick, and let me put this lamb in the water.' I felt a little vexed to be hindered with my washing, and told him I didn't believe he could make it live; but in an hour or two he had it running around the room, and calling loudly for its mother. The next year he came from the barn and said to me, 'Ruth, that lamb I hindered you with when you were washing, I have just sold for one hundred dollars.' It was a pure-blooded Saxony lamb."*

By 1845 wealth again seemed all but within the grasp of John Brown. The country was entering fully upon one of the most remarkable of many noteworthy periods of industrial expansion and the situation in the wool business was particularly favorable. The flock of Saxony sheep owned by Perkins and Brown was "said to be the finest and most perfect flock in the United States and worth about $20,000." The only apparent danger to the prosperity of the western wool-growers was the increasing power of the manufacturers and their desire for cheap wool. The tariff on woolen goods was lower than formerly, but until wartime, remained at about twenty to thirty per cent. *ad valorem,* which afforded sufficient protection. The tariff on cheap wool decreased until, in 1857, all wool costing less than twenty cents a pound came in free and in 1854 Canadian wool of all grades was admitted without duty. This meant practically free trade in wool. The manufacturers of hosiery and carpets increased and the demand for domestic wool was continually growing. There were, however, many difficulties in realizing just prices for domestic wool: it was bought up by the manufacturer's agents, dealing with isolated, untrained farmers and offering the lowest prices; it was bought in bulk ungraded and as wool differs enormously in quality and price, the lowest grade often set the price for all. No sooner did John Brown grasp the details of the wool business than he began to work out plans of amelioration.

* Ruth Brown in Sanborn, p. 95.

And he conceived of this amelioration not as measured simply in personal wealth. To him business was a philanthropy. We have not even to-day reached this idea, but, urged on by the Socialists, we are faintly perceiving it. Brown proposed nothing Quixotic or unpractical, but he did propose a more equitable distribution of the returns of the whole wool business between the producers of the raw material and the manufacturers. He proceeded first to arouse and organize the wool-growers. He traveled extensively among the farmers of Pennsylvania and Ohio. "I am out among the wool-growers, with a view to next summer's operations," he writes March 24, 1846; "our plan seems to meet with general favor." And then thinking of greater plans he adds: "Our unexampled success in minor affairs might be a lesson to us of what unity and perseverance might do in things of some importance."* For what indeed were sheep as compared with men, and money weighed with liberty?

The plan outlined by Brown before a convention of wool-growers involved the placing of a permanent selling agent in the East, the grading and warehousing of the wool, and a pooling of profits according to the quality of the fleece. The final result was that in 1846 Perkins and Brown sent out a circular, saying: "The undersigned, commission wool-merchants, wool-graders, and exporters, have completed arrangements for receiving wool of growers and holders, and for grading and selling the same for cash at its real value, when quality and condition are considered."**

John Brown was put in special charge of this business while his son ran the sheep farm in Ohio. The idea underlying this movement was excellent and it was soon started successfully. John Brown went to live in Springfield with his family. In December, 1846, he writes: "We are getting along with our business slowly, but prudently, I trust, and

* Letter to John Brown, Jr., 1846, in Sanborn, p. 62.
** Circular issued in 1846, quoted in Sanborn, p. 63.

as well as we could reasonably expect under all the circumstances; and so far as we can discover, we are in favor with this people, and also with the many we have had to do business with."*

In two weeks during 1847 he has "turned about four thousand dollars' worth of wool into cash since I returned; shall probably make it up to seven thousand by the 16th."**

Yet great as was this initial prosperity, the business eventually failed and was practically given up in 1851. Why? It was because of one of those strange economic paradoxes which bring great moral questions into the economic realm; — questions which we evaded yesterday and are trying to evade to-day, but which we must answer to-morrow. Here was a man doing what every one knew was for the best interests of a great industry, — grading and improving the quality of its raw material and systematizing its sale. His methods were absolutely honest, his technical knowledge was unsurpassed and his organization efficient. Yet a combination of manufacturers forced him out of business in a few months. Why? The ordinary answer of current business ethics would be that John Brown was unable to "corner" the wool market against the manufacturers. But this he never tried to do. Such a policy of financial freebooting never occurred to him, and he would have repelled it indignantly if it had. He wished to force neither buyer nor seller. He was offering worthy goods at a fair price and making a just return for them. That this system was best for the whole trade every one knew, yet it was weak. It was weak in the same sense that the merchants of the Middle Ages were weak against the lawless onslaughts of robber barons. Any compact organization of manufacturers could force John Brown to take lower prices for his wool — that is, to allow the farmer a smaller proportion of the profit of the business of clothing human beings. In other words, well-

* Letter to Owen Brown, 1846, in Sanborn, p. 22.
** Letter to John Brown, Jr., 1847, in Sanborn, p. 143.

organized industrial highwaymen could hold up the wool farmer and make him hand over some of his earnings. But John Brown knew, as did, indeed, the manufacturing gentlemen of the road that the farmers were getting only moderate returns. It was the millmen who made fortunes. Now it was possible to oppose the highwaymen's demand by counter organization like the Middle-Age Hanse. The difficulty here would be to bring all the threatened parties into an organization. They could be forced in by killing off or starving out the ignorant or recalcitrant. This is the modern business method. Its result is arraying two industrial armies in a battle whose victims are paupers and prostitutes, and whose victory comes by compromising, whereby a half-dozen millionaires are born to the philanthropic world.

On the other hand, to offer no opposition to organized economic aggression is to depend on the simple justice of your cause in an industrial world that recognizes no justice. It means industrial death and that was what it meant to John Brown. The Tariff of 1846 had cut the manufacturers' profits. The growing woolen trade would more than recoup them in a few years, but they "were not in business for their health"; that is, they recognized no higher moral law than money-making and therefore determined to keep present profits where they were, and add possible future profits to them. They continued their past efforts to force down the price of wool and got practical free trade in wool by 1854. Meantime local New England manufacturers began to boycott John Brown. They expected him to see his danger and lower his prices on the really fine grades he carried. He was obdurate. His prices were right and he thought justice counted in the wool business. The manufacturers objected. He was not playing according to the rules of the game. He was, as a fellow merchant complained, "no *trader:* he waited until his wools were graded and then fixed a price; if this suited the manufacturers they took the fleeces; if not, they bought elsewhere. ... Yet he was a scrupulously honest and upright man — hard and inflexible, but everybody had just what belonged to him. Brown was in a position to make a fortune and a regular bred merchant would have done so."*

Thereupon the combination turned the screws a little closer. Brown's clerks were bribed, and other "competitive" methods resorted to. But Brown was inflexible and serene. The prospect of great wealth did not tempt but rather repelled him. Indeed this whole warehouse business, successful and important as it had hitherto been, was drawing him away from his plans of larger usefulness. It took his time and thought, and his surroundings more and more made it mere money-getting. The manufacturers were after dollars, of course; his clients were waiting simply for returns, and his partner was ever anxiously scanning the balance-sheet. This whole aspect of things more and more disquieted Brown. He therefore writes soberly in December, 1847:

"Our business seems to be going on middling well and will not probably be any the worse for the pinch in the money concerns. I trust that getting or losing money does not entirely engross our attention; but I am sensible that it quite occupies too large a share in it. To get a little property together to leave, as the world would have done, is really a low mark to be firing at through life.

"'A nobler toil may I sustain,
A nobler satisfaction gain.'"**

The next year, however, came a severe money pressure, "one of the severest known for many years. The consequence to us has been, that some of those who have contracted for wool of us are as yet unable to pay for and take the wool as they agreed, and we are on that account unable to close our business."*** This brought a fall in the price and complaint on all sides: on the part of the wool-growers, because their profits were not continuing to rise; and from manufacturers

* E. C. Leonard in Sanborn, p. 65.
** Letter to Owen Brown, 1847, in Sanborn, pp. 23–24.
*** Letter to Owen Brown, 1849, in Sanborn, p. 25

who demurred more and more clamorously at the prices demanded by Brown.

He writes early in 1849: "We have been selling wool middling fast of late, on contract, at 1847 prices"; but he adds, scenting the coming storm: "We have in this part of the country the strongest proofs that the great majority have made gold their hope, their only hope."*

Evidently a crisis was approaching. The boycott against the firm was more evident and the impatience of wool farmers growing. The latter kept calling for advances on their stored wool. If they had been willing to wait quietly, there was still a chance, for Perkins and Brown had undoubtedly the best in the American market and as good as the better English grades. But the growers were restive and in some cases poor. The result was shown in the balance-sheet of 1849. Brown had bought 130,000 pounds of wool and paid for it, including freight and commissions, $57,884.48. His sales had amounted to $49,902.67, leaving him $7,981.81 short, and 200,000 pounds of wool in the warehouse.** Perkins afterward thought Brown was stubborn. It would have been easily possible for them to have betrayed the growers and accepted a lower price. Their commissions would have been larger, the manufacturers were friendly, and the sheepmen too scattered and poor to protest. Indeed, low prices and cash pleased them better than waiting. But John Brown conceived that a principle was at stake. He knew that his wool was worth even more than he asked. He knew that English wool of the same grade sold at good prices. Why not, then, he argued, take the wool to England and sell it, thus opening up a new market for a great American product? Then, too, he had other and, to him, better reasons for wishing to see Europe. He decided quickly and in August, 1849, he took his 200,000 pounds of wool to England. He had graded every bit himself, and packed it in new

---

* Letter to Owen Brown, 1849, in Sanborn, p. 25.
** Memoranda by John Brown, in Sanborn, p. 65; Redpath, p. 56.

sacks: "The bales were firm, round, hard and true, almost as if they had been turned out in a lathe."*

In this English venture John Brown showed one weakness of his character: he did not know or recognize the subtler twistings of human nature. He judged it ever from his own simple, clear standpoint and so had a sort of prophetic vision of the vaster and the eternal aspects of the human soul. But of its kinks and prejudices, its little selfishnesses and jealousies and dishonesties, he knew nothing. They always came to him as a sort of surprise, uncalculated for and but partially comprehended. He could fight the devil and his angels, and he did, but he could not cope with the million misbirths that hover between heaven and hell.

Thus to his surprise he found his calculations all at fault in England. His wool was good, his knowledge of the technique of sorting and grading unsurpassed and yet because Englishmen believed it was not possible to raise good wool in America, they obstinately refused to take the evidence of their own senses. They "seemed highly pleased"; they said that they "had never seen superior wools" and that they "would see me again" but they did not offer decent prices. Then, too, American woolen men had long arms and they were tipped with gold. They fingered busily across the seas about this prying Yankee, and English wool-growers responded very willingly, so that John Brown acknowledged mournfully late in September, "I have a great deal of stupid obstinate prejudice to contend with, as well as conflicting interests both in this country and from the United States."** In the end the wool was sacrificed at prices fifty per cent. below its American value and some of it actually resold in America. The American woolen men chuckled audibly:

"A little incident occurred in 1850. Perkins and Brown's clip had come forward, and it was beautiful; the little compact Saxony fleeces were as nice as possible. Mr. Musgrave

* Sanborn, pp. 67–68.
** Letter to John Brown, Jr., 1849, Sanborn, p. 73

of the Northampton Woolen Mill, who was making shawls and broadcloths, wanted it, and offered Uncle John (Brown) sixty cents a pound for it. 'No, I am going to send it to London.' Musgrave, who was a Yorkshire man, advised Brown not to do it, for American wool would not sell in London, — not being thought good. He tried hard to buy it, but without avail. ... Some little time after, long enough for the purpose, news came that it was sold in London, but the price was not stated. Musgrave came into my counting-room one forenoon all aglow, and said he wanted me to go with him, — he was going to have some fun. Then he went to the stairs and called Uncle John, and told him he wanted him to go over to the Hartford depot and see a lot of wool he had bought. So Uncle John put on his coat, and we started. When we arrived at the depot, and just as we were going into the freight-house, Musgrave says: 'Mr. Brune, I want you to tell me what you think of this lot of wull that stands me in just fifty-two cents a pund.' One glance at the bags was enough. Uncle John wheeled, and I can see him now as he 'put back' to the lofts, his brown coat-tails floating behind him, and the nervous strides fairly devouring the way. It was his own clip, for which Musgrave, some three months before, had offered him sixty cents a pound as it lay in the loft. It had been graded, new bagged, shipped by steamer to London, sold, and reshipped, and was in Springfield at eight cents in the pound less than Musgrave offered."*

It was a great joke and it made American woolen men smile.

This English venture was a death-blow to the Perkins and Brown wool business. It was not entirely wound up until four years later, but in 1849 Brown removed his family from Springfield up to the silent forests of the farthest Adirondacks, where the great vision of his life unfolded itself. It was, however, not easy for him to extricate himself from the web wound about him. Two currents set for his com-

* E. C. Leonard, in Sanborn, pp. 67–68.

plete undoing: the wool-growers whom he had over-advanced and who did not deliver the promised wool; and certain manufacturers to whom the firm had contracted to deliver this wool which they could not get. Claims and damages to the amount of $40,000 appeared and some of these got into court; while, on the other hand, the scattered and defaulting wool-growers were scarcely worth suing by the firm. Long drawn-out legal battles ensued, intensely distasteful to Brown's straightforward nature and seemingly endless. Collections and sales continued hard and slow and Perkins began to get restless. John Brown sighed for the older and simpler life of his young manhood with its love and dreams: "I can look back to our log cabin at the centre of Richfield with a supper of porridge and johnny cake as a place of far more interest to me than the Massasoit of Springfield."* He says to his children on the Ohio sheep farm: "I am much pleased with the reflection that you are all three once more together, and all engaged in the same calling that the old patriarchs followed. I will say but one word more on that score, and that is taken from their history: 'See that ye fall not out by the way; and all will be exactly right in the end.' I should think matters were brightening a little in this direction in regard to our claims, but I have not yet been able to get any of them to a final issue. I think, too, that the prospect for the fine wool business rather improves. What burdens me most of all is the apprehension that Mr. Perkins expects of me in the way of bringing matters to a close, what no living man can possibly bring about in a short time and that he is getting out of patience and becoming distrustful."**

Meantime Brown was racing from court to court in Boston, New York, Troy and elsewhere, seeking to settle up the business and know where he stood financially, and, above all, to keep peace with and do justice to his partner. Cases were now settled and now appealed and the progress was

* Letter to his wife, 1850, in Sanborn, p. 107.
** Letter to his children, 1850, in Sanborn, pp. 75–76.

"miserably slow. My journeys back and forth this winter have been very tedious." Then, too, his mind was elsewhere. The nation was in turmoil and so was he. At the time Anthony Burns was arrested in Boston he was advising with his lawyers at Troy. Redpath says:

"The morning after the news of the Burns affair reached here, Brown went at his work immediately after breakfast; but in a few minutes started up from his chair, walked rapidly across the room several times, then suddenly turned to his counsel, and said, 'I am going to Boston.' 'Going to Boston!' said the astonished lawyer. 'Why do you want to go to Boston?' Old Brown continued walking vigorously, and replied, 'Anthony Burns must be released, or I will die in the attempt.' The counsel dropped his pen in consternation. Then he began to remonstrate; told him the suit had been in progress a long time, and a verdict just gained. It was appealed from, and that appeal must be answered in so many days, or the whole labor would be lost; and no one was sufficiently familiar with the whole case except himself. It took a long earnest talk with old Brown to persuade him to remain. His memory and acuteness in that long and tedious lawsuit — not yet ended, I am told — often astonished his counsel. While here he wore an entire suit of snuff-colored cloth, the coat of a decidedly Quakerish cut in collar and skirt. He wore no beard, and was a clean-shaven, scrupulously neat, well-dressed, quiet old gentleman. He was, however, notably resolute in all that he did."*

He spent the time not taken up by his lawsuits at Akron, and in the manner of a patriarch of old, temporarily brought his family back to Ohio. "I wrote you last week that the family is on the road: the boys are driving on the cattle, and my wife and little girls are at Oneida depot waiting for me to go on with them."** He returned to farming again with interest, taking prizes for his stock at state fairs and raising

* Redpath, p. 58.
** Letter to his son, in Sanborn, p. 145.

many sheep. He had 550 lambs in 1853 and Perkins is urging him to continue with him, but things changed and on January 25, 1854, he writes: "This world is not yet freed from real malice and envy. It appears to be well settled now that we go back to North Elba in the spring. I have had a good-natured talk with Mr. Perkins about going away and both families are now preparing to carry out that plan."*

His departure was delayed a year, but he was finally able to remove with a little surplus on hand.

Back then to the crests and forests of the Alleghanies came John Brown at the age of fifty-four. "A tall, gaunt, dark-complexioned man ... a grave, serious man ... with a marked countenance and a natural dignity of manner, — that dignity which is unconscious, and comes from a superior habit of mind."**

---

* Letter to his children, 1854, in Sanborn, p. 155.
** R. H. Dana, in the *Atlantic Monthly*, 1871.

V

The Vision of the Damned

"Remember them that are in bonds as bound with them."

There was hell in Hayti in the red waning of the eighteenth century, in the days when John Brown was born. The dark wave of the French Revolution had raised the brilliant sinister Napoleon to its crest. Already he had stretched greedy arms toward American empire in the rich vale of the Mississippi, when in a flash, out of the dirt and sloth and slavery of the West Indies, the black inert and heavy cloud of African degradation writhed to sudden life and lifted up the dark figure of Toussaint. Ten thousand Frenchmen gasped and died in the fever-haunted hills, while the black men in sudden frenzy fought like devils for their freedom and won it. Napoleon saw his gateway to the Mississippi closed; armed Europe was at his back. What was this wild and empty America to him, anyway? So he sold Louisiana for a song and turned to the shame of Trafalgar and the glory of Austerlitz.

John Brown was born just as the shudder of Hayti was running through all the Americas, and from his earliest boyhood he saw and felt the price of repression — the fearful cost that the western world was paying for slavery. From his earliest boyhood he had dimly conceived, and the conception grew with his growing, that the cost of liberty was less than the price of repression. Perhaps he was so near the humanistic enthusiasm of the French Revolution that he undervalued the cost of liberty. But yet he was right, for it was scarce possible to overrate the price of repression. True, in these latter days men and women of the South, and honest ones, too, have striven feverishly to paint Negro slavery in bright alluring colors. They have told of childlike devotion, faithful service and light-hearted irresponsibility, in the fine old aristocracy of the plantation. Much they have said is true. But when all is said and granted, the awful fact remains congealed in law and indisputable record that American slavery was the foulest and filthiest blot on nineteenth century civilization. As a school of brutality and human suffering, of female prostitution and male debauchery; as a mockery of marriage and defilement of family life; as a darkening of reason, and spiritual death, it had no parallel in its day. It took millions upon millions of men — human men and lovable, light and liberty-loving children of the sun, and threw them with no sparing of brutality into one rigid mold: humble, servile, dog-like devotion, surrender of body, mind and soul, and unaspiring animal content — toward this ideal the slave might strive, and did. Wonderful, even beautiful examples of humble service he brought forth and made the eternal heritage of men. But beyond this there was nothing. All were crushed to this mold and of them that did not fit, the sullen were cowed. the careless brutalized and the rebellious killed. Four things make life worthy to most men: to move, to know, to love, to aspire. None of these was for Negro slaves. A white child could halt a black man on the highway and send him slinking to his kennel. No black slave could legally learn to read. And love? If a black slave loved a lass, there was not a white man from the Potomac to the Rio Grande that could not prostitute her to his lust. Did the proud sons of Virginia and Carolina stoop to such bestial tyranny? Ask the grandmothers of the two million mulattoes that dot the states to-day. Ask the suffering and humiliated wives of the master caste. If a Negro married a wife, there was not a master in the land that could not take her from him.

John Brown's father, Owen Brown, saw such a power stretched all the way from Virginia to Connecticut. A Southern slaveholding minister, Thomson by name, had brought his slaves North and preached in the local church. Then he attempted to take the unwilling chattels back South. Of what followed, Owen Brown says: "There was some excitement amongst the people, some in favor and some against Mr.

Thomson; there was quite a debate, and large numbers to hear. Mr. Thomson said he should carry the woman and children, whether he could get the man or not. An old man asked him if he would part man and wife, contrary to their minds. He said: 'I married them myself, and did not enjoin obedience on the woman.'" Owen Brown added, "Ever since I have been an Abolitionist."*

If a slave begat children, there was not a law south of the Ohio that could stop their eventual sale to any brute with the money. Aspiration in a slave was suspicious, dangerous, fatal. For him there was no inviting future, no high incentive, no decent reward. The highest ambition to which a black woman could aspire was momentarily to supplant the white man's wife as a concubine; and the ambition of black men ended with the carelessly tossed largess of a kinglet. To reduce the slave to this groveling, what was the price which the master paid? Tyranny, brutality, and lawlessness reigned and to some extent still reign in the South. The sweeter, kindlier feelings were blunted: brothers sold sisters to serfdom and fathers debauched even their own dark daughters. The arrogant, strutting bully, who shot his enemy and thrashed his dogs and his darkies, became a living, moving ideal from the cotton-patch to the United States Senate from 1808 onward. No worthy art nor literature, nor even the commerce of daily life could thrive in this atmosphere.

Society there was of a certain type — courtly and lavish, but quarrelsome; seductive and lazy; with a half Oriental sheen and languor spread above peculiar poverty of resource; a fineness and delicacy in certain details, coupled with coarseness and self-indulgence in others; a mingling of the sexes only in play and seldom in work, with its concomitant tendency toward seclusion and helplessness among its whiter women. Withal a society strong indeed, but wholly without vigor or invention.

It was not all as dark as it might have been. Human life,

* Owen Brown, in Sanborn, pp. 10–11.

thank God, is never as bad as it may be, but it is too often desperately bad. Nor do men easily realize how bad life about them is. The full have scant sympathy with the empty, — the rich know all the faults of the poor, and the master sees the horrors of slavery with unseeing eyes. True, there were flashes of light and longing here and there — noble sacrifice, eager help, determined emancipation. But all this was local, spasmodic and exceptional. The unrelenting dead brutality of human bondage to a thousand tyrants, petty wills and caprice was the rule from Florida to Missouri and from the Mississippi to the sea. Under it the wretched writhed like some great black and stricken beast. The flaming fury of their mad attempts at vengeance echoes all down the blood-swept path of slavery. In Jamaica they upturned the government and harried the land until England crept and sued for peace. In the Danish Isles they started a whirlwind of slaughter; in Hayti they drove their masters into the sea; and in South Carolina they rose twice like a threatening wave against the terror-stricken whites, but were betrayed. Such outbreaks here and there foretold the possibility of coördinate action and organic development. To be sure, the successful outbreaks were few and spasmodic; but the flare of Hayti lighted the night and made the world remember that these, too, were men.

Among these black men, changes significant and momentous, were coming. The native born Africans were passing away, with their native tongues and their wild customs. Such were the slaves of John Brown's father's time. "When I was a child four or five years old," writes Owen Brown, "one of the nearest neighbors had a slave that was brought from Guinea. In the year 1776 my father was called into the army at New York, and left his work undone. In August, our good neighbor, Captain John Fast, of West Simsbury, let my mother have the labor of his slave to plough a few days. I used to go out into the field with this slave, — called Sam, — and he used to carry me on his back, and I fell in love with him. He worked but a few days, and went home sick with the pleurisy, and died very suddenly. When told that he would die, he said he should go to Guinea, and wanted victuals put up for the journey. As I recollect, this was the first funeral I ever attended in the days of my youth."

Such slaves and others went into the Revolutionary army and three thousand of them fought for their masters' freedom. After the war, their bravery, the upheaval in Hayti, and the new enthusiasm for human rights, led to a wave of emancipation which started in Vermont during the Revolution and swept through New England and Pennsylvania, ending finally in New York and New Jersey early in the nineteenth century. This freeing of the Northern slaves led to new complications, for in the South, after a hesitating pause, the opposite course was pursued and the thumbscrews were applied; the plantations were isolated, the roads were guarded, the refractory were whipped till they screamed and crawled, and the ringleaders were lynched. A long awful process of selection chose out the listless, ignorant, sly, and humble and sent to heaven the proud, the vengeful and the daring. The old African warrior spirit died away of violence and a broken heart.

Thus the great black mass of Southern slaves were cowed, but they were not conquered. Stretched as they were over wide miles of land, and isolated; guarded in speech and religion; peaceful and light-hearted as was their nature, still the fire of liberty burned in them. In Louisiana and Tennessee and twice in Virginia they raised the night cry of revolt, and once slew fifty Virginians, holding the state for weeks at bay there in those same Alleghanies which John Brown loved and listened to. On the ships of the sea they rebelled and murdered; to Florida they fled and turned like beasts on their pursuers till whole armies dislodged them and did them to death in the everglades; and again and again over them and through them surged and quivered a vast unrest which only the eternal vigilance of the masters kept down. Yet the fear of that great bound beast was ever there — a nameless, haunting dread that never left the South and never ceased, but ever nerved the remorseless cruelty of the master's arm.

One thing saved the South from the blood-sacrifice of Hayti — not, to be sure, from so successful a revolt, for the disproportion of races was less, but from a desperate and bloody effort — and that was the escape of the fugitive.

Along the Great Black Way stretched swamps and rivers, and the forests and crests of the Alleghanies. A widening, hurrying stream of fugitives swept to the havens of refuge, taking the restless, the criminal and the unconquered — the natural leaders of the more timid mass. These men saved slavery and killed it. They saved it by leaving it to a false seductive dream of peace and the eternal subjugation of the laboring class. They destroyed it by presenting themselves before the eyes of the North and the world as living speci-mens of the real meaning of slavery. What was the system that could enslave a Frederick Douglass? They saved it too by joining the free Negroes of the North, and with them organizing themselves into a great black phalanx that worked and schemed and paid and finally fought for the freedom of black men in America.

Thus it was that John Brown, even as a child, saw the puzzling anomalies and contradictions in human right and liberty all about him. Ever and again he saw this in the North, leading to concerted action among the free Negroes, especially in cities where they were brought in contact with one another, and had some chance of asserting their nominal freedom. Just at the close of the eighteenth century, first in Philadelphia and then in New York, small groups of them withdrew from the white churches to escape disgraceful discrimination and established churches of their own, which still live with millions of adherents. In the year of John Brown's birth, 1800, Gabriel planned his formidable uprising in Virginia, and the year after his marriage, 1821, Denmark Vesey of South Carolina went grimly to the scaffold, after one of the shrewdest Negro plots that ever frightened the South into hysterics. Of all this John Brown, the boy and young man, knew little. In after years he learned of Gabriel and Vesey and Turner, and told of their exploits and studied their plans; but at the time he was far off from the world, carrying on his tannery and marrying a wife. Perhaps as a lad he heard some of the oratory that celebrated the act of 1808, stopping the slave trade, as the beginning of the end of slavery. Perhaps not, for the act did little good until it was reënforced in 1820. All the time, however, John Brown's keen eyes were searching for the way of life and his tender heart was sensitive to injustice and wrong everywhere. Indeed, it is not unlikely that the first black folk to gain his aid and sympathies and direct his thoughts to what afterward became his life-work, were the fugitive slaves from the South.

Three paths were opened to the slaves: to submit, to fight or to run away. Most of them submitted as do most people everywhere to force and fate. To fight singly meant death and to fight together meant plot and insurrection — a difficult thing but one often tried. Easiest of all was to run away, for the land was wide and bare and the slaves were many. At first, they ran to the swamps and mountains, and starved and died. Then they ran to the Indians and in Florida founded a nation to overthrow which cost the United States $20,000,000 and more in slave raids known as Seminole "wars." Then gradually, after the War of 1812 had used so many black sailors to fight for free trade that the Negroes learned of the North and Canada as cities of refuge, they fled northward. While John Brown was a tanner at Hudson, he began helping these dark panting refugees who flitted by in the night. His eldest son says:

"When I was four or five years old, and probably no later than 1825, there came one night a fugitive slave and his wife to father's door — sent, perhaps, by some townsman who knew John Brown's compassion for such wayfarers, then but few. They were the first colored people I had seen; and when the woman took me upon her knee and kissed me, I ran away as quick as I could, and rubbed my face 'to get the black off'; for I thought she would 'crock' me, like mother's kettle. Mother gave the poor creatures some supper; but they thought themselves pursued and were uneasy. Presently father heard the trampling of horses crossing a bridge on one of the main roads, half a mile off; so he took his guests out the back door and down into the swamp near the brook to hide, giving them arms to defend themselves, but returning to the house to await the event. It proved a false alarm; the horsemen were people of the neighborhood going to Hudson village. Father then went out into the dark wood, — for it was night, — and had some difficulty in finding his fugitives; finally he was guided to the spot by the sound of the man's heart throbbing for fear of capture. He brought them into the house again, sheltered them a while, and sent them on their way."*

The atmosphere in these days was becoming more and more charged with the slavery problem. That same Louisiana which Toussaint had given America, was gradually filling with settlers until the question of admitting parts of it as states faced the nation, and led to the Missouri Compromise. The discussion of the measure was fierce in John Brown's neighborhood, and it must have strengthened his dislike of slavery and turned his earnest mind more and more toward the Negroes.

In the very year that death first entered his family and took a boy of four, and just before the sombre days when his earnest young wife died demented in childbirth and was buried with her babe, occurred the Nat Turner insurrection in Virginia, the most successful and bloody of slave uprisings since Hayti.

Squire Hudson, the father of the town where John Brown lived and one of the founders of Western Reserve University, heard the news in stern joy; a neighbor met him "one day in September, 1831, coming from his post-office, and reading a newspaper he had just received, which seemed to

* John Brown, Jr., in Sanborn, p. 35.

excite him very much as he read. As Mr. Wright came within hearing, the old Calvinist was exclaiming, 'Thank God for that! I am glad of it! Thank God they have risen at last!' Inquiring what the news was, Squire Hudson replied, 'Why, the slaves have risen down in Virginia, and are fighting for their freedom as we did for ours. I pray God that they may get it.'"*

They did not get freedom but death. And yet there on the edge of Dismal Swamp they slaughtered fifty whites, held the land in terror for more than a month, and set going a tremendous wave of reaction. In the South, Negro churches and free Negro schools were sternly restricted, just at the time Great Britain was freeing her West Indian slaves. In the North, came two movements: a determined anti-slavery campaign, and an opposing movement which disfranchised Negroes, burned their churches and schools, and robbed them of their friends. The Negroes rushed together for counsel and defense, and held their first national meeting in Philadelphia, where they deliberated earnestly on migration to Canada and on schools. But schools for Negroes were especially feared North as well as South, and in John Brown's native state of Connecticut a white woman was shamefully persecuted for attempting to teach Negroes. All this aroused John Brown's antipathy to slavery and made it more definite and purposeful. In November of the year which witnessed the burning of Prudence Crandall's school, and a year after his second marriage, he wrote to his brother:

"Since you have left me, I have been trying to devise some means whereby I might do something in a practical way for my poor fellow men who are in bondage; and having fully consulted the feelings of my wife and my three boys, we have agreed to get at least one Negro boy or youth, and bring him up as we do our own, — viz., give him a good English education, learn him what we can about the history of the world, about business, about general subjects, and,

* Sanborn, p. 34.

67

above all, try to teach him the fear of God. We think of three ways to obtain one: First, to try to get some Christian slaveholder to release one to us. Second, to get a free one, if no one will let us have one that is a slave. Third, if that does not succeed, we have all agreed to submit to considerable privation in order to buy one. This we are now using means in order to effect, in the confident expectation that God is about to bring them all out of the house of bondage.

"I will just mention that when this subject was first introduced, Jason had gone to bed; but no sooner did he hear the thing hinted, than his warm heart kindled, and he turned out to have a part in the discussion of a subject of such exceeding interest. I have for years been trying to devise some way to get a school a-going here for blacks, and I think that on many accounts it would be a most favorable location. Children here would have no intercourse with vicious people of their own kind, nor with openly vicious persons of any kind. There would be no powerful opposition influence against such a thing; and should there be any, I believe the settlement might be so effected in future as to have almost the whole influence of the place in favor of such a school. Write me how you would like to join me, and try to get on from Hudson and thereabouts some first-rate Abolitionist families with you. I do honestly believe that our united exertions alone might soon, with the good hand of our God upon us, effect it all."*

Nothing came of this project, except that John Brown grew more deeply interested. He was now worth $20,000, a man of influence and he felt more and more moved toward definite action to help the Negroes. They were keeping up their conventions and the stream of fugitives was augmenting. The problem, however, was not simply one of slavery. The plight of the free Negro was particularly pitiable. He was liable to be seized and sold South whether an actual slave or not; he was discriminated against and de-

* Letter to his brother Frederick, 1834, in Sanborn, pp. 40–41.

spised in all walks. This was bad enough in every-day life, but to a straightforward religious soul like John Brown it was simply intolerable in the church of God. His eldest daughter says:

"One evening after he had been singing to me, he asked me how I would like to have some poor little black children that were slaves (explaining to me the meaning of slaves) come and live with us; and asked me if I would be willing to divide my food and clothes with them. He made such an impression on my sympathies, that the first colored person that I ever saw (it was a man I met on the street in Meadville, Pa.) I felt such pity for, that I wanted to ask him if he did not want to come and live at our house. When I was six or seven years old, a little incident took place in the church at Franklin, O. (of which all the older part of our family were members), which caused quite an excitement."*

His son tells the details of this incident·

"About 1837, mother, Jason, Owen and I, joined the Congregational Church at Franklin, the Rev. Mr. Burritt, pastor. Shortly after, the other societies, including Methodists and Episcopalians, joined ours in an undertaking to hold a protracted meeting under the special management of an evangelist preacher from Cleveland, named Avery. The house of the Congregationalists being the largest, it was chosen as the place for this meeting. Invitations were sent out to church folks in adjoining towns to 'come up to the help of the Lord against the mighty'; and soon the house was crowded, the assembly occupying by invitation the pews of the church generally. Preacher Avery gave us in succession four sermons from one text, — 'Cast ye up, cast ye up! Prepare ye the way of the Lord; make His paths straight!' Soon lukewarm Christians were heated up to a melting condition, and there was a bright prospect of a good shower of grace. There were at that time in Franklin a number of free colored persons and some fugitive slaves. These became interested and

* Ruth Brown, in Sanborn, p. 37.

69

came to the meetings, but were given seats by themselves, where the stove had stood, near the door, — not a good place for seeing ministers or singers. Father noticed this, and when the next meeting (which was at evening) had fairly opened, he arose and called attention to the fact that, in seating the colored portion of the audience, a discrimination had been made, and said that he did not believe God 'is a respecter of persons.' He then invited the colored people to occupy his slip. The blacks accepted, and all of our family took their vacated seats. This was a bombshell, and the Holy Spirit in the hearts of Pastor Burritt and Deacon Beach at once gave up His place to another tenant. The next day father received a call from the deacons to admonish him and 'labor' with him; but they returned with new views of Christian duty. The blacks during the remainder of that protracted meeting continued to occupy our slip, and our family the seats around the stove. We soon after moved to Hudson, and though living three miles away, became regular attendants at the Congregational Church in the centre of the town. In about a year we received a letter from good Deacon Williams, informing us that our relations with the church in Franklin were ended in accordance with a rule made by the church since we left, that 'any member being absent a year without reporting him or herself to that church should be cut off.' This was the first intimation we had of the existence of the rule. Father, on reading the letter, became white with anger. This was my first taste of the proslavery diabolism that had intrenched itself in the church, and I shed a few uncalled for tears over the matter, for instead I should have rejoiced in my emancipation. From that day my theological shackles were a good deal broken, and I have not worn them since (to speak of), — not even for ornament."*

The years of 1837 and 1838 were the years of persecution for the Abolition cause. Lovejoy was murdered in Illinois

* John Brown, Jr., in Sanborn, pp. 52–53.

and mobs raged in Massachusetts and Pennsylvania. Pennsylvania Hall, in Philadelphia, was burned, and Marlborough Chapel in Boston, where John Brown himself seems to have been present fighting back the people, was sacked. Indeed, as he afterward said, he had seen some of the "principal Abolition mobs."

Whatever John Brown may have wished to do at this time was frustrated by the panic, which swept away his fortune, and left him bankrupt. Yet something he must do — he must at least promise God that he and his family would eternally oppose slavery. How, he did not know — he was not sure — but somehow he was determined, and his old idea of educating youth was still uppermost.

It was in 1839, when a Negro preacher named Fayette was visiting Brown, and bringing his story of persecution and injustice, that this great promise was made. Solemnly John Brown arose; he was then a man of nearly forty years, tall, dark and clean-shaven; by him sat his young wife of twenty-two and his oldest boys of eighteen, sixteen and fifteen. Six other children slept in the room back of the dark preacher. John Brown told them of his purpose to make active war on slavery, and bound his family in solemn and secret compact to labor for emancipation. And then, instead of standing to pray, as was his wont, he fell upon his knees and implored God's blessing on his enterprise.

This marks a turning-point in John Brown's life: in his boyhood he had disliked slavery and his antipathy toward it grew with his years; yet of necessity it occupied but little of a life busy with breadwinning. Gradually, however, he saw the gathering of the mighty struggle about him; the news of the skirmish battles of the greatest moral war of the century aroused and quickened him, and all the more when they struck the tender chords of his acquaintanceships and sympathies. He saw his friends hurt and imposed on until at last, gradually, then suddenly, it dawned upon him that he must fight this monster slavery. He did not now plan physical warfare — he was yet a non-resistant, hating war, and did not dream of Harper's Ferry; but he set his face toward the goal and whithersoever the Lord led, he was ready to follow. He still, too, had his living to earn — his family to care for. Slavery was not yet the sole object of his life, but as he passed on in his daily duties he was determined to seize every opportunity to strike it a blow.

This, at least it seems to me, is a fair interpretation of John Brown's thought and action from the evidence at hand. Some have believed that John Brown planned Harper's Ferry or something similar in 1839; others have doubted whether he had any plans against slavery before 1850. The truth probably lies between these extreme views. Human purposes grow slowly and in curious ways; thought by thought they build themselves until in their full panoplied vigor and definite outline not even the thinker can tell the exact process of the growing, or say that here was the beginning or there the ending. Nor does this slow growth and gathering make the end less wonderful or the motive less praiseworthy. Few Americans recognized in 1839 that the great central problem of America was slavery; and of that few, fewer still were willing to fight it as they knew it should be fought. Of this lesser number, two men stood almost alone, ready to back their faith by action — William Lloyd Garrison and John Brown.

These men did not then know each other — they had in these early days scarcely heard each other's names. They never came to be friends or sympathizers. When John Brown was in Boston he never went to *The Liberator* office, and in after years, now and then, he dropped words very like contempt for "non-resistants"; while Garrison flayed the leader of the Harper's Ferry raid. They were alike only in their intense hatred of slavery, and spiritually they crossed each other's paths in curious fashion, Garrison drifting from a willingness to fight slavery in all ways or in any way to a fateful attitude of non-resistance and withdrawal from the contamination of slaveholders; John Brown drifting from non-resistance to the red path of active warfare.

Nowhere did the imminence of a great struggle show itself more clearly than among the Negroes themselves. Organized insurrection ceased in the South, not because of the increased rigors of the slave system, but because the great safety-valve of escape northward was opened wider and wider, and the methods were gradually coördinated into that mysterious system known as the Underground Railroad. The slaves and freedmen started the work and to the end bore the brunt of danger and hardship; but gradually they more and more secured the coöperation of men like John Brown, and of others less radical but just as sympathetic. Here and there the free Negroes in the North began to gain economic footing as servants in cities, as farmers in Ohio and even as *entrepreneurs* in the great catering business of Philadelphia and New York.

The schools were still for the most part closed to them. They made strenuous efforts to counteract this and established dozens of schools of their own all over the land. At last in 1839 Oberlin was founded and certain earnest students of Cincinnati, disgusted with the color line at Lane College, seceded to Oberlin and brought the color question there. It was fairly met and Negroes were admitted.

It was the establishment of Oberlin College in 1839 and the appointment of his father as trustee that gave John Brown a new vision of life and usefulness — of a life which would at once combine the pursuit of a great moral ideal and the honest earning of a good living for a family. Brown proposed to survey the Virginia lands of Oberlin, as we have shown, locate a large farm for himself and settle there with his family. Here he undoubtedly expected to carry out the plan previously laid before his brother Frederick. He consulted the Oberlin authorities concerning "provision for religious and school privileges" and they thought it possible to have these, although nothing was said specifically of Negroes. The position was strategic and John Brown knew it: in the non-slaveholding portion of a slave state, near the river and not far from the foothills of mountains, beyond

73

which lay the Great Black Way, was formed a highway for the Underground Railroad and a place for experiment in the uplift of black men. That he would meet opposition, and strong opposition, John Brown must have known, but probably at this time he counted on the prevalence of law and justice and the stern principles of his religion rather than on the sword of Gideon, which was his later reliance. But it was not the "will of Providence" as we have seen, that Brown should then settle in Virginia, since his increasing financial straits and final bankruptcy overthrew all plans of purchasing the one thousand acres for which he had already bargained.

The slough of despond through which John Brown passed in the succeeding years, from 1842 to 1846, was never fully betrayed by this stern, self-repressing Puritan. Yet the loss of a fortune and the shattering of a dream, the bankruptcy and imprisonment, and the death of five children, while around him whirled the struggle of the churches with slavery and Abolition mobs, all dropped a sombre brooding veil of stern inexorable fate over his spirit — a veil which never lifted. The dark mysterious tragedy of life gripped him with awful intensity — the iron entered his soul. He became sterner and more silent. He brooded and listened for the voice of the avenging God, and girded up his loins in readiness.

"My husband always believed," said his wife in after years, "that he was to be an instrument in the hands of Providence, and I believed it too.... Many a night he had lain awake and prayed concerning it."*

It began to dawn upon him that he had sinned in the selfish pursuit of petty ends: that he must be about his Father's business of giving the death-blow to that "sum of all villanies — slavery." He had erred in making his great work a side object — a secondary thing; it must be his first and only duty, and let God attend to the nurture of his family.

* Redpath, p. 65.

As his conception of his own relation to slavery thus broadened and deepened, so too did his plan of attacking the system become clearer and more definite and he spent hours discussing the matter. In Springfield, "he used to talk much on the subject, and had the reputation of being quite ultra. His bookkeeper tells me that he and his eldest son used to discuss slavery by the hour in his counting-room, and he used to say that it was right for slaves to kill their masters and escape, and thought slaveholders were guilty of a very great wickedness."*

He studied the census returns and the distribution of the Negroes and made maps of fugitive slave routes with roads, plantations, and supplies. He learned of Isaac, Denmark Vesey, Nat Turner and the Cumberland region insurrections in South Carolina, Virginia, and Tennessee; he knew of the organized resistance to slave-catchers in Pennsylvania, and the history of Hayti and Jamaica.

It needed, as he soon saw, something more radical than schools and moral suasion; so deep-seated and radical a disease demanded "Action! Action!" He welcomed his new and long-loved calling of shepherd because of the leisure it gave him to study out his great moral problem. He sought and gained the acquaintance of Negro leaders like Garnet, Loguen, Gloucester and McCune Smith. As his sheep business broadened, he traveled about and probably at this time first saw Harper's Ferry — the mighty pass where Potomac and Shenandoah, hurling aside the mountain masses, rush to their singular wedding.

Thus the distraction of the Springfield wool business came to John Brown almost in the guise of a temptation to be shunned. For a moment about 1845 he looked again on the lure of wealth and dreamed how useful it would be to what was now his great life object. But only for a moment, for when he realized the price he must pay — the time, the chicanery, the petty detail — he turned from it in disgust. It

* Redpath, pp. 53-54.

75

was at this time that he studied the history of insurrection and became familiar with the Abolition movement; as early as 1846 his Harper's Ferry project began to form itself more or less clearly in his mind.

One thing alone reconciled him to his Springfield sojourn and that was the Negroes whom he met there. He had met black men singly here and there all his life, but now he met a group. It was not one of the principal Negro groups of the day — they were in Philadelphia and New York, Cincinnati and Boston, and in Canada, working largely alone with only imperfect intercommunication, but working manfully and effectively for emancipation and full freedom. The Springfield group was a smaller body without conspicuous leadership, and on that account more nearly approximated the great mass of their enslaved race. He sought them in home and church and out on the street, and he hired them in his business. He came to them on a plane of perfect equality — they sat at his table and he at theirs. He neither descended upon them from above nor wallowed with their lowest, and the result was that as Redpath says, "Captain Brown had a higher notion of the capacity of the Negro race than most white men. I have often heard him dwell on this subject, and mention instances of their fitness to take care of themselves, saying, in his quaint way, that 'they behaved so much like "folks" that he almost thought they were so.' He thought that perhaps a forcible separation of the connection between master and slave was necessary to educate the blacks for self-government; but this he threw out as a suggestion merely."[*]

Nor did this appreciation of the finer qualities and capacity of the Negroes blind him to their imperfections. He found them "intensely human," but with their human frailties weakened by slavery and caste; and with perfect faith in their ability to rise above their faults, he criticized and inspired them. In his quaint essay on "Sambo's Mistakes,"

[*] Redpath, pp. 59–60.

putting himself in the black man's place, he enumerates his errors: His failure to improve his time in good reading; his waste of money in indulgent luxuries and societies and consequent lack of capital; his servile occupations; his talkativeness and inaptitude for organization; his sectarian bias. In part of his arraignment, which will bear thoughtful reading to-day by black men as well as white, he makes his Sambo say:

"Another trifling error of my life has been, that I have always expected to secure the favor of the whites by tamely submitting to every species of indignity, contempt, and wrong, instead of nobly resisting their brutal aggressions from principle, and taking mv place as a man, and assuming the responsibilities of a man, a citizen, a husband, a father, a brother, a neighbor, a friend, — as God requires of every one (if his neighbor will allow him to do it); but I find that I get, for all my submission, about the same reward that the Southern slaveocrats render to the dough-faced statesmen of the North, for being bribed and browbeat and fooled and cheated, as Whigs and Democrats love to be, and think themselves highly honored if they may be allowed to lick up the spittle of a Southerner. I say to get the reward. But I am uncommon quick-sighted; I can see in a minute where I missed it."*

No one knew better than John Brown how slavery had contributed to these faults: for how many slaves could read anything, or when had they been taught the use of money or the A.B.C. of organization? Not in condemnation but in faith was this excellent paper written and delicately worded as from one who has learned his own faults and will not repeat those of others.

Not only did John Brown thus criticize, but he led these black folk. As early as 1846 he revealed something of his final plans to Thomas Thomas, his black porter and friend,

* From "Sambo's Mistakes," published in the *Ram's Horn* and printed in Sanborn, p. 130.

with whom he once was photographed in mutual friendly embrace, holding the sign "S.P.W." — "Subterranean Pass Way" of slaves to freedom.

"How early shall I come to-morrow?" asked Thomas one morning.

"We begin work at seven," answered John Brown. "But I wish you would come around earlier so that I can talk with you." Then Brown disclosed a plan of increasing and systematizing the work of the Underground Railroad by running off larger bodies of slaves. This was the first form of his Harper's Ferry plan and it rapidly grew in detail, so that its disclosure to Douglass in 1847 showed thought and advance.

The first national Negro leader, Frederick Douglass, had delivered his wonderful salutatory in New Bedford in 1844. After publishing his biography, he went to England for safety, but returned in 1847, ransomed from slavery and ready to launch his paper, *The North Star*. No sooner had he landed than the black Wise Men of New York told him of the new Star in the East, whispering of the strange determined man of Springfield who flitted silently here and there among the groups of black folk and whose life was devoted to eternal war upon slavery. Both were eager to meet each other — John Brown to become acquainted with the greatest leader of the race which he aimed to free; Frederick Douglass to know an intense foe of slavery. The historic meeting took place in Springfield and is best told in Douglass' own words:

"About the time I began my enterprise [*i. e.*, his newspaper] in Rochester, I chanced to spend a night and a day under the roof of a man whose character and conversation, and whose objects and aims in life, made a very deep impression upon my mind and heart. His name had been mentioned to me by several prominent colored men; among whom were the Rev. Henry Highland Garnet and J. W. Loguen. In speaking of him their voices would drop to a whisper, and what they said of him made me very eager to see and to know him. Fortunately, I was invited to see him at his own house. At the time to which I now refer this man was a respectable merchant in a populous and thriving city, and our first place of meeting was at his store. This was a substantial brick building on a prominent, busy street. A glance at the interior, as well as at the massive walls without, gave me the impression that the owner must be a man of considerable wealth. My welcome was all that I could have asked. Every member of the family, young and old, seemed glad to see me, and I was made much at home in a very little while. I was, however, a little disappointed with the appearance of the house and its location. After seeing the fine store I was prepared to see a fine residence in an eligible locality, but this conclusion was completely dispelled by actual observation. In fact, the house was neither commodious nor elegant, nor its situation desirable. It was a small wooden building on a back street, in a neighborhood chiefly occupied by laboring men and mechanics; respectable enough, to be sure, but not quite the place, I thought, where one would look for the residence of a flourishing and successful merchant.

"Plain as was the outside of this man's house, the inside was plainer. Its furniture would have satisfied a Spartan. It would take longer to tell what was not in this house than what was in it. There was an air of plainness about it which almost suggested destitution. My first meal passed under the misnomer of tea, though there was nothing about it resembling the usual significance of that term. It consisted of beef-soup, cabbage, and potatoes — a meal such as a man might relish after following the plow all day or performing a forced march of a dozen miles over a rough road in frosty weather. Innocent of paint, veneering, varnish, or table-cloth, the table announced itself unmistakably of pine and of the plainest workmanship. There was no hired help visible. The mother, daughters, and sons did the serving, and did it well. They were evidently used to it, and had no thought of any impropriety or degradation in being their own servants. It is said that a house in some measure reflects the character of its occupants; this one certainly did. In it there were no disguises, no illusions, no make-believes. Everything implied stern truth, solid purpose, and rigid economy. I was not long in company with the master of this house before I discovered that he was indeed the master of it, and was likely to become mine too if I stayed long enough with him. His wife believed in him, and his children observed him with reverence. Whenever he spoke his words commanded earnest attention. His arguments, which I ventured at some points to oppose, seemed to convince all; his appeals touched all, and his will impressed all. Certainly I never felt myself in the presence of a stronger religious influence than while in this man's house.

"In person he was lean, strong, and sinewy, of the best New England mold, built for times of trouble and fitted to grapple with the flintiest hardships. Clad in plain American woolen, shod in boots of cowhide leather, and wearing a cravat of the same substantial material, under six feet high, less than 150 pounds in weight, aged about fifty, he presented a figure straight and symmetrical as a mountain pine. His bearing was singularly impressive. His head was not large, but compact and high. His hair was coarse, strong, slightly gray and closely trimmed, and grew low on his forehead. His face was smoothly shaved, and revealed a strong, square mouth, supported by a broad and prominent chin. His eyes were bluish gray, and in conversation they were full of light and fire. When on the street, he moved with a long, springing, race-horse step, absorbed by his own reflections, neither seeking nor shunning observation. Such was the man whose name I had heard in whispers; such was the spirit of his house and family; such was the house in which he lived; and such was Captain John Brown, whose name has now passed into history, as that of one of the most marked characters and greatest heroes known to American fame.

"After the strong meal already described, Captain Brown cautiously approached the subject which he wished to bring to my attention; for he seemed to apprehend opposition to his views. He denounced slavery in look and language fierce and bitter; thought that slaveholders had forfeited their right to live; that the slaves had the right to gain their liberty in any way they could; did not believe that moral suasion would ever liberate the slave, or that political action would abolish the system. He said that he had long had a plan which could accomplish this end, and he had invited me to his house to lay that plan before me. He said he had been for some time looking for colored men to whom he could safely reveal his secret, and at times he had almost despaired of finding such men; but that now he was encouraged, for he saw heads of such rising up in all directions. He had observed my course at home and abroad, and he wanted my coöperation. His plan as it then lay in his mind had much to commend it. It did not, as some suppose, contemplate a general rising among the slaves, and a general slaughter of the slave-masters. An insurrection, he thought, would only defeat the object; but his plan did contemplate the creating of an armed force which should act in the very heart of the South. He was not averse to the shedding of blood, and thought the practice of carrying arms would be a good one for the colored people to adopt, as it would give them a sense of their manhood. No people, he said, could have self-respect, or be respected, who would not fight for their freedom. He called my attention to a map of the United States, and pointed out to me the far-reaching Alleghanies, which stretch away from the borders of New York into the Southern states.

"'These mountains,' he said, 'are the basis of my plan. God has given the strength of the hills to freedom; they were placed here for the emancipation of the Negro race; they are full of natural forts, where one man for defense will be equal to a hundred for attack; they are full also of good hiding-places, where large numbers of brave men could be concealed, and baffle and elude pursuit for a long time. I know these mountains well, and could take a body of men into them and keep them there despite of all efforts of Virginia to dislodge them. The true object to be sought is first of all to destroy the money value of slavery property; and that can only be done by rendering such property insecure. My plan, then, is to take at first about twenty-five picked men, and begin on a small scale; supply them with arms and ammunition and post them in squads of fives on a line of twenty-five miles. The most persuasive and judicious of these shall go down to the fields from time to time, as opportunity offers, and induce the slaves to join them, seeking and selecting the most restless and daring.'

"He saw that in this part of the work the utmost care must be used to avoid treachery and disclosure. Only the most conscientious and skilful should be sent on this perilous duty. With care and enterprise he thought he could soon gather a force of one hundred hardy men, men who would be content to lead the free and adventurous life to which he proposed to train them; when these were properly drilled, and each man had found the place for which he was best suited, they would begin work in earnest; they would run off the slaves in large numbers, retain the brave and strong ones in the mountains, and send the weak and timid to the North by the Underground Railroad. His operations would be enlarged with increasing numbers and would not be confined to one locality.

"When I asked him how he would support these men, he said emphatically that he would subsist them upon the enemy. Slavery was a state of war, and the slave had a right to anything necessary to his freedom. 'But,' said I, 'suppose you succeed in running off a few slaves, and thus impress the Virginia slaveholders with a sense of insecurity in their slaves further south.' 'That,' he said, 'will be what I want first to do; then I would follow them up. If we could drive slavery out of one county, it would be a great gain; it would weaken the system throughout the state.' 'But they would employ bloodhounds to hunt you out of the mountains.' 'That they might attempt,' said he, 'but the chances are, we

82

should whip them, and when we should have whipped one squad, they would be careful how they pursued.' 'But you might be surrounded and cut off from your provisions or means of subsistence.' He thought that this could not be done so that they could not cut their way out; but even if the worst came he could but be killed, and he had no better use for his life than to lay it down in the cause of the slave. When I suggested that we might convert the slaveholders, he became much excited, and said that could never be. He knew their proud hearts and they would never be induced to give up their slaves, until they felt a big stick about their heads.

"He observed that I might have noticed the simple manner in which he lived, adding that he had adopted this method in order to save money to carry out his purposes. This was said in no boastful tone, for he felt that he had delayed already too long, and had no room to boast either his zeal or his self-denial. Had some men made such display of rigid virtue, I should have rejected it as affected, false, and hypocritical, but in John Brown, I felt it to be real as iron or granite. From this night spent with John Brown in Springfield, Mass., 1847, while I continued to write and speak against slavery, I became all the same less hopeful of its peaceful abolition. My utterances became more and more tinged by the color of this man's strong impressions." *

Tremendously impressed as was Douglass in mind and heart with John Brown and his plan, his reason was never convinced even up to the last; and naturally because here two radically opposite characters saw slavery from opposite sides of the shield. Both hated it with all their strength, but one knew its physical degradation, its tremendous power and the strong sympathies and interests that buttressed it the world over; the other felt its moral evil and knowing simply

* Douglass, *Life and Times of Frederick Douglass* (1892), Chap. 8, Part II, pp. 337–342.

that it was wrong, concluded that John Brown and God could overthrow it. That was all — a plain straightforward path; but to the subtler darker man, more worldly-wise and less religious, the arm of the Lord was not revealed, while the evil of this world had seared his vitals. He uncovered himself if not reverently, certainly respectfully before the Seer; he gave him much help and information; he turned almost imperceptibly but surely toward Brown's darker view of the blood-sacrifice of slavery, but he could never quite believe that John Brown's tremendous plan was humanly possible. And this attitude of Douglass was in various degrees and strides the attitude of the leading Negroes of his day. They believed in John Brown but not in his plan. They knew he was right, but they knew that for any failure in his project they, the black men, would probably pay the cost. And the horror of that cost none knew as they.

If John Brown was to carry out his idea as he had now definitely conceived it, he must first find the men who could help him. On this point there seems to have been deliberation and development of plan, particularly as he consulted Douglass and the Negro leaders. His earlier scheme probably looked toward the use of Negro allies almost exclusively outside his own family. This was eminently fitting but impractical, as Douglass and his fellows must have urged. White men could move where they would in the United States, but to introduce an armed band exclusively or mainly of Negroes from the North into the South was difficult, if not impossible. Nevertheless, some Negroes of the right type were needed and to John Brown's mind the Underground Railroad was bringing North the very material he required. It could not, however, be properly trained in cities whither it drifted both for economic reasons and for self-protection. Brown therefore heard of Gerrit Smith's offer of August 1, 1846, with great interest. This wealthy leader of the New York Abolition group took occasion at the celebration of the twelfth anniversary of British emancipation to offer free Negroes 100,000 acres of his lands in the Adirondack region on easy terms. It was not a well thought-out scheme: the climate was bleak for Negroes, the methods of culture then suitable, were unknown to them; while the surveyor who laid out these farms cheated them as cheerily as though philanthropy had no concern with the project. The Gerrit Smith offer was not wholly a failure. It turned out some good Negro farmers, gave some of its best Negro citizens of to-day to northern New York, and trained a bishop of the British African Church. But it did far less than it might have done if better planned, and much if not all of its success was due to John Brown. He saw possibilities here both to shelter his family when he turned definitely to what was now his single object in life, and to train men to help him. He went to Gerrit Smith at Peterboro, N. Y., in April, 1848, and said: "I am something of a pioneer; I grew up among the woods and wild Indians of Ohio and am used to the climate and the way of life that your colony find so trying. I will take one of your farms myself, clear it up and plant it, and show my colored neighbors how such work should be done; will give them work as I have occasion, look after them in all needful ways and be a kind of father to them."*

His offer was gladly accepted and he moved his family there the following year. It was a wild, lonely place. Thomas Wentworth Higginson wrote once: "The Notch seems beyond the world, North Elba and its half-dozen houses are beyond the Notch, and there is a wilder little mountain road which rises beyond North Elba. But the house we seek is not even on that road, but behind it and beyond it; you ride a mile or two, then take down a pair of bars; beyond the bars faith takes you across a half-cleared field, through the most difficult of wood-paths, and after half a mile of forest you come out upon a clearing. There is a little frame house, unpainted, set in a girdle of black stumps, and with all heaven about it for a wider girdle; on a high hillside, forests on north and west, — the glorious line of the Adi-

* Sanborn, p. 97.

rondacks on the east, and on the south one slender road leading off to Westport, a road so straight that you could sight a United States marshal for five miles."*

To his family John Brown's word was usually not merely law but wish. They went to North Elba cheerfully and with full knowledge of the import of the change, for the father was frank. The daughter Ruth writes: "While we were living in Springfield, our house was plainly furnished, but very comfortably, all excepting the parlor. Mother and I had often expressed a wish that the parlor might be furnished too, and father encouraged us that it should be; but after he made up his mind to go to North Elba he began to economize in many ways. One day he called us older ones to him and said: 'I want to plan with you a little; and I want you all to express your minds. I have a little money to spare; and now shall we use it to furnish the parlor, or spend it to buy clothing for the colored people who may need help in North Elba another year?' We all said, 'Save the money.'"**

It was no paradise, even for the enthusiast. Redpath says: "It is too cold to raise corn there; they can scarcely, in the most favorable seasons, obtain a few ears for roasting. Stock must be wintered there nearly six months in every year. I was there on the first of November, the ground was snowy, and winter had apparently begun — and it would last till the middle of May. They never raise anything to sell off that farm, except sometimes a few fleeces. It was well, they said, if they raised their own provisions, and could spin their own wool for clothing."***

Meantime the scattered isolated eddies of the anti-slavery battles were swirling to one great current, and more and more John Brown was becoming the man of one idea. Im-

* Redpath, p. 61.
** Ruth Brown, in Sanborn, p. 100.
*** Redpath, p. 62.

patiently he neglected his pressing wool business. Instead of keeping his eye on his critical London venture, he hastened across Europe perfecting military observations. He returned to America in time to hear all the feverish discussion of the Fugitive Slave Law and see its final passage. In November, 1850, he writes his wife from Springfield: "It now seems that the Fugitive Slave Law was to be the means of making more Abolitionists than all the lectures we have had for years. It really looks as if God had His hand on this wickedness also. I of course keep encouraging my colored friends to 'trust in God and keep their powder dry.' I did so to-day at Thanksgiving meeting publicly."*

His Springfield meetings led to the formation of his "League of Gileadites," the first of his steps toward the armed organization of Negroes. Forty-four Negroes signed the following agreement:

"As citizens of the United States of America, trusting in a just and merciful God, whose spirit and all-powerful aid we humbly implore, we will ever be true to the flag of our beloved country, always acting under it. We, whose names are hereunto affixed, do constitute ourselves a branch of the United States League of Gileadites. That we will provide ourselves at once with suitable implements, and will aid those who do not possess the means, if any such are disposed to join us. We invite every colored person whose heart is engaged in the performance of our business, whether male or female, old or young. The duty of the aged, infirm, and young members of the League shall be to give instant notice to all members in case of an attack upon any of our people. We agree to have no officers except a treasurer and secretary pro tem., until after some trial of courage and talent of able-bodied members shall enable us to elect officers from those who shall have rendered the most important services. Nothing but wisdom and undaunted courage, effi-

* Letter to his wife, 1850, in Sanborn, pp. 106–107.

ciency, and general good conduct shall in any way influence us in electing officers."*

To this was added exhortation and advice by John Brown.

"Nothing so charms the American people as personal bravery," he wrote. "Witness the case of Cinques, of everlasting memory, on board the *Amistad*. The trial for life of one bold and to some extent successful man, for defending his rights in good earnest, would arouse more sympathy throughout the nation than the accumulated wrongs and suffering of more than three millions of our submissive colored population. We need not mention the Greeks struggling against the oppressive Turks, the Poles against Russia, nor the Hungarians against Austria and Russia combined, to prove this. No jury can be found in the Northern states that would convict a man for defending his rights to the last extremity. This is well understood by Southern congressmen, who insisted that the right of trial by jury should not be granted to the fugitive. Colored people have ten times the number of fast friends among the whites than they suppose, and would have ten times the number they have now were they but half as much in earnest to secure their dearest rights as they are to ape the follies and extravagances of their white neighbors, and to indulge in idle show, in ease and luxury. Just think of the money expended by individuals in your behalf for the last twenty years! Think of the number who have been mobbed and imprisoned on your account! Have any of you seen the branded hand? Do you remember the names of Lovejoy and Torrey?"**

He then gives definite advice as to procedure in case the arrest and the deportation of a fugitive slave were attempted:

* Letter of instructions, agreement and resolutions, as given in Sanborn, pp. 124–127.
** Letter of instructions, agreement and resolutions, as given in Sanborn, pp. 124–127.

"Should one of your number be arrested, you must collect together as quickly as possible, so as to outnumber your adversaries, who are taking an active part against you. Let no able-bodied man appear on the ground unequipped, or with his weapons exposed to view: let that be understood beforehand. Your plans must be known only to yourself, and with the understanding that all traitors must die, wherever caught and proven to be guilty. 'Whosoever is fearful or afraid, let him return and depart early from Mount Gilead' (Judges 7:3; Deut. 20:8). Give all cowards an opportunity to show it on condition of holding their peace. Do not delay one moment after you are ready; you will lose all your resolution if you do. Let the first blow be the signal for all to engage; and when engaged do not do your work in halves, but make clean work with your enemies, — and be sure you meddle not with any others. By going about your business quietly, you will get the job disposed of before the number that an uproar would bring together can collect; and you will have the advantage of those who come out against you, for they will be wholly unprepared with either equipments or matured plans; all with them will be confusion and terror. Your enemies will be slow to attack you after you have done up the work nicely; and if they should, they will have to encounter your white friends as well as you; for you may safely calculate on a division of the whites, and may by that means get to an honorable parley.

"Be firm, determined, and cool; but let it be understood that you are not to be driven to desperation without making it an awful dear job to others as well as to you. Give them to know distinctly that those who live in wooden houses should not throw fire, and that you are just as able to suffer as your white neighbors. After effecting a rescue, if you are assailed, go into the houses of your most prominent and influential white friends with your wives; and that will effectually fasten upon them the suspicion of being connected with you, and will compel them to make a common cause with you, whether they would otherwise live up to their profession or not. This would leave them no choice in the matter.

"Some would doubtless prove themselves true of their own choice; others would flinch. That would be taking them at their own words. You may make a tumult in the court room where a trial is going on by burning gunpowder freely in paper packages, if you cannot think of any better way to create a momentary alarm, and might possibly give one or more of your enemies a hoist. But in such case the prisoner will need to take the hint at once, and bestir himself; and so should his friends improve the opportunity for a general rush. A lasso might possibly be applied to a slave-catcher for once with good effect. Hold on to your weapons, and never be persuaded to leave them, part with them, or have them far away from you. Stand by one another and by your friends, while a drop of blood remains; and be hanged if you must, but tell no tales out of school. Make no confession. Union is strength. Without some well digested arrangements, nothing to any good purpose is likely to be done, let the demand be never so great. Witness the case of Hamlet and Long in New York, when there was no well defined plan of operations or suitable preparation beforehand. The desired end may be effectually secured by the means proposed; namely, the enjoyment of our inalienable rights."*

There is evidence that this league did effective rescue work, as did other groups of Negroes in Boston, Philadelphia, Albany, New York and elsewhere. In this service the Negroes could not act alone — it would have meant mob-violence on purely racial lines; — but given a few determined white men to join in, they could and did bear the brunt of the fighting.

John Brown himself was active in such rescue work. He helped in the release of "Jerry" in Syracuse, and writes in

* Letter of instructions, agreement and resolutions, as given in Sanborn, pp. 124–127.

1851 from Springfield: "Since the sending off to slavery of Long from New York, I have improved my leisure hours quite busily with colored people here, in advising them how to act, and in giving them all the encouragement in my power. They very much need encouragement and advice; and some of them are so alarmed that they tell me they cannot sleep on account of either themselves or their wives and children. I can only say I think I have been able to do something to revive their broken spirits. I want all my family to imagine themselves in the same dreadful condition. My only spare time being taken up (often till late hours at night) in the way I speak of, has prevented me from the gloomy homesick feelings which had before so much oppressed me: not that I forget my family at all."*

His hateful lawsuits hung like a weight about John Brown's neck, and a feverish impatience was seizing him: "Father did not close up his wool business in Springfield when he went to North Elba, and had to make several journeys back and forth in 1849–50. He was at Springfield in January, 1851, soon after the passage of the Fugitive Slave Law, and went around among his colored friends there, who had been fugitives, urging them to resist the law, no matter by what authority it should be enforced. He told them to arm themselves with revolvers, men and women, and not to be taken alive. When he got to North Elba, he told us about the Fugitive Slave Law, and bade us resist any attempt that might be made to take any fugitive from our town, regardless of fine or imprisonment. Our faithful boy Cyrus was one of that class; and our feelings were so aroused that we would all have defended him, though the women folks had resorted to hot water. Father at this time said, 'Their cup of iniquity is almost full.' One evening as I was singing, 'The Slave Father Mourning for his Children,' containing these words, —

* Sanborn, p. 132.

> " 'Ye're gone from me, my gentle ones,
> With all your shouts of mirth;
> A silence is within my walls,
> A darkness round my hearth,' —

father got up and walked the floor, and before I could finish the song, he said, 'O Ruth! Don't sing any more; it is too sad!' "*

At the same time his thrifty careful attention to minutiæ did not desert him. He keeps his eye on North Elba even after his wife and part of the family returned to Akron and writes: "The colored families appear to be doing well, and to feel encouraged. They all send much love to you. They have constant preaching on the Sabbath; and intelligence, morality and religion appear to be all on the advance."**

His daughter says: "He did not lose interest in the colored people of North Elba, and grieved over the sad fate of one of them, Mr. Henderson, who was lost in the woods in the winter of 1852 and perished with the cold. Mr. Henderson was an intelligent and good man, and was very industrious and father thought much of him."***

Once we find him saying: "If you find it difficult for you to pay for Douglass' paper, I wish you would let me know, as I know I took liberty in ordering it continued. You have been very kind in helping me and I do not mean to make myself a burden." And again he writes: "I am much rejoiced at the news of a religious kind in Ruth's letter and would be still more rejoiced to learn that all the sects who bear the Christian name would have no more to do with that mother of all abominations — man-stealing."****

And the sects were thinking. All men were thinking. A great unrest was on the land. It was not merely moral leadership from above — it was the push of physical and men-

* Ruth Brown, in Sanborn, pp. 131–132.
** Letter to his wife, 1852, in Sanborn, pp. 108–109.
*** Ruth Brown, in Sanborn, p. 104.
**** Letters to his children, 1852–1853, in Sanborn, pp. 110, 148.

tal pain from beneath; — not simply the cry of the Abolitionist but the upstretching of the slave. The vision of the damned was stirring the western world and stirring black men as well as white. Something was forcing the issue — call it what you will, the Spirit of God or the spell of Africa. It came like some great grinding ground swell, — vast, indefinite, immeasurable but mighty, like the dark low whispering of some infinite disembodied voice — a riddle of the Sphinx. It tore men's souls and wrecked their faith. Women cried out as cried once that tall black sibyl, Sojourner Truth:

"Frederick, is God dead?"

"No," thundered the Douglass, towering above his Salem audience. "No, and because God is not dead, slavery can only end in blood."

VI

The Call of Kansas

"Cry aloud, spare not, lift up thy voice like a trumpet, and shew my people their transgression, and the house of Jacob their sins."

Just three hundred years before John Brown pledged his family to warfare against slavery, a black man stood on the plains of the Southwest looking toward Kansas. It was the Negro Steven, once slave of Dorantes, now leader and interpreter of the Fray Marcos explorers, and the first man of the Old World to look upon the great Southwest, if not upon Kansas itself. Whiter men have since ignored and ridiculed his work, sensualists have charged him with sensuality, lords of greed have called him greedy, and yet withal the plain truth remains: he led the expedition that foreran Coronado, reported back the truth of what he saw and then returned to lay down his life among the savages.*

The land he looked upon in those young years of the sixteenth century was big with the tragic fate of his people. Planted far to the eastward a century later, their dark faces traveled fast westward until slavery was secure in the valley of the Mississippi and in the lower Southwest. Then the slave barons looked behind them, and saw to their own dismay that there could be no backward step. The slavery of the new Cotton Kingdom in the nineteenth century must either die or conquer a nation — it could not hesitate or pause. It was an industrial system built on ignorance, force and the cotton plant. The slaves must be curbed with an iron hand. A moment of relaxation and lo! they would be rising either in revenge or ambition. And slavery had made revenge and ambition one. Such a system could not compete with intelligence, nor with individual freedom, nor with miscellaneous and care-demanding crops. It could not divide territory with

* Compare the *American Anthropologist*, Vol. 4, No. 2, April–June, 1902.

these things; — to do so meant economic death and the sudden, perhaps revolutionary upheaval of a whole social system. This the South saw as it looked backward in the years from 1820 to 1840. Then its bolder vision pressed the gloom ahead, and dreamed a dazzling dream of empire. It saw the slave system triumphant in the great Southwest — in Mexico, in Central America and the islands of the sea. Its softer souls, timid with a fear prophetic of failure, still held half-heartedly back, but bolder leaders like Davis, Toombs and Floyd went relentlessly, ruthlessly on. Three steps they and their forerunners took in that great western wilderness, and other steps were planned. Three steps — that cost uncounted treasure in gold and blood: the first in 1820, when they set foot beyond the Mississippi into Missouri; the second and bolder when they set their seal on the spoils of raped Mexico and made it possible slave soil; and the third and boldest, when on the soil of Kansas they fought to enslave all territory of the Union.

That these steps would cost much the leaders knew, but they did not rightly reckon how much. They risked the upheaval of parties, the enmity of sections and the angry agitation of visionaries. If worse came to worst, they held the trump-card of disrupting the nation and founding a mighty slave aristocracy to stretch from the Ohio to Venezuela and from Cuba to Texas. One thing alone they did not count upon and that was armed force.

The three steps did raise tremendous opposition. The enslaving of Missouri gave birth to the early Abolitionists — the conscience of the nation awakened to find slavery not dead or dying but growing and aggressive; and in these days John Brown, typifying one phase of that terrible conscience, swore blood-feud with this "sum of all villanies." Thus the first step cost.

The second step went some ways awry since California was lost to slavery, but a new law to catch runaways brought compensation and brought too redoubled cost, for it raised in opposition to the whole slave system not only Abolitionists, but Free Soilers — those who hated not slavery but slaves. This was a costlier move, for the sneers that checked philanthropy were powerless against democracy, and when the echoes of this step reached the ears of John Brown, he laid aside all and became the man of one idea, and that idea the extinction of slavery in the United States.

But it was the third step that was costliest — the step that sought to impose slavery by law and blood on free labor lands despite the lands' wish. Of all the steps it was the wildest and most foolish, for it arrayed against slavery not only philanthropy and democracy, but all the world-old forces of plain justice. It compelled those who loved the right to meet law and force by force and lawlessness, and one man that led that lawless fight on the plains of Kansas and struck its bloodiest blow, was John Brown.

John Brown's decision to go to Kansas was sudden. Unexpectedly the centre of the slavery battle had swung westward. A shrewd bidder for the presidency offered the South the unawaited bribe of Kansas territory for their votes and they eagerly sprang at the offer. Stephen Douglas drove the bill through Congress, and Kansas stood ready for its slave population. But not only for slaves — also for freemen as Eli Thayer quickly saw, and the representations of him and his associates aroused the sons of John Brown.

John Brown himself looked on with interest, but he had other plans. He wrote to his son John: "If you or any of my family are disposed to go to Kansas or Nebraska with a view to help defeat Satan and his legions in that direction, I have not a word to say; but I feel committed to operate in another part of the field. If I were not so committed, I would be on my way this fall."*

John Brown's plans were in the Alleghanies. At North Elba lay his northern stronghold, and at Harper's Ferry lay the gates to the Great Black Way. Here he was convinced was the keystone of the slavery arch and here he must strike.

* Letter to John Brown, Jr., 1854, in Sanborn, p. 191.

So in former years Gabriel and Turner believed; so in after years others believed; but it was not till Grant floated down this path in a sea of blood that slavery finally fell.

The sons of John Brown were, however, greatly attracted by the new western lands. His eldest son writes:

"During the years of 1853 and 1854, most of the leading Northern newspapers were not only full of glowing accounts of the extraordinary fertility, healthfulness, and beauty of the territory of Kansas, then newly opened for settlement, but of urgent appeals to all lovers of freedom who desired homes in a new region to go there as settlers, and by their votes save Kansas from the curse of slavery. Influenced by these considerations, in the month of October, 1854, five of the sons of John Brown, — John, Jr., Jason, Owen, Frederick, and Salmon, — then residents of the state of Ohio, made their arrangements to emigrate to Kansas. Their combined property consisted chiefly of eleven head of cattle, mostly young, and three horses. Ten of this number were valuable on account of the breed. Thinking these especially desirable in a new country, Owen, Frederick, and Salmon took them by way of the lakes to Chicago, thence to Meridosia, Ill., where they were wintered; and in the following spring drove them into Kansas to a place selected by these brothers for settlement, about eight miles west of the town of Osawatomie. My brother Jason and his family, and I with my family followed at the opening of navigation in the spring of 1855, going by way of Ohio and Mississippi Rivers to St. Louis. There we purchased two small tents, a plough, and some smaller farming tools, and a hand-mill for grinding corn. At this period there were no railroads west of St. Louis; our journey must be continued by boat on the Missouri at a time of extremely low water, or by stage at great expense. We chose the river route, taking passage on the steamer *New Lucy* which too late we found crowded with passengers, mostly men from the South bound for Kansas. That they were from the South was plainly indicated by their language and dress; while their drinking, profanity, and display of revolvers and bowie-knives — openly worn as an essential part of their make-up — clearly showed the class to which they belonged, and that their mission was to aid in establishing slavery in Kansas.

"A box of fruit trees and grape-vines which my brother Jason had brought from Ohio, our plough, and the few agricultural implements we had on the deck of that steamer looked lonesome; for these were all we could see which were adapted to the occupation of peace. Then for the first time arose in our minds the query: Must the fertile prairies of Kansas, through a struggle at arms, be first secured to freedom before freemen can sow and reap? If so, how poorly we were prepared for such work will be seen when I say that for arms five of us brothers had only two small squirrel rifles and one revolver. But before we reached our destination, other matters claimed our attention. Cholera, which then prevailed to some extent at St. Louis, broke out among our passengers, a number of whom died. Among these brother Jason's son, Austin, aged four years, the elder of his two children, fell a victim to this scourge; and while our boat lay by for repair of a broken rudder at Waverly, Mo., we buried him at night near the panic-stricken town, our lonely way illumined only by the lightning of a furious thunderstorm. True to his spirit of hatred of Northern people, our captain, without warning to us on shore, cast off his lines and left us to make our way by stage to Kansas City to which place we had already paid our fare by boat. Before we reached there, however, we became very hungry, and endeavored to buy food at various farmhouses on the way; but the occupants, judging from our speech that we were not from the South, always denied us, saying, 'We have nothing for you.' The only exception to this answer was at the stage house at Independence, Mo.

"Arrived in Kansas, her lovely prairies and wooded streams seemed to us indeed like a haven of rest. Here in prospect we saw our cattle increased to hundreds and possibly to thousands, fields of corn, orchards and vineyards.

At once we set about the work through which only our visions of prosperity could be realized. Our tents would suffice to shelter until we could plough our land, plant corn and other crops, fruit trees, and vines, cut and secure as hay enough of the waving grass to supply our stock the coming winter. These cheering prospects beguiled our labors through the late spring until midsummer, by which time nearly all of our number were prostrated by fever and ague that would not stay cured; the grass cut for hay mouldered in the wet for the want of the care we could not bestow, and our crop of corn wasted by cattle we could not restrain. If these minor ills and misfortunes were all, they could be easily borne; but now began to gather the dark clouds of war.

"An election for a first territorial legislature had been held on the 30th of March of this year. On that day the residents of Missouri along the borders came into Kansas by thousands, and took forcible possession of the polls. In the words of Horace Greeley, 'There was no disguise, no pretense of legality, no regard for decency. On the evening before and the day of the election, nearly a thousand Missourians arrived at Lawrence in wagons and on horseback, well armed with rifles, pistols and bowie-knives, and two pieces of cannon loaded with musket balls. Although but 831 legal electors in the Territory voted, there were no less than 6,320 votes polled. They elected all the members of the legislature, with a single exception in either house, — the two Free Soilers being chosen from a remote district which the Missourians overlooked or did not care to reach.'

"Early in the spring and summer of this year the actual settlers at their convention repudiated this fraudulently chosen legislature, and refused to obey its enactments. Upon this, the border papers of Missouri in flaming appeals urged the ruffian horde that had previously invaded Kansas to arm, and otherwise prepare to march again into the territory when called upon, as they soon would be, to 'aid in enforcing laws.' War of some magnitude, at least, now appeared to us brothers to be inevitable; and I wrote to our father, whose home was in North Elba, N. Y., asking him to procure and send us, if he could, arms and ammunition, so that we could be better prepared to defend ourselves and our neighbors."*

John Brown hesitated. His fighting blood was stirred and yet there was the plan of years yet unrealized. Then a new vision dawned in his mind. Perhaps this was the call of the Lord and the path to Virginia might lie through Kansas. He hurriedly consulted his friends — Douglass, McCune Smith, the cultured Negro physician of New York, and Gerrit Smith, and in November, 1854, wrote home: "I feel still pretty much determined to go back to North Elba; but expect Owen and Frederick will set out for Kansas on Monday next, with cattle belonging to John, Jason and themselves, intending to winter somewhere in Illinois. . . . Gerrit Smith wishes me to go back to North Elba; from Douglass and Dr. McCune Smith I have not yet heard."**

His business delayed him in Ohio and he still wrote of his going to North Elba. Then followed the Syracuse convention of Abolitionists and a new revelation to John Brown. For the first time he came into contact with the great Abolition movement. He found that money was forthcoming. Here were men willing to pay if others would work. It was the call of God and he answered:"Here am I."

Redpath says: "When in session John Brown appeared in that convention and made a very fiery speech, during which he said he had four sons in Kansas, and had three others who were desirous of going there, to aid in fighting the battles of freedom. He could not consent to go unless he could go armed, and he would like to arm all his sons; but his poverty prevented him from doing so. Funds were contributed on the spot; principally by Gerrit Smith."***

He writes joyfully home:

* John Brown, Jr., in Sanborn, pp. 188–190.
** Letter to his children, 1854, in Sanborn, pp. 110–111.
*** Redpath, p. 81.

"Dear wife and children,—I reached here on the first day of the convention, and I have reason to bless God that I came; for I have met with a most warm reception from all, so far as I know, and except by a few sincere, honest, peace friends, a most hearty approval of my intention of arming my sons and other friends in Kansas. I received to-day donations amounting to a little over sixty dollars,—twenty from Gerrit Smith, five from an old British officer; others giving smaller sums with such earnest and affectionate expression of their good wishes as did me more good than money even. John's two letters were introduced, and read with such effect by Gerrit Smith as to draw tears from numerous eyes in the great collection of people present. The convention has been one of the most interesting meetings I ever attended in my life; and I made a great addition to the number of warm-hearted and honest friends."*

The die was cast and John Brown left for Kansas. Instead of sending the money and arms, says his son John, "he came on with them himself, accompanied by his brother-in-law, Henry Thompson, and my brother Oliver. In Iowa he bought a horse and covered wagon; concealing the arms in this and conspicuously displaying his surveying implements, he crossed into Missouri near Waverly, and at that place disinterred the body of his grandson, and brought all safely through to our settlement, arriving there about the 6th of October, 1855."**

His daughter says: "On leaving us finally to go to Kansas that summer, he said, 'If it is so painful for us to part with the hope of meeting again, how dreadful must be the feelings of hundreds of poor slaves who are separated for life.' "***

So John Brown reached Kansas to strike the blow for freedom. Not that he was the central figure of Kansas terri-

* Letter to his wife, 1855, in Sanborn, pp. 193–194.
** John Brown, Jr., in Sanborn, pp. 190–191.
*** Ruth Thompson, in Sanborn, p. 105.

torial history so far as casual eyes could see, or the acknowledged leader of men and measures; rather he seemed and
was but a humble co-worker, appearing and disappearing
here and there, — now startling men with the grim decision
of his actions, now lost and hidden from public view. But
it is not always the apparent leaders who do the world's
work. More often those who sit in high places, whom men
see and hear, do but represent or mask public opinion and
the social conscience, while down in the blood and dust of
battle stoop those who delivered the master-stroke — the
makers of the thoughts of men. So in Kansas Robinson,
Lane, Atchison and Geary were the conspicuous public leaders: Robinson, the canny Yankee, whose astute reading of
the signs of the times proved in the end wise and correct but
left him always the opportunist and politician; Lane, whose
impetuous daring and rough devotion led thousands of immigrants out of the North and drove hundreds of slaveholders back to Missouri; Atchison, who led the determination
and ruffianism of the South; and Geary, who voiced the
saner nation. And yet one cannot read Kansas history without feeling that the man who in all this bewildering broil
was least the puppet of circumstances — the man who most
clearly saw the real crux of the conflict, most definitely
knew his own convictions and was readiest at the crisis for
decisive action, was a man whose leadership lay not in his
office, wealth or influence, but in the white flame of his utter
devotion to an ideal.

To comprehend this, one must pick from the confused
tangle of Kansas territorial history the main thread of its
unraveling and then show how Brown's life twined with it.
And this is no easy task. Some time before or after 1850
Southern leaders had tacitly fixed the westward extension
of the Compromise line of 1820 at the northern line of Missouri. When, then, the bill for organizing this western territory appeared innocently in Congress, it was hustled back to
committee, and appeared finally as the celebrated Kansas
Nebraska Bill which formed two territories, Kansas and

Nebraska. It was the secret understanding of the promoters of the bill that Kansas would become slave territory and Nebraska free, and this tacit compact was expressed in the formula that the people of each territory should have the right "to form and regulate their domestic institutions in their own way, subject only to the Constitution of the United States." But the game was so easy, and the price so cheap that the Southern leaders and their office-hunting Northern tools were not satisfied, even with the gain of territory, and so juggled the bill as virtually to leave all territory open to slavery even against the will of its people, while eventually they fortified their daring by a Supreme Court decision.

The North, on the other hand, angry enough at even the necessity of disputing slavery north of the long established line, nevertheless began in good faith to prepare to vote slavery out of Kansas by pouring in free settlers.

Thereupon ensued one of the strangest duels of modern times — a political battle between two economic systems: On the one side were all the machinery of government, close proximity to the battle-field and a deep-seated social ideal which did not propose to abide by the rules of the game; on the other hand were strong moral conviction, pressing economic necessity and capacity for organization. It took four years to fight the battle — from the middle of 1854, when the Kansas-Nebraska Bill was passed and the Indians were hustled out of their rights, until 1858, when the pro-slavery constitution was definitely buried under free state votes.

In the beginning, the fall of 1854, the fatal misunderstanding of the two sections was clear: The New England Emigrant Aid Society assumed that the contest was simply a matter of votes, and that if they hurried settlers to Kansas from the North a majority for freedom was reasonably certain. Missouri and the South, on the other hand, assumed that Kansas was already of right a slave state and resented as an impertinence the attempt to make it free by any means.

Thus at Lawrence, on August 1st, the bewildered and unarmed Northern settlers and their immediate successors, such as John Brown's sons, were literally pounced upon by the furious Missourians, who crossed the border like an invading army. "To those who have qualms of conscience as to violating laws, state or national, the time has come when such impositions must be disregarded, as your rights and property are in danger," cried Stringfellow of Missouri. Thereupon 5,000 Missourians proceeded to elect a pro-slavery legislature and Congressional delegate; and led by what Sumner called "hirelings, picked from the drunken spew and vomit of an uneasy civilization," flourished their pistols and bowie-knives, driving some of the free state immigrants back home and the rest into apprehensive inaction and silence.

Snatching thus the whip-hand, with pro-slavery governor, judges, marshal and legislature, they then proceeded in 1855 to deliver blow upon blow to the free state cause until it seemed inevitable that Kansas should become a slave state, with a code of laws which made even an assertion against the right of slaveholding a felony punishable with imprisonment.

The free state settlers hesitatingly began to take serious counsel. They found themselves in three parties: a few who hated slavery, more who hated Negroes, and many who hated slaves. Easily the political *finesse,* afterward unsuccessfully attempted, might now have pitted the parties against one another in such irreconcilable difference as would slip even slavery through. But unblushing force and fraud united them to an appeal for justice at Big Springs in the fall of 1855 — where John Brown's sons were present and active — and a declaration of passive, with a threat of active, resistance to the "bogus" legislature. A peace program was laid down: they would ignore the patent fraud, organize a state and appeal to Congress and the nation. This they did in October and November, 1855, making Topeka their nominal and Lawrence their real capital.

The pro-slavery party, however, was quick to see the weakness of this program and they took the first opportunity to force the free state men into collision with the authorities. A characteristic occasion soon arose: a peaceful free state settler was brutally killed and instead of arresting the murderer, the pro-slavery sheriff arrested the chief witness against him. A few of the bolder free state neighbors released the prisoner and took him to Lawrence. Immediately the sheriff gathered an army of 1,500 deputies from Missouri, and surrounded 500 free state men in Lawrence just after John Brown arrived in Kansas. Things looked serious enough even to the drunken governor, and with the aid of some artifice, liquor and stormy weather, the threatened clash was temporarily averted. The wild and icebound winter that fell on Kansas gave a moment's pause, but with the opening spring the pro-slavery forces gathered themselves for a last crushing blow. Armed bands came out of the South with flying banners, the Missouri River was blockaded to Northern immigrants, and the border ruffians rode unhindered over the Missouri line. The free state men, alarmed, appealed to the East and immigrants were hurried forward; but slavery "with the chief justice, the tamed and domesticated chief justice who waited on him like a familiar spirit," declared the passive resistance movement "constructive treason" and the pro-slavery marshal arrested the free state leaders from the governor down, and clapped them into prison. Two thousand Missourians then surrounded Lawrence and while the hesitating free state men were striving to keep the peace, sacked and half burned the town on the day before Brooks broke Sumner's head in the Senate chamber, for telling the truth about Kansas.

The deed was done. Kansas was a slave territory. The free state program had been repudiated by the United States government and had broken like a reed before the assaults of the pro-slavery party. There were mutterings in the East but the cause of freedom was at its lowest ebb. Then suddenly there came the flash of an awful stroke — a deed of retaliation from the free state side so bloody, relentless and cruel that it sent a shudder through all Kansas and Missouri, and aroused the nation. In one black night, John Brown, four of his sons, a son-in-law and two others, the chosen executors of the boldest free state leaders, seized and killed five of the worst of the border ruffians who were harrying the free state settlers, and practically swept out of existence the "Dutch Henry" pro-slavery settlement in the Swamp of the Swan. The rank and file of the free state men themselves recoiled at first in consternation and loudly, then faintly, disclaimed the deed. Suddenly they saw and laid the lie aside, and seized their Sharps rifles. There was war in Kansas — a quick sweeping change from the passive appeal to law and justice which did not respond, to the appeal to force and blood. The deed did not make Kansas free — no one, least of all John Brown, dreamed that it would. But it brought to the fore in free state councils the men who were determined to fight for freedom, and it meant the end of passive resistance. The carnival of crime and rapine that ensued was a disgrace to civilization but it was the cost of freedom, and it was less than the price of repression. There were pitched battles, the building and besieging of forts, the burning of homes, stealing of property, raping of women and murder of men, until the scared governor signed a truce, exchanged prisoners and fled for his life. The wildest pro-slavery elements, now loosed from all restraint, planned a last desperate blow. Nearly 3,000 men were mustered in Missouri. The new governor, whose *cortège* barely escaped highway robbery, found "desolation and ruin" on every hand; "homes and firesides were deserted; the smoke of burning dwellings darkened the atmosphere; women and children, driven from their habitations, wandered over the prairies and among the woodlands, or sought refuge and protection even among the Indian tribes; the highways were infested with numerous predatory bands, and the towns were fortified and garrisoned by armies of conflicting partisans, each excited almost to frenzy, and determined upon mutual extermination." Not only that, but the territorial "treasury was bankrupt, there were no pecuniary resources within herself to meet the exigencies of the time; the Congressional appropriations intended to defray the expenses of a year, were insufficient to meet the demands of a fortnight; the laws were null, the courts virtually suspended and the civil arm of the government almost entirely powerless."*

Governor Geary came in the nick of time and he came with peremptory orders from the frightened government at Washington, who saw that they must either check the whirlwind they had raised, or lose the presidential election of 1856. For not only was there "hell in Kansas" but the North was aflame — the very thing which John Brown and Lane and their fellows designed. A great convention met at Buffalo and mass-meetings were held everywhere. Clothes, money, arms, and men began to pour out of the North. It was no longer a program of peaceful voting; it was fight. The Southern party was certain to be swamped by an army of men, who, though most of them had few convictions as to slavery, did not propose to settle among slaves. The wilder pro-slavery men did not heed. When Shannon ran away and before Geary came, they planned to strike their blow at the free state forces. An army of nearly three thousand was collected; one wing sacked Osawatomie and the main body was to capture and destroy Lawrence. No sooner was this done than the force of the United States army was to be called in to keep the conquered down. The success of the plan at this juncture might have precipitated Civil War in 1856 instead of 1861, and Geary hurried breathlessly to ward off the mad blow. He succeeded, and by strenuous exertions he was able with some truth to report in Washington before election time: "Peace now reigns in Kansas."

The news, though it helped to elect Buchanan, was re-

* Farewell address of Governor Geary, *Transactions* of the Kansas State Historical Society, Vol. IV, p. 739.

ceived but coldly in Washington, for the Southerners knew how high a price Geary had paid. So evidently was the governor out of favor that before the spring of 1857, the third governor fled in mad haste from his post because of the enmity of his own supporters. It was clear to Washington that Geary's recognition of the free state cause, with the heavy immigration, had already destroyed the possibility of making Kansas a slave state. There were still, however, certain possibilities for *finesse* and political maneuvering. Slaves were already in Kansas and the Dred Scott Decision on March 6, 1857, legalized them there. Moreover, southeast Kansas, thanks to one of the most brutal raids in its history, in the fall of 1856, was still strongly pro-slavery. The constitutional convention was also in that party's hands. By gracefully yielding the legislature therefore to the patent free state majority, it seemed possible that political manipulation might legalize the slaves already in the state. Once this was conceded, there was still a chance to make Kansas a slave state. The pro-slavery men, however, trained in the upheaval of 1856, were poor material to follow and support the astute Governor Walker. They itched for the law of the club, and made but bungling work of the Lecompton constitution. Then too the more determined spirits in the Territory, together with many naturally lawless elements, saw the pro-slavery danger in southeast Kansas, and proceeded to wage guerrilla warfare against the squatters on claims whence free state men had been driven. It was a cruel relentless battle on both sides with murder and rapine — the last expiring flame of the four years' war dying down to sullen peace in the fall of 1858, after the English bill with its bribe of land for slaves had been killed in the spring.

So Kansas was free. In vain did the sullen Senate in Washington fume and threaten and keep the young state knocking for admission; the game had been played and lost and Kansas was free. Free because the slave barons played for an imperial stake in defiance of modern humanity and economic development. Free because strong men had suffered and fought not against slavery but against slaves in Kansas. Above all, free because one man hated slavery and on a terrible night rode down with his sons among the shadows of the Swamp of the Swan — that long, low-winding and sombre stream "fringed everywhere with woods" and dark with bloody memory. Forty-eight hours they lingered there, and then of a pale May morning rode up to the world again. Behind them lay five twisted, red and mangled corpses. Behind them rose the stifled wailing of widows and little children. Behind them the fearful driver gazed and shuddered. But before them rode a man, tall, dark, grim-faced and awful. His hands were red and his name was John Brown. Such was the cost of freedom.

But behind it was greater cost: a million Indians lived in North America when the white man came, with a world of cultures behind them and many beginnings of civilization. But again and again catastrophe struck and the last was the discovery of America by Columbus. They received the white Europeans with curiosity and kindness. They gave them food and gold. In turn the white man stole and killed and tried to enslave, and their last theft was land. They stole the land of America from the Indians, used its wealth of fruit and gave it over to the rape of aristocrat, Puritan, slave and immigrant. Kansas was the last chapter of this great theft.

VII

The Swamp of the Swan

"And his fellow answered and said, This is nothing else save the sword of Gideon the son of Joash, a man of Israel: for into his hands hath God delivered Midian, and all the host."

"Did you go out under the auspices of the Emigrant Aid Society?" asked the Inquisition of John Brown in after years. He answered grimly: "No, sir, I went out under the auspices of John Brown." In broad outline the story of his coming to Kansas has been told in the last chapter, but the picture needs now to be filled in with the details of his personal fortunes, and a more careful study of the development of his personal character in this critical period of his career. The place of his coming was storied and romantic. French-fathered Indians wheeling onward in their swift canoes saw stately birds in the reedy lowlands of eastern Kansas and called the marsh the Swamp of the Swan. Up from the dark sluggish rivers rose rolling goodly lands over which John Brown's brother Edward had passed to California in 1849, and on which his brother-in-law had settled as early as 1854. Here, too, naturally had followed the five pioneering sons in April, 1855. They came hating slavery and yet peacefully, unarmed, and in all good faith, with cattle and horses and trees and vines to settle in a free land. In Missouri they met hatred and inhospitality, and in Kansas sickness and freezing weather. Nevertheless they were stout-hearted and hopeful, and went bravely to work until the political storm broke, when they wrote home hastily for arms to defend themselves. John Brown, as we have seen, brought the arms himself, taking his son Oliver and his son-in-law Henry with him. "We reached the place where the boys are located one week ago, late at night," he wrote October 13, 1855. "We had between us all, sixty cents in cash when we arrived. We found our folks in a most uncomfortable situation, with no houses to

110

shelter one of them, no hay or corn fodder of any account secured, shivering over their little fires, all exposed to the dreadful cutting winds, morning, evening and stormy days." All went to work to build cabins and secure fodder, keeping at the same time a careful eye on the political developments. On free state election day, October 9th, "hearing that there was a prospect of difficulty, we all turned out most thoroughly armed," but "no enemy appeared" and Brown was encouraged to think that the prospect of Kansas becoming free "is brightening every day."

By November the settlers, he wrote, "have made but little progress, but we have made a little. We have got a shanty three logs high, chinked and mudded, and roofed with our tent, and a chimney so far advanced that we can keep a fire in it for Jason. John has his shanty a little better fixed than it was, but miserable enough now; and we have got their little crop of beans secured, which together with johnny-cake, mush and milk, pumpkins and squashes, constitute our fare." And he adds, "After all God's tender mercies are not taken from us. . . . I feel more and more confident that slavery will soon die out here — and to God be the praise!"

On November 23d he writes: "We have got both families so sheltered that they need not suffer hereafter; have got part of the hay (which had been in cocks) secured; made some progress in preparation to build a house for John and Owen; and Salmon has caught a prairie wolf in a steel trap. We continue to have a good deal of stormy weather — rains with severe winds, and forming into ice as they fall, together with cold nights that freeze the ground considerably. Still God has not forsaken us!" *

It was thus that John Brown came to Kansas and stood ready to fight for freedom. No sooner had he stepped on Kansas soil, however, than it was plain to him and to others that the cause for which he was fighting was far different from that for which most of the settlers were willing to risk life and

* Letters to his family, 1855, in Sanborn, pp. 201 and 205.

property. The difference came out at the first meeting of settlers in the little Osawatomie township. Redpath says: "The politicians of the neighborhood were carefully pruning resolutions so as to suit every variety of anti-slavery extensionists; and more especially that class of persons whose opposition to slavery was founded on expediency — the selfishness of race, and caste, and interest: men who were desirous that Kansas should be consecrated to free white labor only, not to freedom for all and above all. The resolution which aroused the old man's anger declared that Kansas should be a free white state, thereby favoring the exclusion of Negroes and mulattoes, whether slave or free. He rose to speak, and soon alarmed and disgusted the politicians by asserting the manhood of the Negro race, and expressing his earnest, anti-slavery convictions with a force and vehemence little likely to suit the hybrids."*

Nothing daunted by the cold reception of his radical ideas here, Brown strove to extend them when a larger opportunity came at the first beleaguering of Lawrence. It was in December, 1855, when rumors of the surrounding of Lawrence by the governor and his pro-slavery followers came to the Browns. The old man wrote home: "These reports appeared to be well authenticated, but we could get no further accounts of the matters; and I left this for the place where the boys are settled, at evening, intending to go to Lawrence to learn the facts the next day. John was, however, started on horseback; but before he had gone many rods, word came that our help was immediately wanted. On getting this last news, it was at once agreed to break up at John's camp, and take Wealthy and Johnnie to Jason's camp (some two miles off), and that all the men but Henry, Jason, and Oliver should at once set off for Lawrence under arms; those three being wholly unfit for duty. We then set about providing a little corn bread and meat, blankets, and cooking utensils, running bullets and loading all our guns, pistols, etc. The five set

* Redpath, pp. 103–104.

112

off in the afternoon, and after a short rest in the night (which was quite dark), continued our march until after daylight; next morning, when we got our breakfast, started again, and reached Lawrence in the forenoon, all of us more or less lamed by our tramp." *

The band approached the town at sunset, looming strangely on the horizon: an old horse, a homely wagon and seven stalwart men armed with pikes, swords, pistols and guns. John Brown was immediately put in command of a company. He found that already "negotiations had commenced between Governor Shannon (having a force of some fifteen or sixteen hundred men) and the principal leaders of the free state men, they having a force of some five hundred men at that time. These were busy, night and day, fortifying the town with embankments and circular earthworks, up to the time of the treaty with the governor, as an attack was constantly looked for, notwithstanding the negotiations then pending. This state of things continued from Friday until Sunday evening," ** when Governor Shannon was induced to enter the town and after some parley a treaty was announced. Immediately Brown's suspicions were aroused. He surmised that the governor's party had not thus lightly given up the fight for slavery, and he feared that the leading free state politicians had sacrificed the principles for which he was fighting for the sake of the temporary truce. Already the drunken governor was making conciliatory remarks to the crowd in front of the free state hotel, the free state Governor Robinson replying, when John Brown, mounting a piece of timber at the corner of the house, began a fiery speech. "He said that the people of Missouri had come to Kansas to destroy Lawrence; that they had beleaguered the town for two weeks, threatening its destruction; that they came for blood; that he believed, 'without the shedding of blood there is no remission'; and asked for volunteers to go under

* Letter to his family, 1855, in Sanborn, pp. 217–221.
** Letter to his wife, 1855, in Sanborn, pp. 217–221.

113

his command, and attack the pro-slavery camp stationed near Franklin, some four miles from Lawrence. . . . He demanded to know what the terms were. If he understood Governor Shannon's speech, something had been conceded, and he conveyed the idea that the territorial laws were to be observed. Those laws he denounced and spit upon, and would never obey — no! The crowd was fired by his earnestness and a great echoing shout arose: 'No! No! Down with the bogus laws. Lead us out to fight first!' For a moment matters looked serious to the free state leaders who had so ingeniously engineered the compromise, and they hastened to assure Brown that he was mistaken; that there had been no surrendering of principles on their side." * The real terms of the treaty were kept secret, but Brown with his usual loyalty accepted their word as true and wrote exultingly home: "So ended this last Kansas invasion, — the Missourians returning with flying colors, after incurring heavy expenses, suffering great exposure, hardships, and privations, not having fought any battles, burned or destroyed any infant towns or Abolition presses; leaving the free state men organized and armed, and in full possession of the Territory; not having fulfilled any of all their dreadful threatenings, except to murder one unarmed man, and to commit some robberies and waste of property upon the defenseless families, unfortunately within their power. We learn by their papers that they boast of a great victory over the Abolitionists; and well they may. Free state men have only hereafter to retain the footing they have gained, and Kansas is free." **

The Wakarusa "treaty," however, was but a winter's truce as John Brown soon saw; his distrust of the compromisers and politicians grew, and he tried to get his own channels of news from the seat of government at Washington. "We are very anxious to know what Congress is doing. We hear

* G. W. Brown, *Reminiscences of Old John Brown*, p. 8; Phillips, *History of Kansas*, quoted in Redpath, p. 90.
** Letter to his family, 1855, in Sanborn, pp. 217–221.

that Frank Pierce means to crush the men of Kansas. I do not know how well he may succeed, but I think he may find his hands full before it is all over." * And Joshua R. Giddings assures him that the President "never will dare to employ the troops of the United States to shoot the citizens of Kansas." ** Yet the President did dare. Not only were regular troops put into the hands of the Kansas slave power, but armed bands from the South appeared, and one in particular from Georgia encamped on the Swamp of the Swan near the Brown settlement. John Brown's procedure was characteristic. With his surveying instruments in hand one May morning, he sauntered into their camp. He was immediately taken for a government surveyor and consequently "sound on the goose," for "every governor sent here, every secretary, every judge, every Indian agent, every land surveyor, every clerk in every office, believed in making Kansas a slave state. All the money sent here by the national government was disbursed by pro-slavery officials to pro-slavery menials." *** Brown took with him, his son says, "four of my brothers, — Owen, Frederick, Salmon, and Oliver, — as chain carriers, axman, and marker, and found a section line which, on following, led through the camp of these men. The Georgians indulged in the utmost freedom of expression. One of them, who appeared to be the leader of the company, said: 'We've come here to stay. We won't make no war on them as minds their own business; but all the Abolitionists, such as them damned Browns over there, we're going to whip, drive out, or kill, — any way to get shut of them, by God!' "****

Many of the intended victims were openly mentioned, and every word said was calmly written down in John

* Letter to his family, 1856, in Sanborn, p. 223.
** Letter of Giddings to John Brown, 1856, in Sanborn, p. 224.
*** D. W. Wilder, in the *Transactions* of the Kansas State Historical Society, Vol. 6, p. 537.
**** E. A. Coleman, in Sanborn, p. 260.

Brown's surveyor's book. Soon this information was corroborated by the Southern camp being moved nearer the Brown settlement. Secret marauding and stealing began. Brown warned the intended victims, and, at a night meeting, it seems to have been decided that at the first sign of a move on the part of the "border ruffians" the ringleaders should be seized and lynched. Not only was this the opinion at Osawatomie, but secret councils throughout the state were beginning to lose faith in conciliation and compromise, and to listen to more radical advice. From Lawrence, too, there came encouragement to John Brown to take the lead in this darker forward movement. There was little open talk or explicit declaration, but it was generally understood that the next aggressive move in the Swamp of the Swan meant retaliation and that John Brown would strike the blow.

While, however, the free state leaders were willing to let this radical hater of slavery thus defend the frontiers of their cause, they themselves deemed it wise still to stick to the policy of passive resistance, and their wisdom cost them dear. On the 21st of May the pro-slavery forces swooped on Lawrence, and burned and sacked it, while its citizens stood trembling by and raised no hand in its defense. John Brown knew nothing of this until it was too late to help. Notwithstanding, he hurried to the scene, and sat down by the smoldering ashes in grim anger. He was "indignant that there had been no resistance; that Lawrence was not defended; and denounced the members of the committee and leading free state men as cowards, or worse." It seemed to Brown nothing less than a crime for men thus to lie down and be kicked by ruffians. "Caution, caution, sir!" he burst out at a discreet old gentleman, "I am eternally tired of hearing that word caution — it is nothing but the word of cowardice." * Yet there seemed nothing to do then, and he was about to break camp when a boy came up riding swiftly. The ruffians at Dutch Henry's crossing, he said, had been

* James Hanway, in Hinton, *John Brown and His Men*, p. 695.

warning the defenseless women in the Brown settlement that the free state families must leave by Saturday or Sunday, else they would be driven out. The Brown women, hastily gathering up their children and valuables, had fled by ox-cart to the house of a kinsman farther away. Two houses and a store in the German settlement had been burned.

John Brown arose. "I will attend to those fellows," he said grimly. "Something must be done to show these barbarians that we too have rights!" * He called four of his sons, Watson, Frederick, Owen and Oliver, his son-in-law, Henry Thompson, and a German, whose home lay in ashes. A neighbor with wagon and horses offered to carry the band, and the cutlasses were carefully sharpened. An uneasy feeling crept through the onlookers. They knew that John Brown was going to strike a blow for freedom in Kansas, but they did not understand just what that blow would be. There were hesitation and whispering, and one at least ventured a mild remonstrance, but Brown shook him off in disgust. As the wagon moved off, a cheer arose from the company left behind.

It was two o'clock on Friday afternoon that the eight men started toward the Swamp of the Swan. Arriving in the neighborhood they spent Saturday in quietly and secretly investigating the situation, and in gathering evidence of the intentions of the "border ruffians." Although the exact facts have never all been told, it seems clear that a meeting of the intended victims was secured at which John Brown himself presided. Probably it was then decided that the seven ringleaders of the projected deviltry must be killed, and John Brown was appointed to see that the deed was done. The men condemned were among the worst of their kind. One was a liquor dealer in whose disreputable dive the United States court was held. His brother, a giant of six feet four, was a thief and a bully whose pastime was insulting free state

* Bondi in *Transactions* of the Kansas State Historical Society, Vol. 8, p. 279; Spring, *Kansas*, p. 143.

women. The third was the postmaster, who managed to avoid direct complicity in the crime, but shared the spoils. Next came the probate judge, who harried the free state men with warrants of all sorts; and lastly, three miserable drunken tools, formerly slave-chasers who had come to Kansas with their bloodhounds and were ready for any kind of evil.

These were not the leaders of the pro-slavery party in Kansas, but rather the dogs which were to worry the free state men to death. The ringleaders sat securely hedged back of United States bayonets and the Missouri militia, but their tools depended for their safety on terrorizing the localities wherein they lived. Here then, said John Brown, was the spot to strike and, once sentence of death had been formally passed, the band hurried to its task. The saloon lay on the creek where the great highway from Leavenworth in the northeastern part of the state crossed on its way to Fort Scott. Around it within an hour's walk were the cabins of the others. In all cases the proceeding was similar: a silent approach and a quick sharp knocking in the night. The inmates leapt startled from their beds, for midnight rappings were ominous there. They hesitated to open the door, but the demand was peremptory and the door was frail. Then the dark room was filled with shadowy figures, the man dressed quickly, the woman whimpered and listened, but the footsteps died away and all was still. Three homes were visited thus; two of the number could not be found, but five men went out into the darkness with their captors and never returned. They were led quickly into the woods and surrounded. John Brown raised his hand and at the signal the victims were hacked to death with broadswords.

The deed inflamed Kansas. The timid rushed to disavow the deed. The free state people were silent and the pro-slavery party was roused to fury. Even the silent co-conspirators of Pottawatomie rushed to pledge themselves "individually and collectively, to prevent a recurrence of a similar tragedy, and to ferret out and hand over to the criminal authorities the perpetrators for punishment." But they took no steps to lay hands on John Brown and as he said, their cowardice did not protect them. Four times in four years the wrath of the avengers flamed in the Swamp of the Swan, and swept the land in fire and blood, and the last red breath of the expiring war in Kansas glowed in these dark ravines.

To this day men differ as to the effect of John Brown's blow. Some say it freed Kansas, while others say it plunged the land back into civil war. Truth lies in both statements. The blow freed Kansas by plunging it into civil war, and compelling men to fight for freedom which they had vainly hoped to gain by political diplomacy. At first it was hard to see this, and even those sons of John Brown whom he had not taken with him, recoiled at the news. One son says: "On the afternoon of Monday, May 26th, a man came to us at Liberty Hill, ... his horse reeking with sweat, and said, 'Five men have been killed on the Pottawatomie, horribly cut and mangled; and they say old John Brown did it.' Hearing this, I was afraid it was true, and it was the most terrible shock that ever happened to my feelings in my life; but brother John took a different view. The next day as we were on the east side of Middle Creek, I asked father, 'Did you have any hand in the killing?' He said, 'I did not, but I stood by and saw it.' I did not ask further for fear I should hear something I did not wish to hear. Frederick said, 'I could not feel as if it was right'; but another of the party said it was justifiable as a means of self-defense and the defense of others. What I said against it seemed to hurt father very much; but all he said was, 'God is my judge, — we were justified under the circumstances.'"*

This was as much as John Brown usually said of the matter, although in later years a friend relates: "I finally said, 'Captain Brown, I want to ask you one question, and you can answer it or not as you please, and I shall not be offended.' He stopped his pacing, looked me square in the face,

* Jason Brown, in Sanborn, p. 273.

and said, 'What is it?' Said I, 'Captain Brown, did you kill those five men on the Pottawatomie, or did you not?' He replied, 'I did not; but I do not pretend to say that they were not killed by my order; and in doing so I believe I was doing God's service.' My wife spoke and said, 'Then, captain, you think that God uses you as an instrument in His hands to kill men?' Brown replied, 'I think He has used me as an instrument to kill men; and if I live, I think He will use me as an instrument to kill a good many more!' "*

No sooner was the deed known than John Brown became a hunted outlaw. Two of his sons who had not been with him at the murders were arrested on Lecompte's "constructive treason" warrants because they had affiliated with the free state movement. Horror at his father's deed and the cruelty of his captors drove the eldest son temporarily insane, while the life of the other was saved only by a scrap of paper which said, "I am aware that you hold my two sons, John and Jason, prisoners — John Brown."** The old man never wavered. He wrote home: "Jason started to go and place himself under the protection of the government troops; but on his way he was taken prisoner by the bogus men, and is yet a prisoner, I suppose. John tried to hide for several days; but from feelings of the ungrateful conduct of those who ought to have stood by him, excessive fatigue, anxiety, and constant loss of sleep, he became quite insane, and in that situation gave up, or, as we are told, was betrayed at Osawatomie into the hands of the bogus men. We do not know all the truth about this affair. He has since, we are told, been kept in irons, and brought to a trial before bogus court, the result of which we have not yet learned. We have great anxiety both for him and Jason, and numerous other prisoners with the enemy (who have all the while had the government troops to sustain them). We can only commend them to God."***

* E. A. Coleman, in Sanborn, p. 259.
** John Brown, Jr., in Sanborn, p. 278.
*** Letter to his family, 1856, in Sanborn, pp. 236–241.

Withdrawing to the forests, John Brown now began to organize his followers. Thirty-five of them adopted this covenant in the summer of 1856:

"We whose names are found on these and the next following pages, do hereby enlist ourselves to serve in the free state cause under John Brown as commander, during the full period of time affixed to our names respectively and we severally pledge our word and our sacred honor to said commander, and to each other, that during the time for which we have enlisted, we will faithfully and punctually perform our duty (in such capacity or place as may be assigned to us by a majority of all the votes of those associated with us, or of the companies to which we may belong as the case may be) as a regular volunteer force for the maintenance of the rights and liberties of the free state citizens of Kansas: and we further agree; that as individuals we will conform to the by-laws of this organization and that we will insist on their regular and punctual enforcement as a first and a last duty: and, in short, that we will observe and maintain a strict and thorough military discipline at all times until our term of service expires."*

A score of by-laws were added, providing for electing officers, trial by jury, disposal of captured property, etc. Then follow these articles:

"Art. XIV. All uncivil, ungentlemanly, profane, vulgar talk or conversation shall be discountenanced.

"Art. XV. All acts of petty theft, needless waste of property of the members or of citizens are hereby declared disorderly; together with all uncivil, or unkind treatment of citizens or of prisoners.

"Art. XX. No person after having first surrendered himself a prisoner shall be put to death, or subjected to corporeal punishment, without first having had the benefit of an impartial trial.

"Art. XXI. The ordinary use or introduction into the camp

* Sanborn, pp. 287–288.

of any intoxicating liquor, as a beverage, is hereby declared disorderly."*

Nor was this ideal of discipline merely on paper. The reporter of the New York *Tribune* stumbled on the camp which the authorities did not dare to find:

"I shall not soon forget the scene that here opened to my view. Near the edge of the creek a dozen horses were tied, all ready saddled for a ride for life, or a hunt after Southern invaders. A dozen rifles and sabres were stacked against the trees. In an open space, amid the shady and lofty woods, there was a great blazing fire with a pot on it; a woman, bareheaded, with an honest sunburnt face, was picking blackberries from the bushes; three or four armed men were lying on red and blue blankets on the grass; and two fine-looking youths were standing, leaning on their arms, on guard near by. One of them was the youngest son of old Brown, and the other was 'Charley,' the brave Hungarian, who was subsequently murdered at Osawatomie. Old Brown himself stood near the fire, with his shirt sleeves rolled up, and a large piece of pork in his hand. He was cooking a pig. He was poorly clad, and his toes protruded from his boots. The old man received me with great cordiality, and the little band gathered about me. But it was a moment only; for the captain ordered them to renew their work. He respectfully but firmly forbade conversation on the Pottawatomie affair; and said that, if I desired any information from the company in relation to their conduct or intentions, he, as their captain, would answer for them whatever it was proper to communicate.

"In this camp no manner of profane language was permitted; no man of immoral character was allowed to stay, excepting as a prisoner of war. He made prayers in which all the company united, every morning and evening; and no food was ever tasted by his men until the divine blessing had been asked on it. After every meal, thanks were re-

* Sanborn, pp. 288–290.

turned to the Bountiful Giver. Often, I was told, the old man would retire to the densest solitudes, to wrestle with his God in secret prayer. One of his company subsequently informed me that, after these retirings, he would say that the Lord had directed him in visions what to do; that for himself he did not love warfare, but peace, — only acting in obedience to the will of the Lord, and fighting God's battles for His children's sake.

"It was at this time that the old man said to me: 'I would rather have the smallpox, yellow fever, and cholera all together in my camp, than a man without principles. It's a mistake, sir,' he continued, 'that our people make, when they think that bullies are the best fighters, or that they are the men fit to oppose those Southerners. Give me men of good principles; God-fearing men; men who respect themselves; and, with a dozen of them, I will oppose any hundred such men as these Buford ruffians.'

"I remained in the camp about an hour. Never before had I met such a band of men. They were not earnest but earnestness incarnate."*

A member of the band says:

"We stayed here up to the morning of Sunday, the first of June, and during these few days I fully succeeded in understanding the exalted character of my old friend. He exhibited at all times the most affectionate care for each of us. He also attended to cooking. We had two meals daily, consisting of bread made of flour, baked in skillets; this was washed down with creek water, mixed with a little ginger and a spoon of molasses to each pint. Nevertheless we kept in excellent spirits; we considered ourselves as one family, allied to one another by the consciousness that it was our duty to undergo all these privations to further the good cause; had determined to share any danger with one another, that victory or death might find us together. We were united as a band of brothers by the love and affection toward the

* Redpath, pp. 112–114.

man who with tender words and wise counsel, in the depth of the wilderness of Ottawa Creek, prepared a handful of young men for the work of laying the foundation of a free commonwealth. His words have ever remained firmly engraved in my mind. Many and various were the instructions he gave during the days of our compulsory leisure in this camp. He expressed himself to us that we should never allow ourselves to be tempted by any consideration to acknowledge laws and institutions to exist as of right, if our conscience and reason condemned them. He admonished us not to care whether a majority, no matter how large, opposed our principles and opinions. The largest majorities were sometimes only organized mobs, whose howlings never changed black into white, or night into day. A minority conscious of its rights, based on moral principles, would, under a republican government, sooner or later become the majority. Regarding the curse and crimes of the institution of slavery, he declared that the outrages committed in Kansas to further its extension had directed the attention of all intelligent citizens of the United States and of the world to the necessity of its abolishment, as a stumbling-block in the path of nineteenth century civilization; that while it was true that the pro-slavery people and their aiders and abettors had the upper hand at present, and the free state organization dwindled to a handful hid in the brush, nevertheless, we ought to be of good cheer, and start the ball to rolling at the first opportunity, no matter whether its starting motion would even crush us to death. We were under a protection of a wise Providence, which might use our feeble efforts.

"Occasionally Captain Brown also gave us directions for our conduct during a fight, for attack and retreat. Time and again he entreated us never to follow the example of the border ruffians, who took a delight in destruction; never to burn houses or fences, so often done by the enemy. Free state people could use them to advantage. Repeatedly he admonished us not to take human life except when absolutely necessary. Plunder taken from the enemy should be common property, to be used for continuance of the struggle; horses to go to recruits, cattle and provision to poor free state people."*

To this band of men the surrounding country, which was already feeling the first retaliatory blows of the pro-slavery party, now looked for aid, and Brown stood ever ready. His men, however, could form but the nucleus of a spirited defense and for a time the settlers hesitated to join the band until Brown threatened to withdraw. "Why did you send Carpenter after us? I am not willing to sacrifice my men without having some hope of accomplishing something,"** he demanded of a hesitating emissary, and turning to his men he said: "If the cowardice and indifference of the free state people compel us to leave Kansas, what do you say, men, if we start south, for instance to Louisiana, and get up a Negro insurrection, and thereby compel them to let go their grip on Kansas, and so bring relief to our friends here?" Frederick Brown jumped up and said: "I am ready."***

The petty outrages of the Georgia guerrillas now so increased in boldness and in frequency that a company was hastily formed which called Brown's men to the defense of a neighboring village. "We will be with you," cried Brown, and thus he told the story of what followed to the folks at home:

"The cowardly mean conduct of Osawatomie and vicinity did not save them; for the ruffians came on them, made numerous prisoners, fired their buildings, and robbed them. After this a picked party of the bogus men went to Brown's Station, burned John's and Jason's houses, and their contents to ashes; in which burning we have all suffered more or less. Orson and boy have been prisoners, but we soon set them

* Bondi in the *Transactions* of the Kansas State Historical Society, Vol. 8, pp. 282–284.
** Bondi in the *Transactions* of the Kansas State Historical Society, Vol. 8, p. 285.
*** *Ibid.*, p. 284.

at liberty. They are well, and have not been seriously injured. Owen and I have just come here for the first time to look at the ruins. All looks desolate and forsaken, — the grass and weeds fast covering up the signs that these places were lately the abodes of quiet families. After burning the houses, this self-same party of picked men, some forty in number, set out as they supposed, and as was the fact, on the track of my little company, boasting with awful profanity, that they would have our scalps. They, however, passed the place where we hid, and robbed a little town some four or five miles beyond our camp in the timber. I had omitted to say that some murders had been committed at the time Lawrence was sacked.

"On learning that this party was in pursuit of us, my little company, now increased to ten in all, started after them in company of a Captain Shore, with eighteen men, he included (June 1st). We were all mounted as we traveled. We did not meet them on that day, but took five prisoners, four of whom were of their scouts, and well armed. We were out all night, but could find nothing of them until about six o'clock next morning, when we prepared to attack them at once, on foot, leaving Frederick and one of Captain Shore's men to guard the horses. As I was much older than Captain Shore, the principal direction of the fight devolved on me. We got to within about a mile of their camp before being discovered by their scouts, and then moved at a brisk pace, Captain Shore and men forming our left, and my company the right. When within about sixty rods of the enemy, Captain Shore's men halted by mistake in a very exposed situation, and continued the fire, both his men and the enemy being armed with Sharps rifles. My company had no long shooters. We (my company) did not fire a gun until we gained the rear of a bank, about fifteen or twenty rods to the right of the enemy, where we commenced, and soon compelled them to hide in a ravine. Captain Shore, after getting one man wounded, and exhausting his ammunition, came with part of his men to the right of my position, much discouraged. The balance of his men, including the one wounded, had left the ground. Five of Captain Shore's men came boldly down and joined my company, and all but one man, wounded, helped to maintain the fight until it was over. I was obliged to give my consent that he should go after more help, when all his men left but eight, four of whom I persuaded to remain in a secure position, and there busied them in the horses and mules of the enemy, which served for a show of fight. After the firing had continued for some two to three hours, Captain Pate with twenty-three men, two badly wounded, laid down their arms to nine men, myself included, — four of Captain Shore's men and four of my own. One of my men (Henry Thompson) was badly wounded, and after continuing his fire for an hour longer, was obliged to quit the ground. Three others of my company (but not of my family) had gone off. Salmon was dreadfully wounded by accident, soon after the fight; but both he and Henry are fast recovering.

"A day or two after the fight, Colonel Sumner of the United States army came suddenly upon us, while fortifying our camp and guarding our prisoners (which, by the way, it had been agreed mutually should be exchanged for as many free state men, John and Jason included), and compelled us to let go our prisoners without being exchanged, and to give up their horses and arms. They did not go more than two or three miles before they began to rob and injure free state people. We consider this in good keeping with the cruel and unjust course of the administration and its tools throughout this whole Kansas difficulty. Colonel Sumner also compelled us to disband; and we, being only a handful, were obliged to submit.

"Since then we have, like David of old, had our dwellings with the serpents of the rocks and wild beasts of the wilderness, being obliged to hide away from our enemies. We are not disheartened, though nearly destitute of food, clothing, and money. God, who has not given us over to the will of our enemies, but has moreover delivered them into our hand, will, we humbly trust, still keep and deliver us. We feel assured that He who sees not as men see, does not lay the guilt of innocent blood to our charge."*

It was John Brown's hope that the courage engendered by the striking success of the fight at Black Jack, would spread the spirit of resistance to the whole free state party. Lawrence, then the capital, was still surrounded by a chain of forts held by bands of pro-slavery marauders: one at Franklin just east of the city; another just south and known as Fort Saunders; and a third between Lawrence and the pro-slavery capital, Lecompton, known as Fort Titus. When it was rumored that the United States troops would disperse the free state legislature about to meet at Topeka, John Brown hurried thither, hoping that resistance would begin here and sweep the Territory. One of the free state leaders met him at Lawrence and journeyed with him toward Topeka. Brown and he took the main road as far as Big Springs, he says, and continues:

"There we left the road, going in a southwesterly direction for a mile, when we halted on a hill, and the horses were stripped of their saddles, and picketed out to graze. The grass was wet with dew. The men ate of what provision they had with them, and I received a portion from the captain, — dry beef (which was not so bad), and bread made from corn bruised between stones, then rolled in balls and cooked in the ashes of the camp-fire. Captain Brown observed that I nibbled it very gingerly, and said, 'I am afraid you will be hardly able to eat a soldier's harsh fare.'

"We next placed our two saddles together, so that our heads lay only a few feet apart. Brown spread his blanket on the wet grass, and when we lay together upon it, mine was spread over us. It was past eleven o'clock, and we lay

* Bondi in the *Transactions* of the Kansas State Historical Society, Vol. 8, p. 286; John Brown to his family, 1856, in Sanborn, pp. 236–241.

there until two in the morning, but we slept none. He seemed to be as little disposed to sleep as I was, and we talked; or rather he did, for I said little. I found that he was a thorough astronomer; he pointed out the different constellations and their movements. 'Now,' he said, 'it is midnight,' as he pointed to the finger-marks of his great clock in the sky. The whispering of the wind on the prairie was full of voices to him, and the stars as they shone in the firmament of God seemed to inspire him. 'How admirable is the symmetry of the heaven; how grand and beautiful! Everything moves in sublime harmony in the government of God. Not so with us poor creatures. If one star is more brilliant than others, it is continually shooting in some erratic way into space.'

"He criticized both parties in Kansas. Of the pro-slavery men he said that slavery besotted everything, and made men more brutal and coarse — nor did the free state men escape his sharp censure. He said that we had many noble and true men, but too many broken-down politicians from the older states, who would rather pass resolutions than act, and who criticized all who did real work. A professional politician, he went on, you never could trust; for even if he had convictions, he was always ready to sacrifice his principles for his advantage. One of the most interesting things in his conversation that night, and one that marked him as a theorist, was his treatment of our forms of social and political life. He thought that society ought to be organized on a less selfish basis; for while material interests gained something by the deification of pure selfishness, men and women lost much by it. He said that all great reforms, like the Christian religion, were based on broad, generous, self-sacrificing principles. He condemned the sale of land as a chattel, and thought that there was an indefinite number of wrongs to right before society would be what it should be, but that in our country slavery was the 'sum of all villanies,' and its abolition the first essential work. If the American people did not take courage and end it speedily, human freedom and republican liberty would soon be empty names in these United States."

Early next morning the party pressed on until they came in sight of the town. Brown would not enter but sent a messenger ahead, and the narrator continues:

"As he wrung my hand at parting, he urged that we should have the legislature meet, resist all who should interfere with it, and fight, if necessary, even the United States troops. He had told me the night before of his visit to many of the fortifications in Europe, and criticized them sharply, holding that modern warfare did away with them, and that a well-armed brave soldier was the best fortification. He criticized all the arms then in use, and showed me a fine repeating-rifle which he said would carry eight hundred yards; but he added, 'The way to fight is to press to close quarters.'"*

The Topeka journey was in vain. The legislature quietly dispersed at the command of Colonel Sumner, and John Brown saw that his only hope of stirring up effective resistance lay in Lane's "army" of immigrants, then approaching the northern boundaries of Kansas, with whom was his son-in-law's brother. Taking, therefore, his wounded son-in-law and leaving his band, he pressed forward alone on a dangerous and wearisome way of one hundred and fifty miles through the enemy's country. Hinton saw him as he rode into one of the camps and says:

"'Have you a man in your camp named William Thompson? You are from Massachusetts, young man, I believe, and Mr. Thompson joined you at Buffalo.' These words were addressed to me by an elderly man, riding a worn-looking, gaunt gray horse. It was on a late July day, and in its hottest hours. I had been idly watching a wagon and one horse, toiling slowly northward across the prairie, along the emigrant trail that had been marked out by free state men under command of 'Sam' Walker and Aaron D. Stevens, who was

* W. A. Phillips, in Sanborn, pp. 306–308.

130

then known as 'Colonel Whipple.' John Brown, whose name the young and ardent had begun to conjure with and swear by, had been described to me. So, as I heard the question, I looked up and met the full, strong gaze of a pair of luminous, questioning eyes. Somehow I instinctively knew this was John Brown, and with that name I replied, saying that Thompson was in our company. It was a long, rugged-featured face I saw. A tall, sinewy figure, too (he had dismounted), five feet eleven, I estimated, with square shoulders, narrow flank, sinewy and deep-chested. A frame full of nervous power, but not impressing one especially with muscular vigor. The impression left by the pose and the figure was that of reserve, endurance, and quiet strength. The questioning voice-tones were mellow, magnetic, and grave. On the weather-worn face was a stubby, short, gray beard, evidently of recent growth. ... This figure, — unarmed, poorly clad, with coarse linen trousers tucked into high, heavy cowhide boots, with heavy spurs on their heels, a cotton shirt opened at the throat, a long torn linen duster, and a bewrayed chip straw hat he held in his hand as he waited for Thompson to reach us, made up the outward garb and appearance of John Brown when I first met him. In ten minutes his mounted figure disappeared over the north horizon."*

Pushing on northward, Brown found asylum for his wounded follower at Tabor, Ia. Returning, he joined the main body of Lane's men at Nebraska City. Here again arose divided counsels. Radical leaders like Lane and Brown were proscribed men, and United States troops stood on the borders of Iowa to prevent the entrance of armed bodies. It was decided, therefore, that Lane must not enter with the immigrants, and a letter to this effect was brought to him by Samuel Walker, a free state leader. Walker says:

"After reading it he sat for a long time with his head bowed and the tears running down his cheeks. Finally he

* Hinton, pp. 201–204.

looked up and said: 'Walker, if you say the people of Kansas don't want me, it's all right, and I'll blow my brains out. I can never go back to the states, and look the people in the face, and tell them that as soon as I got these Kansas friends of mine fairly into danger I had to abandon them. I can't do it. No matter what I say in my own defense, no one will believe it. I'll blow my brains out and end the thing right here.' 'General,' said I, 'the people of Kansas would rather have you than all the party at Nebraska City. I have got fifteen good boys that are my own. If you will put yourself under my orders I'll take you through all right.' "*

Thus Walker, Lane, and John Brown with a party of thirty stole into Kansas and started anew the flame of civil war.

Brown's old company, organized early in 1858, was mounted and brought to the front, and a systematic effort was made by Lane to free Lawrence from its beleaguering forts. The first attack was directed against Franklin on the night of August 12th, and as ex-Senator Atchison of Missouri indignantly reported: "Three hundred Abolitionists, under this same Brown, attacked the town of Franklin, robbed, plundered and burned, took all the arms in town, broke open and destroyed the post-office, captured the old cannon 'Sacramento,' which our gallant Missourians captured in Mexico, and are now turning its mouth against our friends."** Two days later the little army turned southward to Fort Saunders. Lane deployed his forces before it with John Brown's cavalry on his right wing. A charge was ordered and the garrison fled to the woods, leaving an untasted dinner and large stores of goods. On August 16th, Fort Titus on the road to Lecompton was besieged with cannon, and finally fired by a load of hay; Colonel Titus, a Georgian, was captured and John Brown and other leaders wanted to

---

* Samuel Walker in *Transactions* of the Kansas State Historical Society, Vol. 6, p. 267.

** Appeal to the citizens of Lafayette County, Mo., Sanborn, p. 309.

hang him, for he was one of the most brutal of the border-ruffian commanders. Sam Walker, however, saved his neck.

So furious had been this short campaign that the proslavery party sued for a truce. Walker tells how "on the following day Governor Shannon and Major Sedgwick came to Lawrence to negotiate an exchange of prisoners. They held about thirty of our men and we forty of theirs. It was agreed to 'swap even,' we surrendering all their men, including Titus; they to hand over all our men and cannon they had captured at the sacking of Lawrence. I insisted very strongly on this last point of the contract, for when the gun was taken I swore I would have it back within six months. I had the pleasure of escorting our prisoners to Sedgwick's camp, and receiving the cannon and the prisoners held by the enemy there, in exchange."*

The whirlwind of guerrilla warfare now swept back to the dark ravines of the Swamp of the Swan. After the murders of May came the first counter attack of early June, culminating in the battle of Black Jack. This check quelled the proslavery party a while and they began manning the forts around Lawrence. On August 5th the free state men struck a retaliating blow while John Brown was absent in Nebraska, although he was credited with being present by the Missouri newspapers. Similar skirmishes followed, and the advantage was now so completely with the free state forces, that a final crushing blow was planned by the slave party of Missouri. Manifestoes swept the state, and "No quarter" was the motto. The Missourians responded with alacrity and a great mass crossed the border divided into two wings. The lesser attacked Osawatomie and a newspaper in Missouri said:

"The attack on Osawatomie was by part of an army of eleven hundred and fifty men, of whom Atchison was major-general. General Reid with two hundred and fifty

* Samuel Walker in *Transactions* of the Kansas State Historical Society, Vol. 6, pp. 272–273.

men and one piece of artillery, moved on to attack Osawatomie; he arrived near that place and was attacked by two hundred Abolitionists under the command of the notorious John Brown, who commenced firing upon Reid from a thick chaparral four hundred yards off. General Reid made a successful charge, killing thirty-one, and taking seven prisoners. Among the killed was Frederick Brown. The notorious John Brown was also killed, by a pro-slavery man named White, in attempting to cross the Marais des Cygnes. The pro-slavery party have five wounded. On the same day Captain Hays, with forty men, attacked the house of the notorious Ottawa Jones, burned it, and killed two Abolitionists. Jones fled to the cornfield, was shot by Hays, and is believed to be dead."[*]

But John Brown was not dead and was ever after known as "Osawatomie" Brown. He wrote home September 7th saying:

"I have one moment to write to you, to say that I am yet alive, that Jason and family were well yesterday; John and family, I hear, are well (he being yet a prisoner). On the morning of the 30th of August an attack was made by the ruffians on Osawatomie, numbering some four hundred, by whose scouts our dear Frederick was shot dead without warning, — he supposing them to be free state men, as near as we can learn. One other man, a cousin of Mr. Adair, was murdered by them about the same time that Frederick was killed, and one badly wounded at the same time. At this time I was about three miles off, where I had some fourteen or fifteen men over night that I had just enlisted to serve under me as regulars. These I collected as well as I could, with some twelve or fifteen more; and in about three-quarters of an hour I attacked them from a wood with thick undergrowth. With this force we threw them into confusion for about fifteen or twenty minutes, during which time we killed or wounded from seventy to eighty of the enemy, —

* Quoted in Sanborn, p. 321.

as they say, — and then we escaped as well as we could, with one killed while escaping, two or three wounded, and as many more missing. Four or five free state men were butchered during the day in all. Jason fought bravely by my side during the fight, and escaped with me, he being unhurt. I was struck by a partly-spent grape, canister, or rifle shot, which bruised me some, but did not injure me seriously. Hitherto the Lord has helped me."*

A cheer went up from all free Kansas over this vigorous defense, and for once there was unanimity among the leaders of the free state cause. Robinson, the wariest of them, wrote: "I cheerfully accord to you my heartfelt thanks for your prompt, efficient, and timely action against the invaders of our rights and the murderers of our citizens. History will give your name a proud place on her pages, and posterity will pay homage to your heroism in the cause of God and humanity."**

Meantime the Missourians, after their hard-won victory, hastened back to join the larger wing of the invaders, and so disconcerting was their report, that when Lane made a feint against them, they started to retreat. Governor Woodson's call for the "territorial militia," however, heartened them and gave them legal standing. By September 15th they were threatening Kansas again with nearly 3,000 men. The nation, however, was now aroused and the new governor, Geary, with orders to make peace at all costs, was hurrying forward. Among the first whom he summoned to secret conference was John Brown. Brown came to Lawrence and was leaving, satisfied with Geary's promises, when the invading army of Missourians suddenly appeared before the city. He immediately returned to the town, where there were only 200 fighting men. He was asked to take command of the defense but declined, preferring to act with his usual independ-

* John Brown to his family, 1856, Sanborn, pp. 317–318.
** Charles Robinson to John Brown, 1856, in Sanborn, pp. 330–331.

ence. About five o'clock Monday, the 15th, he mounted a dry-goods box on Main Street opposite the post-office and spoke to the people:

"Gentlemen, — it is said that there are twenty-five hundred Missourians down at Franklin, and that they will be here in two hours. You can see for yourselves the smoke they are making by setting fire to the houses in that town. Now is probably the last opportunity you will have of seeing a fight, so that you had better do your best. If they should come up and attack us, don't yell and make a great noise, but remain perfectly silent and still. Wait until they get within twenty-five yards of you; get a good object; be sure you see the hind sight of your gun, — then fire. A great deal of powder and lead and very precious time is wasted by shooting too high. You had better aim at their legs than at their heads. In either case, be sure of the hind sights of your guns. It is from this reason that I myself have so many times escaped; for if all the bullets which have ever been aimed at me had hit me, I would have been as full of holes as a riddle."*

It was a desperate situation. The free state forces were scattered, leaving but a handful to face an army. But in that handful was John Brown, and the invaders knew it, and advanced cautiously. Redpath who was with Brown says: "About five o'clock in the afternoon, their advance-guard, consisting of four hundred horsemen, crossed the Wakarusa, and presented themselves in sight of the town, about two miles off, when they halted, and arrayed themselves for battle, fearing, perhaps, to come within too close range of Sharps rifle balls. Brown's movement now was a little on the offensive order; for he ordered out all the Sharps riflemen from every part of the town, — in all not more than forty or fifty, — marched them a half mile into the prairie, and arranged them three paces apart, in a line parallel with that of the enemy; and then they lay down upon their faces in the grass, awaiting the order to fire."**

* Speech of John Brown, Redpath, pp. 163–164.
** Redpath, pp. 164–165.

The invaders hesitated, halted and then retired. John Brown says:

"I know of no possible reason why they did not attack and burn that place except that about one hundred free state men volunteered to go out on the open plain before the town and there give them the offer of a fight, which they declined after getting some few scattering shots from our men, and then retreated back toward Franklin. I saw that whole thing. The government troops at this time were with Governor Geary at Lecompton, a distance of twelve miles only from Lawrence, and, notwithstanding several runners had been to advise him in good time of the approach or of the setting out of the enemy, who had to march some forty miles to reach Lawrence, he did not on that memorable occasion get a single soldier on the ground until after the enemy had retreated back to Franklin, and had been gone for about five hours. He did get the troops there about midnight afterward; and that is the way he saved Lawrence, as he boasts of doing in his message to the bogus legislature!

"This was just the kind of protection the administration and its tools have afforded the free state settlers of Kansas from the first. It has cost the United States more than a half million, for a year past, to harass poor free state settlers in Kansas, and to violate all law, and all right, moral and constitutional, for the sole and only purpose of forcing slavery upon that territory. I challenge this whole nation to prove before God or mankind the contrary. Who paid this money to enslave the settlers of Kansas and worry them out? I say nothing in this estimate of the money wasted by Congress in the management of this horrible, tyrannical, and damnable affair."*

The withdrawal, however, was but temporary and it seems hardly possible that Lawrence could have escaped a second capture and burning had not Geary thrown himself into the breach with great earnestness. As he reported:

* Paper by John Brown, Sanborn, pp. 332–333.

"Fully appreciating the awful calamities that were impending, I hastened with all possible dispatch to the encampment, assembled the officers of the militia, and in the name of the President of the United States demanded a suspension of hostilities. I had sent, in advance, the secretary and adjutant-general of the Territory, with orders to carry out the letter and spirit of my proclamations; but up to the time of my arrival, these orders had been unheeded, and I discovered but little disposition to obey them. I addressed the officers in command at considerable length, setting forth the disastrous consequences of such a demonstration as was contemplated, and the absolute necessity of more lawful and conciliatory measures to restore peace, tranquillity, and prosperity to the country. I read my instructions from the President, and convinced them that my whole course of procedure was in accordance therewith, and called upon them to aid me in my efforts, not only to carry out these instructions, but to support and enforce the laws and the Constitution of the United States."*

Without doubt Geary especially emphasized the fact that another sacking of Lawrence would possibly defeat Buchanan and elect Frémont. What chance would there be then for the pro-slavery party?

The Missourians were thus induced to retreat, partly by Geary's logic, partly perhaps by John Brown's resolute handling of his patently inadequate but nevertheless efficient force. They marched back home, leaving a trail of flame and ashes — the last and largest Missouri invasion of Kansas, the culmination and failure of the pro-slavery policy of force.

Geary now began successfully to cope with the Kansas situation. His most puzzling problem was John Brown and his ilk. His experience soon led him to see the righteousness of the free state cause, but he had to insist on law and order

* Executive minutes of Governor Geary in *Transactions* of the Kansas State Historical Society, Vol. 4, p. 537.

even under the "bogus" laws, promising equitable treatment in the future. Immediately the free state party split into its old divisions: the small body of irreconcilables like John Brown, who were fighting slavery in Kansas and everywhere; and the far larger mass of compromisers like Robinson, whose only object was to make a free state of Kansas, and who were willing to concede all else. Under such circumstances the best move was to get rid of John Brown. To have sought to arrest him would have precipitated civil war again. Could he not be induced quietly to leave on promise of immunity? Accordingly, Geary issued a warrant against Brown, but gave it into the hands of the friendly Samuel Walker whom he had previously asked to warn the old man. Brown was not loath. His work in Kansas, so far as he could then see, was done. The state was bound to be free and further than that few Kansans cared. They had no enmity toward slavery as such which called them to a crusade; far from regarding Negroes as brothers, they disliked them and were willing to disfranchise them and crowd them from the state.

Among such folk there was no place for John Brown. His greater mission called him. Kansas had been an interlude only, although for a time he hoped to make it the chief battleground. Now he knew better and again the Alleghanies beckoned. To be sure, he owed Kansas much. Here he had passed through his baptism of fire, and had offered the sacrifice of blood to his God. He was sterner stuff now, ready to go whithersoever the Master called; and he heard Him calling. Not only had he learned a method of warfare in Kansas — he had learned to know a band of simple honest young fellows, hot with the wine of youth, hero-worshipers ready to do and dare in a great cause. Thus the worst difficulties of the past disappeared and the way lay clear. Only one thing oppressed him — he was old and sick, a tired, toil-racked man. Could he live and do the Lord's will?

His company of regulators was formally disbanded but left spiritually intact, and he started north late in September, 1856, taking with him his four sons, John, Jr., who had at last been released, Jason, Salmon, and Oliver, and also, true to his cause, a fugitive slave whom he had chanced upon. As he moved northward the United States troops, unaware of Geary's diplomacy, shadowed and all but captured him. Yet he passed safely through their very midst with his old wagon and cow and the hidden slave, displaying his surveyor's instruments. Thus silently John Brown disappeared from Kansas, and for a year nothing was heard of him in his former haunts. Only his near friends knew that he had gone eastward, and a few of them hinted at his great mission. Matters moved swiftly in Kansas. There was more and more evident a free state majority. But would the pro-slavery administration let it be counted? The new governor was trying to save something for his masters, but the irreconcilables of the Lane and John Brown type doubted it.

"I bless God," wrote Brown in April, "that He has not left the free state men of Kansas to pollute themselves by the foul and loathsome embrace. . . . I have been trembling all along lest they might 'back down' from the high and holy ground they had taken. I say in view of the wisdom, firmness and patience of my friends and fellow sufferers in the cause of humanity, let the Lord's name be eternally praised!"* Notwithstanding this attitude of many of the free state party, they were prevailed upon to vote in the state election of October, 1857. As a concession, however, Lane was appointed to guard the ballot-boxes and, hearing that John Brown was back again in Iowa, he sent for him in hot haste. His messengers found the old man sick and disappointed among his staunch Quaker friends at Tabor. Brown offered to come if supplied with "three good teams, with well-covered wagons, and ten really ingenious, industrious (not gassy) men, with about one hundred and fifty dollars in cash."** These demands were not met until too late, so

* Letter to Augustus Wattles, 1857, in Sanborn, p. 391.
** Correspondence of Lane and Brown, in Sanborn, pp. 401–402.

that Brown returned the money and did not appear in Kansas until the election was over, and the free state forces had triumphed. This had now but passing interest for him. He had other objects in Kansas and flitted noiselessly about among the picked men who had promised their aid. Then he disappeared again. Eight months passed away, when suddenly another Kansas outrage startled the nation. It was the last vengeful echo of that first night of murder in the Swamp of the Swan. In 1856 Linn and Bourbon counties, some miles below the original Brown settlement, had been cleared of free state settlers. In 1857 these settlers ventured to return and found the pro-slavery forces centred at Fort Scott, waiting for Congress to pass the Lecompton constitution. Thus in 1857 and 1858 the expiring horror of Kansas guerrilla warfare centred in southeast Kansas. The pro-slavery forces saw the state slipping from them, but they determined by desperate blows to plant slavery so deeply in the counties next Missouri that no free state majority could possibly uproot it. To accomplish this it was necessary again to drive off the free state settlers. The settlers objected and led by James Montgomery, there ensued a series of bloody reprisals culminating in May, 1858, two years after the first May massacre. A Georgian with a remnant of Buford's band again rode down amid the calm silent beauty of the Swamp of the Swan. They gathered eleven unarmed farmers from their fields and homes and marched them to a gloomy ravine near Snyder's blacksmith shop; there the party killed four and badly wounded six others, leaving them all for dead.

The echoes of this last desperate blow had scarcely died before John Brown appeared on the scene and attempted to buy and fortify the very blacksmith shop where the murders were done. He writes to Eastern friends:

"I am here with about ten of my men, located on the same quarter-section where the terrible murders of the 19th of May were committed, called the Hamilton or trading-post murders. Deserted farms and dwellings lie in all directions for some miles along the line, and the remaining inhabitants watch every appearance of persons moving about, with anxious jealousy and vigilance. Four of the persons wounded or attacked on that occasion are staying with me. The blacksmith Snyder, who fought the murderers, with his brother and son are of the number. Old Mr. Hairgrove, who was terribly wounded at the same time, is another. The blacksmith returned here with me and intends to bring back his family on to his claim within two or three days. A constant fear of new trouble seems to prevail on both sides of the line, and on both sides are companies of armed men. Any little affair may open the quarrel afresh. Two murders and cases of robbery are reported of late. I have also a man with me who fled from his family and farm in Missouri but a day or two since, his life being threatened on account of being accused of informing Kansas men of the whereabouts of one of the murderers, who was lately taken and brought to this side. I have concealed the fact of my presence pretty much, lest it should tend to create excitement; but it is getting leaked out, and will soon be known to all. As I am not here to seek or secure revenge, I do not mean to be the first to reopen the quarrel. How soon it may be raised against me, I cannot say; nor am I over-anxious."*

He quickly had fifteen of his former companions in arms organized as "Shubel Morgan's Company" under the old regulations, and he eagerly sought out and coöperated with Captain Montgomery. The vigil was long and wearisome. "I had lain every night without shelter," he writes, "suffering from cold rains and heavy dews, together with the oppressive heat of the days."** Hinton met Brown at this time and found him not only unwell but "somewhat more impatient and nervous in his manner than I had ever before observed. Soon after my arrival, he remarked again in conversation as to the various public men in the Territory. Cap-

* Letter to F. B. Sanborn and others, 1858, in Sanborn, pp. 474-477.
** *Ibid.*

tain Montgomery's name was introduced, and I inquired how Mr. Brown liked him. The captain was quite enthusiastic in praise of him, avowing a most perfect confidence in his integrity and purposes. 'Captain Montgomery,' he said, 'is the only soldier I have met among the prominent Kansas men. He understands my system of warfare exactly. He is a natural chieftain, and knows how to lead.'

"Of his own early treatment at the hands of ambitious 'leaders,' to which I alluded in bitter terms, he said:

"'They acted up to their instincts, as politicians. They thought every man wanted to lead, and therefore supposed I might be in the way of their schemes. While they had this feeling, of course they opposed me. Many men did not like the manner in which I conducted warfare, and they too opposed me. Committees and councils could not control my movements; therefore they did not like me. But politicians and leaders soon found that I had different purposes and forgot their jealousy. They have all been kind to me since.'

"Further conversation ensued relative to the free state struggle, in which I, criticizing the management of it from an anti-slavery point of view, pronounced it, 'an abortion.' Captain Brown looked at me with a peculiar expression in the eyes, as if struck by the word and in a musing manner remarked, 'Abortion! — yes, that's the word!'

"'For twenty years,' he said, 'I have never made any business arrangement which would prevent me at any time answering the call of the Lord. I have kept my business in such a condition, that in two weeks I could always wind up my affairs, and be ready to obey the call. I have permitted nothing to be in the way of my duty, neither my wife, children, nor worldly goods. Whenever the occasion offered, I was ready. The hour is very near at hand, and all who are willing to act should be ready.'"*

During the fall John Brown coöperated with Montgomery in his guerrilla warfare, and laid out miniature fortifications

* Hinton in Redpath, pp. 199–206.

with his men. While he himself was not personally present in Montgomery's fights, he usually helped plan them and sent his men along. Meantime winter set in and John Brown knew that hostilities would cease. Once again he turned to his long and exasperatingly interrupted life-work. Just after the famous raid on Fort Scott, he had a chance not only to begin his greater work but to strike a blow at slavery right in Kansas. Hinton says: "On the Sunday following the expedition of Fort Scott, as I was scouting down the line, I ran across a colored man, whose ostensible purpose was the selling of brooms. He soon solved the problem as to the propriety of making a confidant of me, and I found that his name was Jim Daniels; that his wife, self, and babies belonged to an estate, and were to be sold at administrator's sale in the immediate future. His present business was not selling of brooms particularly, but to find help to get himself, family, and a few friends in the vicinity away from these threatened conditions. Daniels was a fine-looking mulatto. I immediately hunted up Brown, and it was soon arranged to go the following night and give what assistance we could. I am sure that Brown, in his mind, was just waiting for something to turn up; or, in his way of thinking, was expecting or hoping that God would provide him a basis of action. When this came, he hailed it as heaven-sent."*

John Brown himself told the story in the New York *Tribune:*

"Not one year ago eleven quiet citizens of this neighborhood, — William Robertson, William Colpetzer, Amos Hall, Austin Hall, John Campbell, Asa Snyder, Thomas Stillwell, William Hairgrove, Asa Hairgrove, Patrick Ross, and B. L. Reed, — were gathered up from their work and their homes by an armed force under one Hamilton, and without trial or opportunity to speak in their own defense were formed into line, and all but one shot, — five killed and five wounded. One fell unharmed, pretending to be dead.

* George B. Gill in Hinton, p. 218.

All were left for dead. The only crime charged against them was that of being free state men. Now, I inquire what action has ever, since the occurrence in May last, been taken by either the President of the United States, the governor of Missouri, the governor of Kansas, or any of their tools, or by any pro-slavery or administration man, to ferret out and punish the perpetrators of this crime.

"Now for the other parallel. On Sunday, December 19th, a Negro man called Jim came over to Osage settlement, from Missouri, and stated that he, together with his wife, two children, and another Negro man, was to be sold within a day or two, and begged for help to get away. On Monday (the following) night, two small companies were made up to go to Missouri and forcibly liberate the five slaves, together with other slaves. One of these companies I assumed to direct. We proceeded to the place, surrounding the buildings, liberated the slaves, and also took certain property supposed to belong to the estate. We, however, learned before leaving that a portion of the articles we had belonged to a man living on the plantation as a tenant, and who was supposed to have no interest in the estate. We promptly returned to him all we had taken. We then went to another plantation, where we found five more slaves, took some property and two white men. We all moved slowly away into the Territory for some distance, and then sent the white men back, telling them to follow us as soon as they chose to do so. The other company freed one female slave, took some property, and, as I am informed, killed one white man (the master), who fought against the liberation.

"Now for comparison. Eleven persons are forcibly restored to their natural and inalienable rights, with but one man killed, and all 'hell is stirred from beneath.' It is currently reported that the governor of Missouri has made a requisition upon the governor of Kansas for the delivery of all such as were concerned in the last named 'dreadful outrage.' The marshal of Kansas is said to be collecting a posse of Missouri (not Kansas) men at West Point, in Missouri, a little town about ten miles distant, to 'enforce the laws.' All pro-slavery, conservative, free state, and dough-face men and administration tools are filled with holy horror."*

One of the slaves, Samuel Harper, afterward told of this wonderful *katabasis* of a thousand miles in the teeth of the elements and in defiance of the law:

"It was mighty slow traveling. You see there were several different parties amongst our band, and our masters had people looking all over for us. We would ride all night, and then maybe, we would have to stay several days in one house to keep from getting caught. In a month we had only got to a place near Topeka, which was about forty miles from where we started. There was twelve of us at the one house of a man named Doyle, besides the captain and his men, when there came along a gang of slave-hunters. One of Captain Brown's men, Stevens, he went down to them and said: — 'Gentlemen, you look as if you were looking for somebody or something.' 'Aye, yes!' says the leader, 'we think as how you have some of our slaves up yonder in that there house.' 'Is that so?' says Stevens. 'Well, come on right along with me, and you can look them over and see.'

"We were watching this here conversation all the time, and when we see Stevens coming up to the house with that there man, we just didn't know what to make of it. We began to get scared that Stevens was going to give us to them slave-hunters. But the looks of things changed when Stevens got up to the house. He just opened the door long enough for to grab a double-barreled gun. He pointed it at the slave-hunter, and says: 'You want to see your slaves, does you? Well, just look up them barrels and see if you can find them.' That man just went all to pieces. He dropped his gun, his legs went trembling, and the tears most started from his eyes. Stevens took and locked him up in the house. When

* Sanborn, pp. 481–483.

146

the rest of his crowd seen him captured, they ran away as fast as they could go.

"Captain Brown went to see the prisoner, and says to him, 'I'll show you what it is to look after slaves, my man.' That frightened the prisoner awful. He was a kind of old fellow and when he heard what the captain said, I suppose he thought he was going to be killed. He began to cry and beg to be let go. The captain he only smiled a little bit, and talked some more to him, and the next day he was let go.

"A few days afterward, the United States marshal came up with another gang to capture us. There was about seventy-five of them, and they surrounded the house, and we was all afraid we was going to be took for sure. But the captain he just said, 'Get ready, boys, and we'll whip them all.' There was only fourteen of us altogether, but the captain was a terror to them, and when he stepped out of the house and went for them the whole seventy-five of them started running. Captain Brown and Kagi and some others chased them, and captured five prisoners. There was a doctor and lawyer amongst them. They all had nice horses. The captain made them get down. Then he told five of us slaves to mount the beasts and we rode them while the white men had to walk. It was early in the spring, and the mud on the roads was away over their ankles. I just tell you it was mighty tough walking, and you can believe those fellows had enough of slave-hunting. The next day the captain let them all go.

"Our masters kept spies watching till we crossed the border. When we got to Springdale, Ia., a man came to see Captain Brown, and told him there was a lot of friends down in a town in Kansas that wanted to see him. The captain said he did not care to go down, but as soon as the man started back, Captain Brown followed him. When he came back, he said there was a whole crowd coming up to capture us. We all went up to the schoolhouse and got ourselves ready to fight.

"The crowd came and hung around the schoolhouse a few

days, but they didn't try to capture us. The governor of Kansas, he telegraphed to the United States marshal at Springdale: 'Capture John Brown, dead or alive.' The marshal he answered: 'If I try to capture John Brown it'll be dead, and I'll be the one that'll be dead.' Finally those Kansas people went home, and then that same marshal put us in a car and sent us to Chicago. It took us over three months to get to Canada.... What kind of a man was Captain Brown? He was a great big man, over six feet tall, with great big shoulders, and long hair, white as snow. He was a very quiet man, awful quiet. He never even laughed. After we was free we was wild of course, and we used to cut up all kinds of foolishness. But the captain would always look as solemn as a graveyard. Sometimes he just let out the tiniest bit of a smile, and says: 'You'd better quit your fooling and take up your book.'"*

On the 12th of March, 1859, nearly three months after the starting, John Brown landed his fugitives safely in Canada "under the lion's paw." The old man lifted his hands and said: "Lord, permit Thy servant to die in peace; for mine eyes have seen Thy salvation! I could not brook the thought that any ill should befall you, — least of all, that you should be taken back to slavery. The arm of Jehovah protected us."**

* Hamilton, *John Brown in Canada*, pp. 4–5.
** Sanborn, p. 491.

VIII

The Great Plan

"Is not this the fast that I have chosen? To loose the bands of wickedness, to undo the heavy burdens, and to let the oppressed go free, and that ye break every yoke?"

"Sir, the angel of the Lord will camp round about me," said John Brown with stern eyes when the timid foretold his doom.* With a steadfast almost superstitious faith in his divine mission, the old man had walked unscathed out of Kansas in the fall of 1856, two years and a half before the slave raid into Missouri related in the last chapter. In his mind lay a definitely matured plan for attacking slavery in the United States in such a way as would shake its very foundations. The plan had been long forming, and changing in shape from 1828, when he proposed a Negro school in Hudson, until 1859 when he finally fixed on Harper's Ferry. At first he thought to educate Negroes in the North and let them leaven the lump of slaves. Then, moving forward a step, he determined to settle in a border state and educate slaves openly or clandestinely and send them out as emissaries. As gradually he became acquainted with the great work and wide ramifications of the Underground Railroad, he conceived the idea of central depots for running off slaves in the inaccessible portions of the South, and he began studying Southern geography with this in view. He noted the rivers, swamps and mountains, and more especially, the great struggling heights of the Alleghanies, which swept from his Pennsylvania home down to the swamps of Virginia, Carolina and Georgia. His Kansas experiences suggested for a time the southwest pathway to Louisiana by the swamps of the Red and Arkansas Rivers, but this was but a passing thought; he soon reverted to the great spur of the Alleghanies.

* Redpath, p. 48.

"I never shall forget," writes Thomas Wentworth Higginson, "the quiet way in which he once told me that 'God had established the Alleghany Mountains from the foundation of the world that they might one day be a refuge for fugitive slaves.' I did not know then that his own home was among the Adirondacks."*

More and more, as he thought and worked, did his great plan present itself to him clearly and definitely until finally it stood in 1858 as Kagi told it to Hinton:

"The mountains of Virginia were named as the place of refuge, and as a country admirably adapted in which to carry on guerrilla warfare. In the course of the conversation, Harper's Ferry was mentioned as a point to be seized, but not held, — on account of the arsenal. The white members of the company were to act as officers of different guerrilla bands, which, under the general command of John Brown, were to be composed of Canadian refugees, and the Virginia slaves who would join them. A different time of the year was mentioned for the commencement of the warfare from that which had lately been chosen. It was not anticipated that the first movement would have any other appearance to the masters than a slave stampede, or local insurrection, at most. The planters would pursue their chattels and be defeated. The militia would then be called out, and would also be defeated. It was not intended that the movement should appear to be of large dimension, but that, gradually increasing in magnitude, it should, as it opened, strike terror into the heart of the slave states by the amount of the organization it would exhibit, and the strength it gathered. They anticipated, after the first blow had been struck, that, by the aid of the free and Canadian Negroes who would join them, they could inspire confidence in the slaves, and induce them to rally. No intention was expressed of gathering a large body of slaves, and removing them to Canada. On the contrary, Kagi clearly stated, in answer to my in-

* Redpath, p. 71.

quiries, that the design was to make the fight in the mountains of Virginia, extending it to North Carolina, and Tennessee, and also to the swamps of South Carolina if possible. Their purpose was not the extradition of one or a thousand slaves, but their liberation in the states wherein they were born, and were now held in bondage. 'The mountains and swamps of the South were intended by the Almighty,' said John Brown to me afterward, 'for a refuge for the slave, and a defense against the oppressor.' Kagi spoke of having marked out a chain of counties extending continuously through South Carolina, Georgia, Alabama, and Mississippi. He had traveled over a large portion of the region indicated, and from his own personal knowledge, and with the assistance of Canadian Negroes who had escaped from those states, they had arranged a general plan of attack.

"The counties he named were those which contained the largest proportion of slaves, and would, therefore, be the best in which to strike. The blow struck at Harper's Ferry was to be in the spring, when the planters were busy, and the slaves most needed. The arms in the arsenal were to be taken to the mountains, with such slaves that joined. The telegraph wires were to be cut, and the railroad tracks torn up in all directions. As fast as possible other bands besides the original ones were to be formed, and a continuous chain of posts established in the mountains. They were to be supported by provisions taken from the farms of the oppressors. They expected to be speedily and constantly reenforced; first, by the arrival of those men, who, in Canada, were anxiously looking and praying for the time of deliverance, and then by the slaves themselves. The intention was to hold the egress to the free states as long as possible, in order to retreat when that was advisable. Kagi, however, expected to retreat southward, not in the contrary direction. The slaves were to be armed with pikes, scythes, muskets, shotguns, and other simple instruments of defense; the officers, white or black, and such of the men as were skilled and trustworthy, to have the use of the Sharps rifles and revolvers.

They anticipated procuring provisions enough for subsistence by forage, as also arms, horses, and ammunition. Kagi said one of the reasons that induced him to go into the enterprise was a full conviction that at no very distant day forcible efforts for freedom would break out among the slaves, and that slavery might be more speedily abolished by such efforts, than by any other means. He knew by observation in the South, that in no point was the system so vulnerable as in its fear of slave-rising. Believing that such a blow would soon be struck, he wanted to organize it so as to make it more effectual, and also, by directing and controlling the Negroes, to prevent some of the atrocities that would necessarily arise from the sudden upheaval of such a mass as the Southern slaves."*

The knowledge of the country was obtained by personal inspection. Kagi and others of Brown's lieutenants went out on trips; the old man himself had been in western, northern and southern Virginia, and his Negro friends especially knew these places and routes. One of Brown's men writes:

"My object in wishing to see Mr. Reynolds, who was a colored man (very little colored, however), was in regard to a military organization which, I had understood, was in existence among the colored people. He assured me that such was the fact, and that its ramifications extended through most, or nearly all, of the slave states. He, himself, I think, had been through many of the slave states visiting and organizing. He referred me to many references in the Southern papers, telling of this and that favorite slave being killed or found dead. These, he asserted, must be taken care of, being the most dangerous element they had to contend with. He also asserted that they were only waiting for Brown, or some one else to make a successful initiative move when their forces would be put in motion. None but colored persons could be admitted to membership, and, in part to corroborate his assertions, he took me to the room in which they

* Hinton in Redpath, pp. 203–205.

held their meetings and used as their arsenal. He showed me a fine collection of arms. He gave me this under the pledge of secrecy which we gave to each other at the Chatham Convention.

"On my return to Cleveland he passed me through the organization, first to J. J. Pierce, colored, at Milan, who paid my bill over night at the Eagle Hotel, and gave me some money, and a note to E. Moore, at Norwalk, who in turn paid my hotel bill and purchased a railroad ticket through to Cleveland for me."[*]

Speaking of this league, Hinton also says:

"As one may naturally understand, looking at conditions then existing, there existed something of an organization to assist fugitives and for resistance to their masters. It was found all along the borders from Syracuse, New York, to Detroit, Michigan. As none but colored men were admitted into direct and active membership with this 'League of Freedom,' it is quite difficult to trace its workings or know how far its ramifications extended. One of the most interesting phases of slave life, so far as the whites were enabled to see or impinge upon it, was the extent and rapidity of communication among them. Four geographical lines seem to have been chiefly followed. One was that of the coast south of the Potomac, whose almost continuous line of swamps from the vicinity of Norfolk, Va., to the northern border of Florida afforded a refuge for many who could not escape and became 'marooned' in their depths, while giving facility to the more enduring to work their way out to the North Star Land. The great Appalachian range and its abutting mountains were long a rugged, lonely, but comparatively safe route to freedom. It was used, too, for many years. Doubtless a knowledge of that fact, for John Brown was always an active Underground Railroad man, had very much to do, apart from its immediate use strategically considered, with the captain's decision to begin operations there-

---

[*] Reminiscences of George B. Gill, Hinton, pp. 732–733.

in. Harriet Tubman, whom John Brown met for the first time at St. Catherines in March or April, 1858, was a constant user of the Appalachian route."*

The trained leadership John Brown found in his Kansas experience, and his wide acquaintance with colored men; the organization of the Negroes culminated in a convention at Chatham, Canada. The raising of money for this work, as time went on, was more and more the object of his various occupations and commercial ventures. These visions of personal wealth to be expended for great deeds failed because the pressure of work for the ideal overcame the pressure of work for funds to finance it. When once he discovered at Syracuse men of means, ready to pay the expenses of men of deeds, he dropped all further thought of his physical necessities, gave himself to the cause and called on them for money. In his earlier calls he regards this not as charity but as wages. He said once: "From about the 20th of May of last year hundreds of men like ourselves lost their whole time, and entirely failed of securing any kind of crop whatever. I believe it safe to say that five hundred free state men lost each one hundred and twenty-five days, at $1.50 per day, which would be, to say nothing of attendant losses, $90,000. I saw the ruins of many free state men's houses at different places in the Territory, together with stacks of grain wasted and burning, to the amount of, say $50,000; making, in lost time and destruction of property, more than $150,000."**

And again: "John Brown has devoted the service of himself and two minor sons to the free state cause for more than a year; suffered by the fire before named and by robbery; has gone at his own cost for that period, except that he and his company together have received forty dollars in cash, two sacks of flour, thirty-five pounds bacon, thirty-five do. sugar, and twenty pounds rice.

* Hinton, pp. 171–172.
** Notes by John Brown, in Sanborn, p. 244.

154

"I propose to serve hereafter in the free state cause (provided my needful expenses can be met), should that be desired; and to raise a small regular force to serve on the same condition. My own means are so far exhausted that I can no longer continue in the service at present without the means of defraying my expenses are furnished me."*

Finally, however, he had to appeal more directly to philanthropy. He was especially encouraged by the Kansas committees. These committees had sprung up in various ways and places in 1854, but had nearly all united in Thayer's New England Emigrant Aid Company in 1855. This company proposed to aid free state emigration as an investment, but it failed in this respect because of the political troubles, and the panic of 1857. It did, however, arouse great interest throughout the nation. The National Kansas Committee, formed after the sacking of Lawrence, was more belligerent than philanthropic in its projects, while the Boston Relief Committee was distinctly radical. John Brown had some connection with Thayer's company, but his hopes were especially built on the National Kansas Committee, which Lane had done so much to bring into being, and to which Gerrit Smith contributed many thousands of dollars.

Leaving Kansas secretly in October, 1856, John Brown hastened to the Chicago headquarters of this National Kansas Committee with a proposal that they equip a company for him. The Chicago committee referred this proposal to a full meeting of the members to be held in New York in January. John Brown immediately started East, clad in new clothes which the committee furnished and armed with letters from the governors of Kansas and Ohio. Gerrit Smith welcomed him and said: "Captain John Brown, — you did not need to show me letters from Governor Chase and Governor Robinson to let me know who and what you are. I have known you for many years, and have highly esteemed you as long as I have known you. I know your unshrinking

* Paper by John Brown, in Sanborn, pp. 241–242.

bravery, your self-sacrificing benevolence, your devotion to the cause of freedom, and have long known them. May Heaven preserve your life and health, and prosper your noble purpose!"*

But his half-brother in Ohio wrote:

"Since the trouble growing out of the settlement of the Kansas Territory, I have observed a marked change in brother John. Previous to this, he devoted himself entirely to business; but since these troubles he has abandoned all business, and has become wholly absorbed by the subject of slavery. He had property left him by his father, and of which I had the agency. He has never taken a dollar of it for the benefit of his family, but has called for a portion of it to be expended in what he called the Service. After his return to Kansas he called on me, and I urged him to go home to his family and attend to his private affairs; that I feared his course would prove his destruction and that of his boys. . . . He replied that he was sorry that I did not sympathize with him; that he knew that he was in the line of his duty, and he must pursue it, though it should destroy him and his family. He stated to me that he was satisfied that he was a chosen instrument in the hands of God to war against slavery. From his manner and from his conversation at this time, I had no doubt he had become insane upon the subject of slavery, and gave him to understand that this was my opinion of him!"**

Mrs. George L. Stearns, the wife of the Massachusetts anti-slavery leader, writes:

"At this juncture, Mr. Stearns wrote to John Brown, that if he would come to Boston and consult with the friends of freedom, he would pay his expenses. They had never met, but 'Osawatomie Brown' had become a cherished household name during the anxious summer of 1856. Arriving in Boston they were introduced to each other in the street by a

* Letter from Gerrit Smith to John Brown, in Sanborn, p. 364.
** Jeremiah Brown in Redpath, pp. 174–175.

Kansas man, who chanced to be with Mr. Stearns on his way to the committee rooms in Nilis's Block, School Street. Captain Brown made a profound impression on all who came within the sphere of his moral magnetism. Emerson called him 'the most ideal of men, for he wanted to put all his ideas into action.' His absolute superiority to all selfish aims and narrowing pride of opinion touched an answering chord in the self-devotion of Mr. Stearns. A little anecdote illustrates the modest estimate of the work he had in hand. After several efforts to bring together certain friends to meet Captain Brown at his home, in Medford, he found that Sunday was the only day that would serve their several conveniences, and being a little uncertain how it might strike his ideas of religious propriety, he prefaced his invitation with something like an apology. With characteristic promptness came the reply: 'Mr. Stearns, I have a little ewe-lamb that I want to pull out of the ditch, and the Sabbath will be as good a day as any to do it.'

"It may not be out of place to describe the impression he made upon the writer on this first visit. When I entered the parlor, he was sitting near the hearth, where glowed a bright, open fire. He rose to greet me, stepping forward with such an erect, military bearing, such fine courtesy of demeanor and grave earnestness, that he seemed to my instant thought some old Cromwellian hero suddenly dropped down before me; a suggestion which was presently strengthened by his saying (proceeding with the conversation my entrance had interrupted), 'Gentlemen, I consider the Golden Rule and the Declaration of Independence one and inseparable; and it is better that a whole generation of men, women, children should be swept away than that this crime of slavery should exist one day longer.' These words were uttered like rifle balls; in such emphatic tones and manner that our little Carl, not three years old, remembered it in manhood as one of his earliest recollections. The child stood perfectly still, in the middle of the room, gazing with his beautiful eyes on this new sort of a man, until his absorption arrested the attention of Captain Brown, who soon coaxed him to his knee, though the look and childlike wonder remained. His dress was of some dark brown stuff, quite coarse, but its exactness and neatness produced a singular air of refinement. At dinner, he declined all dainties, saying that he was unaccustomed to luxuries, even to partaking of butter.

"The 'friends of freedom,' with whom Mr. Stearns had invited John Brown to consult, were profoundly impressed with his sagacity, integrity, and devotion; notably among these were R. W. Emerson, Theodore Parker, H. D. Thoreau, A. Bronson Alcott, F. B. Sanborn, Dr. S. G. Howe, Col. T. W. Higginson, Governor Andrew, and others."[*]

Sanborn says:

"He came to me with a note of introduction from George Walker of Springfield — both of us being Kansas committee men, working to maintain the freedom of that Territory, and Brown had been one of the fighting men there in the summer of 1856, just before. His theory required fighting in Kansas; it was the only sure way, he thought, to keep that region free from the curse of slavery. His mission now was to levy war on it, and for that to raise and equip a company of a hundred well-armed men who should resist aggression in Kansas, or occasionally carry the war into Missouri. Behind that purpose, but not yet disclosed, was his intention to use the men thus put into the field for incursions into Virginia or other slave states. Our State Kansas Committee, of which I was secretary, had a stock of arms that Brown wished to use for this company, and these we voted to him. They had been put in the custody of the National Committee at Chicago, and it was needful to follow up our vote by similar action in the National Committee. For this purpose I was sent to a meeting of that committee at the Astor House, in New York, as the proxy of Dr. Howe and Dr. Samuel Cabot — both members of the National Committee.

---

[*] Reminiscences of Mrs. Mary E. Stearns, in Hinton, pp. 719–727.

I met Brown there, and aided him in obtaining from the meeting an appropriation of $5,000 for his work in Kansas, of which, however, he received only $500. The committee also voted to restore the custody of two hundred rifles to the Massachusetts committee which bought them, well knowing that we should turn them over to John Brown, as we did. He found them at Tabor, Ia., in the following September, and took possession; it was with part of these rifles that he entered Virginia two years later.

"At this Astor House meeting Brown was closely questioned by some of the National Committee, particularly by Mr. Hurd of Chicago, as to what he would do with money and arms. He refused to pledge himself to use them solely in Kansas, and declared that his past record ought to be a sufficient guarantee that he should employ them judiciously. If we chose to trust him, well and good, but he would neither make pledges nor disclose his plans. Mr. Hurd had some inkling that Brown would not confine his warfare to Kansas, but the rest of us were willing to trust Brown, and the money was voted."*

John Brown immediately made a careful estimate of the cost of the necessary equipment which with "two weeks of provisions for men and horses" amounted to $1,774. The funds of the committee, however, were low and the officers suspicious; in April they informed Brown: "The committee are at present out of money, and compelled to decline sending you the five hundred dollars you speak of. They are sorry this has become the case, but it was unavoidable. I need not state to you all the reasons why. The country has stopped sending us contributions, and we have no means of replenishing our treasury. We shall need to have aid from some quarter to enable us to meet our present engagements."**

Immediately Brown set out to raise his own funds and for

---

* Sanborn, *John Brown and his Friends*, p. 8.
** Letter of H. B. Hurd to John Brown, 1857, in Sanborn, p. 367.

three months worked fervently. Just before the Dred Scott Decision he spoke to the Massachusetts legislature from which his friends hoped to secure an appropriation for Kansas. This failed, and Brown started on a tour in New England. He spoke at his old home and made a contract for securing one thousand pikes near there. He showed a Kansas bowie-knife and said: "Such a blade as this, mounted upon a strong shaft, or handle, would make a cheap and effective weapon. Our friends in Kansas are without arms or money to get them; and if I could put such weapons into their hands, they could make them very useful. A resolute woman, with such a pike, could defend her cabin door against man or beast."*

In Hartford he spoke and said:

"I am trying to raise from twenty to twenty-five thousand dollars in the free states to enable me to continue my efforts in the cause of freedom. Will the people of Connecticut, my native state, afford me some aid in this undertaking? Will the gentlemen and ladies of Hartford, where I make my appeal in this state, set the example of an earnest effort? Will some gentleman or lady take hold and try what can be done by small contributions from counties, cities, towns, societies, or churches, or in some other way? I think the little beggar children in the street are sufficiently interested to warrant their contributing, if there was any need of it, to secure the object.

"I was told that the newspapers in a certain city were dressed in mourning on hearing that I was killed and scalped in Kansas, but I did not know of it until I reached the place. Much good it did me. In the same place I met a more cool reception than in any other place where I have stopped. If my friends will hold up my hands while I live, I will freely absolve them from any expense over me when I am dead. I do not ask for pay, but shall be most grateful for all the assistance I can get."**

* Sanborn, pp. 375–376.
** Speech of John Brown, Sanborn, p. 379.

On the day that Buchanan was inaugurated and two days before the Dred Scott Decision, he published a similar appeal in the New York *Tribune* "with no little sacrifice of personal feeling." Once he writes: "I am advised that one of Uncle Sam's hounds is on my track, and I have kept myself hid for a few days to let my track get cold. I have no idea of being taken, and intend (if God will) to go back with irons in, rather than upon, my hands."*

Dr. Wayland met him in Worcester where a Frederick Douglass meeting was being arranged just after Taney's decision and says: "I called at the house of Eli Thayer, afterward member of Congress from that district, to ask him to sit on the platform. Here I found a stranger, a man of tall, gaunt form, with a face smooth-shaven, destitute of full beard, that later became a part of history. The children were climbing over his knees; he said, 'The children always come to me.' I was then introduced to John Brown of Osawatomie. How little one imagined then that in less than three years the name of this plain homespun man would fill America and Europe! Mr. Brown consented to occupy a place on the platform, and at the urgent request of the audience, spoke briefly. It is one of the curious facts, that many men who *do* it are utterly unable to *tell* about it. John Brown, a flame of fire in action, was dull in speech."**

Later in the same month Brown accompanied Sanborn and Conway to ex-Governor Reeder's home in Pennsylvania to induce him to return to Kansas, but he declined. April 1st found Brown back in Massachusetts, where for a week or more he was again in hiding from United States officers, probably among his Negro friends in Springfield. It was in April, too, that he took another step in his plan, namely, toward securing military training for his band. He stated according to Realf that, "for twenty or thirty years the idea had possessed him like a passion of giving liberty to the

* Letter to Eli Thayer, 1857, in Sanborn, p. 382.
** Reminiscences of Dr. Wayland, Sanborn, p. 381.

slaves; that he made a journey to England, during which he made a tour upon the European continent, inspecting all fortifications, and especially all earthwork forts which he could find, with a view of applying the knowledge thus gained, with modifications and inventions of his own, to a mountain warfare in the United States. He stated that he had read all the books upon insurrectionary warfare, that he could lay his hands on: the Roman warfare, the successful opposition of the Spanish chieftains during the period when Spain was a Roman province, — how, with ten thousand men, divided and subdivided into small companies, acting simultaneously, yet separately, they withstood the whole consolidated power of the Roman Empire through a number of years. In addition to this he had become very familiar with the successful warfare waged by Schamyl, the Circassian chief, against the Russians; he had posted himself in relation to the wars of Toussaint L'Ouverture; he had become thoroughly acquainted with the wars in Hayti and the islands round about."*

Despite his own knowledge, however, he felt the need of expert advice, and meeting a former lieutenant of Garibaldi, one Hugh Forbes, he was captivated by him, and forthwith hired him to drill his men. Forbes was an excitable, ill-balanced Englishman, who had fought in Italy and at last landed penniless in New York. He thought Brown simply an agent of wealthy and powerful interests and that the whole North was ready to attack slavery. He proposed translating and publishing a manual of guerrilla warfare and John Brown gave him $600 for this work. He was then to join the leader and they would together go to the West and gather and drill a company. This large outlay left John Brown but little in his purse, for, after all, his efforts had been disappointing, and he departed from New England with a quaint half-sarcastic "Farewell to the Plymouth

* Reports of Senate Committees, 36th Congress, 1st Session, No. 278, Testimony of Richard Realf, p. 96.

Rocks, Bunker Hill monuments, Charter Oaks and Uncle Tom's Cabins." He wrote:

"He has left for Kansas; has been trying since he came out of the Territory to secure an outfit, or, in other words, the means of arming and thoroughly equipping his regular minutemen, who are mixed up with the people of Kansas. And he leaves the states with the deepest sadness, that after exhausting his own small means, and with his family and with his brave men suffering hunger, cold, nakedness, and some of them sickness, wounds, imprisonment in irons with extreme cruel treatment, and others death; that, lying on the ground for months in the most sickly, unwholesome, and uncomfortable places, some of the time with the sick and wounded, destitute of shelter, hunted like wolves, and sustained in part by Indians; that after all this, in order to sustain a cause which every citizen of this 'glorious Republic' is under equal moral obligation to do, and for the neglect of which he will be held accountable by God, — a cause in which every man, woman, and child of the entire human family has a deep and awful interest, — that when no wages are asked or expected, he cannot secure, amid all wealth, luxury, and extravagance of this 'heaven-exalted' people, even the necessary supplies of the common soldier. 'How are the mighty fallen!'

"I am destitute of horses, baggage wagons, tents, harness, saddles, bridles, holsters, spurs, and belts; camp equipage, such as cooking and eating utensils, blankets, knapsacks, intrenching tools, axes, shovels, spades, mattocks, crowbars; have not a supply of ammunition; have not money sufficient to pay freight and traveling expenses; and left my family poorly supplied with common necessaries."*

Forbes also disappointed him by his delay, lingering in New York and not appearing in Iowa until August. Brown, who had been sick again, was nevertheless pushing matters among his Kansas friends. He wrote in June: "There are

* Hinton, pp. 614–615.

some half-dozen men I want a visit from at Tabor, Ia., to come off in the most quiet way; ... I have some very important matters to confer with some of you about. Let there be no words about it."*

Arriving at Tabor early in August, Brown's first business was to secure the arms voted him. Because of a previous failure to equip emigrants at points further east, the Massachusetts Kansas State Committee had sent 200 Sharps rifles to Tabor, Ia. Here they were stored in a minister's barn until John Brown called for and removed them. Hugh Forbes finally arrived August 9th, bringing with him copies of his "Manual for the Patriotic Volunteer." Brown wrote home that he and his son Owen were "beginning to take lessons and have, we think, a capable teacher."

Differences, however, soon arose. Forbes wanted $100 per month in addition to the $600 previously paid, while Brown apparently considered that he had already advanced a half year's wage. Then too matters were on a meaner scale than Forbes had dreamed; there was no money, few followers and little glory in sight. He felt himself duped; he despised Brown's ability and proposed taking full command himself, projecting slave-raids into Missouri and other states. Brown was obdurate, and early in November, the foreign tactician suddenly left for the East. This disturbed Brown's plans. He had intended to establish two or three military schools, one in Iowa, one in northern Ohio and one in Canada. Forbes's desertion made him determine to give up the Iowa school and hasten to Ohio. He therefore passed quickly to Kansas, arriving in the vicinity of Lawrence, November 5, 1857.

Cook says:

"I met him at the house of E. B. Whitman, about four miles from Lawrence, K. T., which, I think, was about the first of November following. I was told that he intended to organize a company for the purpose of putting a stop to the

* Letter to Augustus Wattles, 1857, in Sanborn, p. 393.

aggressions of the pro-slavery men. I agreed to join him and was asked if I knew of any other young men who were perfectly reliable whom I thought would join also. I recommended Richard Realf, L. F. Parsons, and R. J. Hinton. I received a note on the next Sunday morning, while at breakfast in the Whitney House, from Captain Brown, requesting me to come up that day, and to bring Realf, Parsons, and Hinton with me. Realf and Hinton were not in town, and therefore I could not extend to them the invitation. Parsons and myself went and had a long talk with Captain Brown. A few days afterward I received another note from Captain Brown, which read, as near as I can recollect, as follows:

"'*Captain Cook*: — Dear Sir — You will please get everything ready to join me at Topeka by Monday night next. Come to Mrs. Sheridan's, two miles south of Topeka, and bring your arms, ammunition, clothing and other articles you may require. Bring Parsons with you if he can get ready in time. Please keep very quiet about this matter. Yours, etc., *John Brown.*'

"I made all my arrangements for starting at the time appointed. Parsons, Realf, and Hinton could not get ready. I left them at Lawrence, and started in a carriage for Topeka. Stopped at a hotel over night, and left early next morning for Mrs. Sheridan's to meet Captain Brown. Staid a day and a half at Mrs. S.'s — then left for Topeka, at which place we were joined by Whipple, Moffett, and Kagi. Left Topeka for Nebraska City, and camped at night on the prairie northeast of Topeka. Here, for the first, I learned that we were to leave Kansas to attend a military school during the winter. It was the intention of the party to go to Ashtabula County, Ohio."*

In this way Brown enlisted John E. Cook, whom he had met about the time of the turn of the battle of Black Jack; Luke F. Parsons, who was a member of his old Kansas

* Confession of John E. Cook in Hinton, pp. 700–701.

company; and Richard Realf, a newspaper man. At Topeka Aaron D. Stevens, a veteran free state fighter, joined, with Charles W. Moffett, an Iowa man, and John Henry Kagi, who became his right hand. With these six he returned to Tabor, where he found William H. Leeman and Charles Plummer Tidd, two of his former followers; Richard Richardson, an intelligent Negro fugitive; and his son Owen. This party of eleven started hurriedly for Ashtabula, O., late in November. "Good-bye," said John Brown, "you will hear from me. We've had enough talk about 'bleeding Kansas.' I will make a bloody spot at another point to be talked about."[*]

So the band started and pressed on their lonely way over two hundred and fifty miles across the wild wastes of Iowa until they came to the village of Springdale, about fifty miles from the Missouri. This was a little settlement intensely anti-slavery in sentiment. Here Brown had planned to stop long enough to sell his teams and then proceed by railroad, east-ward. The panic of this year, beginning late in August, was by December in full swing, and he found himself without funds, and with no remittances from the East. He therefore decided to have his men spend the winter at Springdale while he went East alone. The Quakers received them gladly and they were quartered at a farmhouse three miles from the village, where they paid only a dollar a week for board. The winter passed pleasantly but busily.

Stevens was made drill-master; all arose at five, break-fasted, studied until ten and drilled from ten to twelve. In the afternoon they practiced gymnastics and shooting at targets. Five nights in the week a mock legislature was held either at the home or in the schoolhouse near by. Sometimes Realf and others listened to the townspeople, and there was much visiting. Before John Brown left for the East, he re-vealed his plans in part to his landlord and two other citizens of Springdale.

* Richman, *John Brown Among the Quakers*, pp. 20–21.

"Some time toward spring, John Brown came to my house one Sunday afternoon," said this man. "He informed me that he wished to have some private talk with me; we went into the parlor. He then told me his plans for the future. He had not then decided to attack the armory at Harper's Ferry, but intended to take some fifty to one hundred men into the hills near the Ferry and remain there until he could get together quite a number of slaves, and then take what conveyances were needed to transport the Negroes and their families to Canada. And in a short time after the excitement had abated, to make a strike in some other Southern state; and to continue on making raids, as opportunity offered, until slavery ceased to exist. I did my best to convince him that the probabilities were that all would be killed. He said that, as for himself, he was willing to give his life for the slaves. He told me repeatedly, while talking, that he believed he was an instrument in the hands of God through which slavery would be abolished. I said to him: 'You and your handful of men cánnot cope with the whole South.' His reply was: 'I tell you, Doctor, it will be the beginning of the end of slavery.' He also told me that but two of his men, Kagi and Stevens, knew what his intentions were."*

The landlord several times sat late into the night arguing with Brown about his plans. Some of the neighbors were persuaded to join the band, among them the two Coppocs, and George B. Gill, a Canadian. Stewart Taylor also enlisted there. Hinton, however, still supposed the battleground would be Kansas. He says:

"There was no attempt to make a secret of their drilling, and as Gill shows and Cook stated in his 'confession,' the neighborhood folks all understood that this band of earnest young men were preparing for something far out of the ordinary. Of course Kansas was presumed to be the objective point. But generally the impression prevailed that when the party moved again, it would be somewhere in the direction

* Richman, pp. 28–29.

of the slave states. The atmosphere of those days was charged with disturbance. It is difficult to determine how many of the party actually knew that John Brown designed to invade Virginia. All the testimony goes to show that it is most probable that not until after the assembling at the Maryland farm in 1859 was there a full, definite announcement of Harper's Ferry as the objective point. That he fully explained his purpose to make reprisals on slavery wherever the opportunity offered is without question, but except to Owen, who was vowed to work in his early youth, and Kagi, who informed me at Osawatomie in July, 1858, that Brown gave him his fullest confidence upon their second interview at Topeka in 1857, there is every reason to believe that among the men the details of the intended movement were matters of after confidence. My own experience illustrates this. I was absent from Lawrence when John Brown recruited his little company. He had left already for Iowa before I returned. I met Realf just as he was leaving, and we talked without reserve, he assuring me that the purpose was just to prepare a fighting nucleus for resisting the enforcement of the Lecompton Constitution, which it was then expected Congress might try to impose upon us. Through this, advantage was to be taken of the agitation to prepare for a movement against slavery in Missouri, Arkansas, the Indian Territory and possibly Louisiana. At Kagi's request (with whom I maintained for nearly two years an important, if irregular, correspondence), I began a systematic investigation of the conditions, roads and topography of the Southwest, visiting a good deal of the Indian Territory, with portions of southwest Missouri, western Arkansas, and northern Texas, also, under the guise of examining railroad routes, etc."*

Forbes in the meantime hurried East, nursing his wrath. He had all of a foreigner's difficulty in following the confused threads of another nation's politics at a critical

* Hinton, pp. 156–157.

time. He classed Seward, Wilson, Sumner, Phillips and John Brown together as anti-slavery men who were ready to attack the institution *vi et armis*. This movement which he proposed to lead had been started, and then, as he supposed, shamelessly neglected by its sponsors while he had been thrust upon the tender mercies of John Brown. He was angry and penniless and he intended to have reparation. He first sought out Frederick Douglass, but was received coldly. He appears to have been more successful with Mc Cune Smith and the New York group of Negro leaders. He immediately, too, began to address letters to prominent Republicans.

John Brown was annoyed at Forbes's behavior but seems at first not to have taken it seriously. He left his men at Springdale, and started East in January, arriving at Douglass's Rochester home in February. Douglass says:

"He desired to stop with me several weeks, but added, 'I will not stay unless you will allow me to pay board.' Knowing that he was no trifler, but meant all he said, and desirous of retaining him under my roof, I charged him three dollars a week. While here he spent most of his time in correspondence. He wrote often to George L. Stearns, of Boston, Gerrit Smith, of Peterboro, and many others, and received many letters in return. When he was not writing letters, he was writing and revising a constitution, which he meant to put in operation by means of the men who should go with him in the mountains. He said that to avoid anarchy and confusion there should be a regularly constituted government, which each man who came with him should be sworn to honor and support. . . . His whole time and thought were given to this subject. It was the first thing in the morning and the last thing at night till, I confess, it began to be something of a bore to me. Once in a while he would say he could, with a few resolute men, capture Harper's Ferry and supply himself with arms belonging to the government at that place; but he never announced his intention to do so.

"It was, however, very evidently passing in his mind as a thing that he might do. I paid but little attention to such remarks, although I never doubted that he thought just what he said. Soon after his coming to me he asked me to get for him two smoothly planed boards, upon which he could illustrate, with a pair of dividers, by a drawing, the plan of fortification which he meant to adopt in the mountains. These forts were to be so arranged as to connect one with the other by secret passages, so that if one was carried, another could easily be fallen back upon, and be the means of dealing death to the enemy at the very moment when he might think himself victorious. I was less interested in these drawings than my children were; but they showed that the old man had an eye to the means as well as to the end, and was giving his best thought to the work he was about to take in hand."*

From Rochester went letters sounding his friends, as he was uncertain of the real devotion of the many types of Abolitionists. He wrote Theodore Parker:

"I am again out of Kansas and at this time concealing my whereabouts; but for very different reasons, however, from those I had for doing so at Boston last spring. I have nearly perfected arrangements for carrying out an important measure in which the world has a deep interest, as well as Kansas; and only lack from five to eight hundred dollars to do so, — the same object for which I asked for the secret-service money last fall. It is my only errand here; and I have written to some of my mutual friends in regard to it, but they none of them understand my views so well as you do, and I cannot explain without their first committing themselves more than I know of their doing. I have heard that Parker Pillsbury, and some others in your quarters hold out ideas similar to those on which I act; but I have no personal acquaintance with them, and know nothing of their influence or means. Cannot you either by direct or indirect action do

* Douglass, *Life and Times of Frederick Douglass*, pp. 385–386.

something to further me? Do you know of some parties whom you could induce to give their Abolition theories a thoroughly practical shape? I hope that this will prove to be the last time I shall be driven to harass a friend in such a way. Do you think any of my Garrisonian friends, either at Boston, Worcester, or any other place, can be induced to supply a little 'straw,' if I will absolutely make 'brick'? I have written George L. Stearns, of Medford, and Mr. F. B. Sanborn, of Concord; but I am not informed as to how deeply-dyed Abolitionists those friends are, and must beg you to consider this communication strictly confidential, unless you know of parties who will feel and act, and hold their peace. I want to bring the thing about during the next sixty days."*

To Higginson he wrote: "Railroad business on a somewhat extended scale is the identical object for which I am trying to get means. I have been connected with that business, as commonly conducted, from my childhood, and never let an opportunity slip. I have been operating to some purpose the past season; but I know I have a measure on foot that I feel sure would awaken in you something more than a common interest if you could understand it. I have just written to my friends G. L. Stearns, and F. B. Sanborn, asking them to meet me for consultation at Peterboro, N. Y. I am very anxious to have you come along, as I feel certain that you will never regret having been one of the council."**

The Boston folk hesitated and suggested that Brown come there. He demurred on account of his being too well known. Finally Sanborn alone went to meet Brown and thus relates his experience:

"After dinner, and after a few minutes spent with our guests in the parlor, I went with Mr. Smith, John Brown, and my classmate Morton, to the room of Mr. Morton in

* Letter to Theodore Parker, 1858, in Sanborn, pp. 434–435.
** Letter to Higginson, 1858, in Sanborn, p. 436.

the third story. Here, in the long winter evening which followed, the whole outline of Brown's campaign in Virginia was laid before our little council, to the astonishment and almost the dismay of those present. The constitution which he had drawn for the government of his men, and of such territory as they might occupy, was exhibited by Brown, its provisions recited and explained, the proposed movements of his men indicated, and the middle of May was named as the time of the attack. To begin his hazardous adventure he asked for but eight hundred dollars, and would think himself rich with a thousand. Being questioned and opposed by his friends, he laid before them in detail his methods of organization and fortification; of settlement in the South, if that were possible, and of retreat through the North, if necessary; and his theory of the way in which such an invasion would be received in the country at large. He desired from his friends a patient hearing of his statements, a candid opinion concerning his plan, and, if that were favorable, then such aid in money and support as we could give him. We listened until after midnight, proposing objections and raising difficulties; but nothing could shake the purpose of the old Puritan. Every difficulty had been foreseen and provided against in some manner; the grand difficulty of all, — the manifest hopelessness of undertaking anything so vast with such slender means, — was met with the text of Scripture: 'If God be for us, who can be against us?' He had made nearly all his arrangements: he had so many men enlisted, so many hundred weapons; all he now wanted was the small sum of money. With that he would open his campaign in the spring, and he had no doubt that the enterprise 'would pay' as he said.

"On the 23d of February the discussion was renewed, and, as usually happened when he had time enough, Captain Brown began to prevail over the objections of his friends. At any rate, they saw that they must either stand by him, or leave him to dash himself alone against the fortress he was determined to assault. To withhold aid would only delay, not prevent him; nothing short of betraying him to the enemy would do that. As the sun was setting over the snowy hills of the region where we met, I walked for an hour with Gerrit Smith among those woods and fields (then included in his broad manor) which his father had purchased of the Indians and bequeathed to him. Brown was left at home by the fire, discussing the points of theology with Charles Stewart, an old captain under Wellington, who also happened to be visiting at the house. Mr. Smith restated in his eloquent way the daring propositions of Brown, whose import he understood fully; and then said in substance: 'You see how it is; our dear old friend has made up his mind to this course, and cannot be turned from it. We cannot give him up to die alone; we must support him. I will raise so many hundred dollars for him; you must lay the case before your friends in Massachusetts and perhaps they will do the same. I see no other way.' For myself, I had reached the same conclusion, and engaged to bring the scheme at once to the attention of the three Massachusetts men to whom Brown had written, and also of Dr. S. G. Howe, who had sometimes favored action almost as extreme as this proposed by Brown. I returned to Boston on the 25th of February, and on the same day communicated the enterprise to Theodore Parker and Wentworth Higginson. At the suggestion of Parker, Brown, who had gone to Brooklyn, N. Y., was invited to visit Boston secretly, and did so on the 4th of March, taking a room at the American House, in Hanover Street, and remaining for the most part in his room during the four days of his stay. Mr. Parker was deeply interested in the project, but not very sanguine of its success. He wished to see it tried, believing that it must do good even if it failed. Brown remained at the American House until Monday, March 8th, when he departed for Philadelphia."

On the 6th of March he wrote to his son John from Boston: "My call here has met with a hearty response, so that I feel assured of at least tolerable success. I ought to be thankful for this. All has been effected by quiet meeting of a few

173

choice friends, it being scarcely known that I have been in the city."*

Leaving the money-raising to Sanborn and Smith, Brown turned to his Negro friends, saying to his eldest son, meantime: "I have been thinking that I would like to have you make a trip to Bedford, Chambersburg, Gettysburg, and Uniontown in Pennsylvania, traveling slowly along, and inquiring of every man on the way, or every family of the right stripe, and getting acquainted with them as much as you could. When you look at the location of those places, you will readily perceive the advantage of getting some acquaintance in those parts."**

And then he wrote two touching letters; one to his eldest daughter and one to his staunch friend, Sanborn.

To Ruth Brown he wrote: "The anxiety I feel to see my wife and children once more I am unable to describe. I want exceedingly to see my big baby Ruth's baby, and to see how that little company of sheep look about this time. The cries of my poor sorrow-stricken, despairing children, whose 'tears on their cheeks' are ever in my eyes, and whose sighs are ever in my ears, may however prevent my enjoying the happiness I so much desire. But, courage, courage, courage! — the great work of my life (the unseen hand that 'guided me, and who had indeed holden my right hand, may hold it still,' though I have not known Him at all as I ought) I may yet see accomplished (God helping), and be permitted to return, and 'rest at evening.'

"Oh, my daughter Ruth! Could any plan be devised whereby you could let Henry go 'to school' (as you expressed it in your letter to him while in Kansas), I would rather now have him 'for another term' than to have a hundred average scholars. I have a particular and very important, but not dangerous, place for him to fill in the 'school,' and I know of no man living so well adapted to fill it. I am

* Sanborn, pp. 438–440.
** Letter to John Brown, Jr., 1858, in Sanborn, pp. 450–451.

quite confident some way can be devised so that you and your children could be with him, and be quite happy even, and safe; but God forbid me to flatter you in trouble!"*

To his friend Sanborn he said: "I believe when you come to look at the ample field I labor in, and the rich harvest which not only this entire country but the whole world during the present and future generations may reap from its successful cultivation, you will feel that you are in it, an entire unit. What an inconceivable amount of good you might so effect by your counsel, your example, your encouragement, your natural and acquired ability for active service! And then, how very little we can possibly lose! Certainly the cause is enough to live for, if not to — for. I have only had this one opportunity, in a life of nearly sixty years; and could I be continued ten times as long again, I might not again have another equal opportunity. God has honored but comparatively a very small part of mankind with any possible chance for such mighty and soul-satisfying rewards. But, my dear friend, if you should make up your mind to do so, I trust it will be wholly from the promptings of your own spirit, after having thoroughly counted the cost. I would flatter no man into such a measure, if I could do it ever so easily.

"I expect nothing but to endure hardness; but I expect to effect a mighty conquest, even though it be like the last victory of Samson. I felt for a number of years, in earlier life, a steady, strong desire to die; but since I saw any prospect of becoming a 'reaper' in the great harvest, I have not only felt quite willing to live, but have enjoyed life much; and am now rather anxious to live for a few years more."**

* Letter to his family, 1858, in Sanborn, pp. 440–441.
** Letter to F. B. Sanborn, 1858, in Sanborn, pp. 444–445.

IX

The Black Phalanx

"Awake, awake, put on thy strength, O Zion."

The decade 1830 to 1840 was one of the severest seasons of trial through which the black American ever passed. The great economic change which made slavery the corner-stone of the cotton kingdom was definitely finished and all the subtle moral adjustments which follow were in full action. New immigrants took advantage of the growing prejudice which found a profitable place for the Negro in slavery, and was determined to keep him in it. They began to crowd the free Northern Negro in a fierce economic battle. With a precarious social foothold, little economic organization, and no support in public opinion, the Northern free Negro was forced to yield. In Philadelphia from 1829 to 1849 six mobs of hoodlums and foreigners cowed and murdered the Negroes. In the Middle West and, especially in Ohio, severe Black Laws had been enacted in 1804 to 1807 providing that (a) No Negro should be allowed to settle in Ohio unless he could within twenty days give bond to the amount of $500 signed by two bondsmen, who should guarantee his good behavior and support; (b) The fine for harboring or concealing a fugitive was at first $50, then $100, one-half to go to the informer and one-half to the overseer of the poor in the district; (c) No Negro was allowed to give evidence in any case where a white man was a party.*

These laws, however, were dead letters until 1829, when increased Negro immigration induced the Cincinnati authorities to enforce them. The Negroes obtained a respite of thirty days and sent a deputation to Canada. They were absent for sixty days, and when the whites saw no effort to enforce the law further, they organized a riot. For three days Negroes were killed in the streets until they barricaded their

* Hickok, *The Negro in Ohio*, p. 42.

homes and shot back. Meantime the governor of upper Canada sent word that he "would extend to them a cordial welcome." He said: "Tell the republicans on your side of the line that we royalists do not know men of their color. Should you come to us you will be entitled to all the privileges of the rest of His Majesty's subjects."*

On receipt of this, fully two thousand Negroes went to Canada and founded Wilberforce; while a national convention of Negroes was called in Philadelphia in 1830 — the first of its kind. This convention at an adjourned session in 1831 addressed the public as follows:

"The cause of general emancipation is gaining powerful and able friends abroad. Britain and Denmark have performed such deeds as will immortalize them for their humanity, in the breasts of the philanthropists of the present day; whilst as a just tribute to their virtues, after-ages will yet erect imperishable monuments to their memory. (Would to God we could say thus of our own native soil.)

"And it is only when we look to our own native land, to the birthplace of our fathers, to the land for whose prosperity their blood and our sweat have been shed and cruelty extorted, that the convention has had cause to hang its head and blush. Laws as cruel in themselves as they were unconstitutional and unjust, have in many places been enacted against our poor unfriended and unoffending brethren; laws (without a shadow of provocation on our part) at whose bare recital the very savage draws him up for fear of the contagion, looks noble, and prides himself because he bears not the name of a Christian. But the convention would not wish to dwell long on this subject, as it is one that is too sensibly felt to need description. . . .

"This spirit of persecution was the cause of our convention. It was this that induced us to seek an asylum in the Canadas; and the convention feels happy to report to its brethren, that our efforts to establish a settlement in that

* Hickok, *The Negro in Ohio*, p. 44.

province have not been made in vain. Our prospects are cheering; our friends and funds are daily increasing; wonders have been performed far exceeding our most sanguine expectations; already have our brethren purchased eight hundred acres of land — and two thousand of them have left the soil of their birth, crossed the lines, and laid the foundation for a structure which promises to prove an asylum for the colored population of these United States. They have erected two hundred log-houses, and have five hundred acres under cultivation."

A college "on the manual labor system" was planned: "For the present ignorant and degraded condition of many of our brethren in these United States (which has been a subject of much concern to the convention) can excite no astonishment (although used by our enemies to show our inferiority in the scale of human beings); for, what opportunities have they possessed for mental cultivation or improvement? Mere ignorance, however, in a people divested of the means of acquiring information by books, or an extensive connection with the world, is no just criterion of their intellectual incapacity; and it has been actually seen, in various remarkable instances, that the degradation of the mind and character, which has been too hastily imputed to a people kept, as we are, at a distance from those sources of knowledge which abound in civilized and enlightened communities, has resulted from no other causes than our unhappy situation and circumstances."*

The convention met again in 1833 and resolved on further plans for settling in Canada. These conventions continued to assemble annually for five years, when they were succeeded by the convention of the American Moral Reform Society which met two years longer. Meantime Nat Turner had terrorized Virginia and the South and sent a wave of repression over the North that led to the disfranchisement of Pennsylvania Negroes in 1837.

* Williams, *Negro Race in America*, Vol. 2, pp. 65–67.

Notwithstanding all this the Negroes were struggling on. Beside the general conventions arose the Phœnix Societies, which "planned an organization of the colored people in their municipal sub-divisions with the special object of the promotion of their improvement in morals, literature and the mechanic arts." Lewis Tappan refers to them in his biography. The "Mental Feast," which was a social feature, survived thirty years later in some of the interior towns of Pennsylvania and the West.*

The first Negro paper, *Freedom's Journal*, had been established in 1827 and organizations like the Massachusetts General Colored Association were coöperating with the Abolitionists. The news of emancipation in the British West Indies cheered the Negroes, and indeed without the long effective and self-sacrificing efforts of the Northern freed Negroes, the Abolition movement in the United States could not have been successful. Garrison's first subscriber to *The Liberator* was a black man of Philadelphia, and before and after the Negroes were admitted to membership in the anti-slavery societies, their aid was invaluable. In the West, despite proscription, a fight for schools was carried on from 1830 to 1840, which finally resulted in a wide system of Negro schools partially supported by public funds. Toward 1840 signs of promise began gradually to appear. A West Indian endowed a Negro school in Philadelphia in 1837. The Negro population increased from two and one-third to two and nine-tenths millions in the decade, and evidences of economic success were seen among the free Negroes. Philadelphia had in 1838 one hundred small beneficial societies; Ohio Negroes owned ten thousand acres of land in 1840, while the Canada refugees were beginning to prosper. The mutiny on the *Creole*, the establishment of the Negro Odd Fellows, and the doubling, in ten years, of the membership of the African Methodist Episcopal Church, all pointed to an awakening after the long period of distress.

* Occasional Papers of the American Negro Academy, No. 9, p. 10.

The decade of 1840 to 1850 was a new era — an era of self-assertion and rapid advance for the free Northern Negro. For the first time conscious leadership of undoubted ability appeared. In Boston there was De Grasse, a physician, trained in this country and in France and a member of the Massachusetts Medical Society. Robert Morris was a member of the bar, as was E. R. Walker, whose "Appeal" in 1829 startled the country. William Wells Brown and William Nell were writing, while Charles Lennox Remond was one of the first of the Abolition orators. In New York were the gifted preacher, Henry Highland Garnet; the teachers, Reason and Peterson who made the Negro schools effective; and the physician, McCune Smith, one of the best trained men of his day. In Philadelphia were Robert Purvis, the Abolitionist; William Still, of the Underground Railroad; the three men who made the catering business — Dorsey, Jones and Minton; and the rich Negro lumber merchant, Stephen Smith, whose magnificent endowment for aged Negroes stands to-day at the corner of Girard and Belmont Avenues and is valued at $400,000. In western Pennsylvania were Vashon and Woodson, and in the West were Day, librarian of the Cleveland library; the three Langstons of Oberlin, and the merchants Boyd and Wilcox of Cincinnati. Elsewhere appeared the unlettered, but brave and shrewd leaders of the fugitive slaves. It is said that 500 black messengers of this sort were passing backward and forward between the slave and the free states in this decade, and noticeable among them were Harriet Tubman and Josiah Henson, who brought thousands to the North and to Canada. Foremost of all came Frederick Douglass, born in 1817 and re-born to freedom in 1838. He made his first speech in 1841 and took a prominent part in the anti-slavery campaign of the next decade. In 1845-6, he was in England and, returning in 1847, he established his paper and met John Brown. From that time on he was Brown's chief Negro confidant, and in his house Brown's Eastern campaign was started and largely carried on. The churches also were training men in social leadership in the persons of their bishops, like John Brown's friend Loguen and the noble Daniel Payne.

About 1847 new life appeared in the free Negro group. The Odd Fellows, under Peter Ogden, maintained their independence against aggressions of the whites, and the first of a new series of national colored conventions assembled at Troy, N. Y. "The first article in the first number of Frederick Douglass's *North Star*, published January, 1848, was an extended notice of this convention held at the Liberty Street Church, Troy, N. Y., 1847."

The next year, 1848, Cleveland welcomed a similar national convention. Nearly seventy delegates assembled there on September 6th, "the sessions alternating between the Court-House and the Tabernacle. Frederick Douglass was chosen president. As in previous conventions education was encouraged, the importance of statistical information stated and temperance societies urged."*

The representative character of the delegates was shown by the fact that printers, carpenters, blacksmiths, shoemakers, engineers, dentists, gunsmiths, farmers, physicians, plasterers, masons, college students, clergymen, barbers, hairdressers, laborers, coopers, livery-stable keepers, bath-house keepers and grocers were among the members who were present.**

The same year Frederick Douglass attended a Free Soil convention at Buffalo, N. Y., and writes: "I was not the only colored man well known to the country who was present at this convention. Samuel Ringold Ward, Henry Highland Garnet, Charles L. Remond, and Henry Bibb were there and made speeches which were received with surprise and gratification by the thousands there assembled. As a colored man I felt greatly encouraged and strengthened for my cause while listening to these men, in the pres-

* Occasional Papers of the American Negro Academy, No. 9, p. 15.
** *Ibid.*, No. 9, p. 16.

ence of the ablest men of the Caucasian race. Mr. Ward especially attracted attention at that convention. As an orator and thinker he was vastly superior, I thought, to any of us, and being perfectly black and of unmixed African descent, the splendors of his intellect went directly to the glory of race. In depth of thought, fluency of speech, readiness of wit, logical exactness, and general intelligence, Samuel R. Ward has left no successor among the colored men amongst us, and it was a sad day for our cause when he was laid low in the soil of a foreign country."*

The next decade opened with over three and one-half millions of Negroes in the United States — an enormous increase since 1840 — and a remarkable indication of virility and prosperity despite the new Fugitive Slave Law. The Canadian Negroes were being organized in the Elgin and other settlements, the colored Baptists reported 150,000 members, and the Negroes of New York, replying to the Black Law recommendations of Governor Ward Hunt, proved unincumbered ownership of $1,160,000 worth of property. The escape of fugitive slaves was now systematized in the Underground Railroad and in the secret organization known to outsiders variously as the "League of Freedom," "Liberty League," or "American Mysteries." To these were added the fourteen Canadian "True Bands" with several hundred members each.

State conventions were called in many instances, and the most representative and intelligent national convention held up to that time met in Rochester, N. Y., Douglass's home, in 1853. This convention developed definite opposition to any hope of permanent relief for the colored freeman through schemes of emigration. On the contrary, it directed its energies to affirmative constructive action and planned three measures:

(1) An industrial college "on the manual labor plan." Harriet Beecher Stowe, who was to make a visit to England

* Douglass, *Life and Times of Frederick Douglass* (1892), p. 345.

at the instance of friends in that country, was authorized to receive funds in the name of the colored people of the country for that purpose. "The successful establishment and conduct of such an institution of learning would train youth to be self-reliant and skilled workmen, fitted to hold their own in the struggle of life on the conditions prevailing here."

(2) A registry of colored mechanics, artisans, and business men throughout the Union, and also, "of all the persons willing to employ colored men in business, to teach colored boys mechanic trades, liberal and scientific professions and farming; also a registry of colored men and youth seeking employment or instruction."

(3) A committee on publication "to collect all facts, statistics and statements; all laws and historical records and biographies of the colored people and all books by colored authors." This committee was further authorized "to publish replies of any assaults worthy of note, made upon the character or condition of the colored people."*

The radical stand of this assembly against emigration caused a call for a distinct emigration Negro convention in 1854. This convention was held under the presidency of the same man who afterward presided at the Chatham conclave of John Brown, and with some of the same Negroes present. The account of it continues:

"There were three parties in the emigration convention, ranged according to the foreign fields they preferred to emigrate to. Dr. Delaney headed the party that desired to go to the Niger Valley in Africa, Whitfield the party which preferred to go to Central America, and Holly the party which preferred to go to Haiti.

"All these parties were recognized and embraced by the convention. Dr. Delaney was given a commission to go to Africa, in the Niger Valley, Whitfield to go to Central America, and Holly to Haiti, to enter into negotiations with the

* Occasional Papers of the American Negro Academy, No. 9, pp. 16–19.

authorities of these various countries for Negro emigrants and to report to future conventions. Holly was the first to execute his mission, going down to Haiti in 1855, when he entered into relations with the Minister of the Interior, the father of the late President Hyppolite, and by him was presented to Emperor Faustin I. The next emigration convention was held at Chatham, Canada West, in 1856, when the report on Haiti was made. Dr. Delaney went off on his mission to the Niger Valley, Africa, via England, in 1858. There he concluded a treaty signed by himself and eight kings, offering inducements to Negro emigrants to their territories. Whitfield went to California, intending later to go thence to Central America, but died in San Francisco before he could do so. Meanwhile [James] Redpath went to Haiti as a John Brownist after the Harper's Ferry raid, and reaped the first fruits of Holly's mission by being appointed Haitian Commissioner of Emigration in the United States by the Haitian government, but with the express injunction that Rev. Holly should be called to coöperate with him. On Redpath's arrival in the United States, he tendered Rev. Holly a commission from the Haitian government at $1,000 per annum and traveling expenses to engage emigrants to go to Haiti. The first load of emigrants were from Philadelphia in 1861."*

In 1853 when the American Anti-Slavery Society was formed, Negroes like Purvis and Barbadoes, trained in the Negro convention movement, were among its founders. By 1856 the African Methodist Church had 20,000 members and $425,000 worth of property.

Of all this development John Brown knew far more than most white men and it was on this great knowledge that his great faith was based. To most Americans the inner striving of the Negro was a veiled and an unknown tale: they had heard of Douglass, they knew of fugitive slaves, but of the

* Occasional Papers of the American Negro Academy, No. 9, pp. 20–21.

living, organized, struggling group that made both these phenomena possible they had no conception.

From his earliest interest in Negroes, John Brown sought to know individuals among them intimately and personally. He invited them to his home and he went to theirs. He talked to them, and listened to the history of their trials, advised them and took advice from them. His dream was to enlist the boldest and most daring spirits among them in his great plan.

When, therefore, John Brown came East in January, 1858, his object was not simply to further his campaign for funds, but more especially definitely to organize the Negroes for his work. Already he had disclosed his intentions to Thomas Thomas of Springfield and to Frederick Douglass. He now determined to enlist a larger number and he particularly had in mind the Negroes of New York and Philadelphia, and those in Canada. At no time, however, did John Brown plan to begin his foray with many Negroes. He knew that he must gain the confidence of black men first by a successful stroke, and that after initial success he could count on large numbers. His object then was to interest a few leaders like Douglass, organize societies with wide ramifications, and after the first raid to depend on these societies for aid and recruits.

During his stay with Douglass in February, 1858, he wrote to many colored leaders: Henry Highland Garnet and James N. Gloucester in New York; John Jones in Chicago, and J. W. Loguen of the Zion Church. The addresses of Downing of Rhode Island, and Martin R. Delaney were also noted. On February 23d, after he had been in Boston and Peterboro he notes writing to Loguen, one of the closest of his Negro friends: "Think I shall be ready to go with him [to Canada] by the first of March or about that time."*

On March 10th, John Brown and his eldest son, Henry

* Manuscript Diary of John Brown, Boston Public Library, Vol. 2, p. 35.

Highland Garnet, William Still and others met at the house of Stephen Smith, the rich Negro lumber merchant, of 921 Lombard Street, Philadelphia. Brown seems to have stayed nearly a week in that city, and probably had long conferences with all the chief Philadelphia Negro leaders. On March 18th, he was in New Haven where he wrote Frederick Douglass and J. W. Loguen, saying: "I expect to be on the way by the 28th or 30th inst." After a flying visit home, involving a long walk to save expense, he appeared again at Douglass's in April. Gloucester collected a little money for him in New York and he probably received some in Philadelphia; at last he turned his face toward Canada.

He had long wished to see Canada, and had planned a visit as far back as 1846. Hither he had sent one of the earliest of his North Elba refugees, Walter Hawkins, who became Bishop of the British African Church. On April 8th, John Brown writes his son: "I came on here direct with J. W. Loguen the day after you left Rochester. I am succeeding, to all appearance, beyond my expectations. Harriet Tubman hooked on his whole team at once. He (Harriet) is the most of a man, naturally, that I ever met with. There is the most abundant material, and of the right quality, in this quarter, beyond all doubt. Do not forget to write Mr. Case (near Rochester) at once about hunting up every person and family of the reliable kind about, at, or near Bedford, Chambersburg, Gettysburg, and Carlisle, in Pennsylvania, and also Hagerstown and vicinity, Maryland, and Harper's Ferry, Va."*

He stayed at St. Catherines until the 14th or 15th, chiefly in consultation with that wonderful woman, Harriet Tubman, and sheltered in her home. Harriet Tubman was a full-blooded African, born a slave on the eastern shore of Maryland in 1820. When a girl she was injured by having an iron weight thrown on her head by an overseer, an injury that gave her wild, half-mystic ways with dreams, rhapsodies

* Letter to John Brown, Jr., 1858, in Sanborn, p. 452.

and trances. In her early womanhood she did the rudest and hardest man's work, driving, carting and plowing. Finally the slave family was broken up in 1849, when she ran away. Then began her wonderful career as a rescuer of fugitive slaves. Back and forth she traveled like some dark ghost until she had personally led over three hundred blacks to freedom, no one of whom was ever lost while in her charge. A reward of $10,000 for her, alive or dead, was offered, but she was never taken. A dreamer of dreams as she was, she ever "laid great stress on a dream which she had had just before she met Captain Brown in Canada. She thought she was in 'a wilderness sort of place, all full of rocks, and bushes,' when she saw a serpent raise its head among the rocks, and as it did so, it became the head of an old man with a long white beard, gazing at her, 'wishful like, jes as ef he war gwine to speak to me,' and then two other heads rose up beside him, younger than he, — and as she stood looking at them, and wondering what they could want with her, a great crowd of men rushed in and struck down the younger heads, and then the head of the old man, still looking at her so 'wishful!' This dream she had again and again, and could not interpret it; but when she met Captain Brown, shortly after, behold he was the very image of the head she had seen. But still she could not make out what her dream signified, till the news came to her of the tragedy of Harper's Ferry, and then she knew the two other heads were his two sons."*

In this woman John Brown placed the utmost confidence. Wendell Phillips says: "The last time I ever saw John Brown was under my own roof, as he brought Harriet Tubman to me, saying: 'Mr. Phillips, I bring you one of the best and bravest persons on this continent — General Tubman, as we call her.' He then went on to recount her labors and sacrifices in behalf of her race."**

* Bradford, *Harriet, the Moses of Her People*, pp. 118–119.
** Letter of Wendell Phillips, printed in Bradford, *Harriet, the Moses of Her People*, pp. 155–156.

Only sickness, brought on by her toil and exposure, prevented Harriet Tubman from being present at Harper's Ferry.

From St. Catherines John Brown went to Ingersoll, Hamilton and Chatham. He also visited Toronto, holding meetings with Negroes in Temperance Hall, and at the house of the "late Mr. Holland, a colored man, on Queen Street West. On one occasion Captain Brown remained as a guest with his friend, Dr. A. M. Ross, who is distinguished as a naturalist, as well as an intrepid Abolitionist, who risked his life on several occasions in excursions into the South to enable slaves to flee to Canada."*

Having finally perfected plans for a convention, Brown hurried back to Iowa for his men. During his three months' absence they had been working and drilling in the Quaker settlement of Springdale, Ia., as most persons supposed, for future troubles in "bleeding Kansas." On John Brown's arrival they all hurriedly packed up — Owen Brown, Realf, Kagi, Cook, Stevens, Tidd, Leeman, Moffett, Parsons, and the colored man Richardson, together with their recruits, Gill and Taylor. The Coppocs were to come later. "The leave-taking between them and the people of Springdale was one of tears. Ties which had been knitting through many weeks were sundered, and not only so, but the natural sorrow at parting was intensified by the consciousness of all that the future was full of hazard for Brown and his followers. Before quitting the house and home of Mr. Maxon, where they had spent so long a time, each of Brown's band wrote his name in pencil on the wall of the parlor, where the writing still can be seen by the interested traveler." They all immediately started for Canada by way of Chicago and Detroit. At Chicago they had to wait twelve hours, and the first hotel refused to accommodate Richardson at the breakfast table. John Brown immediately sought another place. The company arrived shortly in Chatham and stopped at a

* Hamilton. *John Brown in Canada*, p. 10.

hotel kept by Mr. Barber, a colored man. While at Chatham, John Brown, as Anderson relates, "made a profound impression upon those who saw or became acquainted with him. Some supposed him to be a staid but modernized 'Quaker'; others a solid business man, from 'somewhere,' and without question a philanthropist. His long white beard, thoughtful and reverent brow and physiognomy, his sturdy, measured tread, as he circulated about with hands, portrayed in the best lithograph, under the pendant coat-skirt of plain brown tweed, with other garments to match, revived to those honored with his acquaintance and knowing his history the memory of a Puritan of the most exalted type."*

John Brown's choice of Canada as a centre of Negro culture, was wise. There were nearly 50,000 Negroes there, and the number included many energetic, intelligent and brave men, with some wealth. Settlements had grown up, farms had been bought, schools established and an intricate social organization begun. Negroes like Henson had been loyally assisted by white men like King, and fugitives were welcomed and succored. Near Buxton, where King and the Elgin Association were working, was Chatham, the chief town of the county of Kent, with a large Negro population of farmers, merchants and mechanics; they had a graded school, Wilberforce Institute, several churches, a newspaper, a fire-engine company and several organizations for social intercourse and uplift. One of the inhabitants said:

"Mr. Brown did not overestimate the state of education of the colored people. He knew that they would need leaders, and require training. His great hope was that the struggle would be supported by volunteers from Canada, educated and accustomed to self-government. He looked on our fugitives as picked men of sufficient intelligence, which, combined with a hatred for the South, would make them willing abettors of any enterprise destined to free their race."

* Anderson, *A Voice from Harper's Ferry*, p. 9.

There were many white Abolitionists near by, but they distrusted Brown and in this way he gained less influence among the Negroes than he otherwise might have had. Martin R. Delaney, who was a fervid African emigrationist, was just about to start to Africa, bearing the mandate of the last Negro convention, when John Brown appeared. "On returning home from a professional visit in the country, Mrs. Delaney informed him that an old gentleman had called to see him during his absence. She described him as having a long, white beard, very gray hair, a sad but placid countenance. In speech he was peculiarly solemn. She added, 'He looked like one of the old prophets. He would neither come in nor leave his name, but promised to be back in two weeks' time.'"

Finally Delaney met John Brown who said:

"'I come to Chatham expressly to see you, this being my third visit on the errand. I must see you at once, sir,' he continued, with emphasis, 'and that, too, in private, as I have much to do and but little time before me. If I am to do nothing here, I want to know it at once.'"

Delaney continues:

"Going directly to the private parlor of a hotel near by, he at once revealed to me that he desired to carry out a great project in his scheme of Kansas emigration, which, to be successful, must be aided and countenanced by the influence of a general convention or council. That he was unable to effect in the United States, but had been advised by distinguished friends of his and mine, that, if he could but see me, his object could be attained at once. On my expressing astonishment at the conclusion to which my friends and himself had arrived, with a nervous impatience, he exclaimed, 'Why should you be surprised? Sir, the people of the Northern states are cowards; slavery has made cowards of them all. The whites are afraid of each other, and the blacks are afraid of the whites. You can effect nothing among such people,' he added, with decided emphasis. On assuring him if a council was all that was desired, he could readily obtain it, he replied, 'That is all; but that is a great deal to me. It is men I want, and not money; money I can get plentiful enough, but no men. Money can come without being seen, but men are afraid of identification with me, though they favor my measures. They are cowards, sir! Cowards!' he reiterated. He then fully revealed his designs. With these I found no fault, but fully favored and aided in getting up the convention."*

Meantime John Brown proceeded carefully to sound public opinion, got the views of others, and, while revealing few of his own plans, set about getting together a body who were willing to ratify his general aims. He consulted the leading Negroes in private, and called a series of small conferences to thresh out preliminary difficulties. In these meetings and in the personal visits, many points arose and were settled. A member of the convention says:

"One evening the question came up as to what flag should be used; our English colored subjects, who had been naturalized, said they would never think of fighting under the hated 'Stars and Stripes.' Too many of them thought they carried their emblem on their backs. But Brown said the old flag was good enough for him; under it freedom had been won from the tyrants of the Old World, for white men; now he intended to make it do duty for the black men. He declared emphatically that he would not give up the Stars and Stripes. That settled the question.

"Some one proposed admitting women as members, but Brown strenuously opposed this, and warned the members not to intimate, even to their wives, what was done.

"One day in my shop I told him how utterly hopeless his plans would be if he persisted in making an attack with the few at his command, and that we could not afford to spare white men of his stamp, ready to sacrifice their lives for the salvation of black men. While I was speaking, Mr. Brown

* Rollins, *Life and Public Services of Martin R. Delaney*, pp. 85–90.

walked to and fro, with his hands behind his back, as was his custom when thinking on his favorite subject. He stopped suddenly and bringing down his right hand with great force, exclaimed: 'Did not my Master Jesus Christ come down from Heaven and sacrifice Himself upon the altar for the salvation of the race, and should I, a worm, not worthy to crawl under His feet, refuse to sacrifice myself?' With a look of determination, he resumed his walk. In all the conversations I had with him during his stay in Chatham of nearly a month, I never once saw a smile light upon his countenance. He seemed to be always in deep and earnest thought."*

The preliminary meeting was held in a frame cottage on Princess Street, south of King Street, then known as the "King Street High School." Some meetings were also held in the First Baptist Church on King Street. In order to mislead the inquisitive, it was pretended that the persons assembling were organizing a Masonic Lodge of colored people. The important proceedings took place in "No. 3 Engine House," a wooden building near McGregor's Creek, erected by Mr. Holden and other colored men.

The regular invitations were issued on the fifth:

Chatham, Canada, May 5, 1858.

"My dear friend:

"I have called a quiet convention in this place of true friends of freedom. Your attendance is earnestly requested. . . .

"Your friend,
"John Brown."

The convention was called together at 10 a. m., Saturday, May 8th, and opened without ceremony. There were present the following Negroes: William Charles Monroe, a Baptist clergyman, formerly president of the emigration

* Reminiscences of J. M. Jones, in Hamilton, *John Brown in Canada,* pp. 14–15.

convention and elected president of this assembly; Martin R. Delaney, afterward major in the United States Army in the Civil War; Alfred Whipper, of Pennsylvania; William Lambert and I. D. Shadd, of Detroit, Mich.; James H. Harris, of Cleveland, O., after the war a representative in Congress for two terms from North Carolina; G. J. Reynolds, an active Underground Railroad leader of Sandusky City; J. C. Grant, A. J. Smith, James M. Jones, a gunsmith and engraver, graduate of Oberlin College, 1849; M. F. Bailey, S. Hunton, John J. Jackson, Jeremiah Anderson, James M. Bell, Alfred Ellisworth, James W. Purnell, George Aiken, Stephen Dettin, Thomas Hickerson, John Cannel, Robinson Alexander, Thomas F. Cary, Thomas M. Kinnard, Robert Van Vauken, Thomas Stringer, John A. Thomas, believed by some to be John Brown s earlier confidant and employee at Springfield, Mass., afterward employed by Abraham Lincoln in his Illinois home and at the White House also; Robert Newman, Charles Smith, Simon Fislin, Isaac Holden, a merchant and surveyor and John Brown's host; James Smith, and Richard Richardson.

Hinton says: "There is no evidence to show that Douglass, Loguen, Garnet, Stephen Smith, Gloucester, Langston, or others of the prominent men of color in the states who knew John Brown, were invited to the Chatham meeting. It is doubtful if their appearance would have been wise, as it would assuredly have been commented on and aroused suspicion."*

The white men present were: John and Owen Brown, father and son; John Henri Kagi, Aaron Dwight Stevens, still known as Charles Whipple; John Edwin Cook, Richard Realf, George B. Gill, Charles Plummer Tidd, William Henry Leeman, Charles W. Moffett, Luke F. Parsons, all of Kansas; and Steward Taylor of Canada, twelve in all. It has been usually assumed that Jeremiah Anderson was white but the evidence makes it possible that he was a mulatto.

* Hinton, p. 178.

John J. Jackson called the meeting to order and Monroe was chosen president. Delaney then asked for John Brown, and Brown spoke at length, followed by Delaney and others.

The constitution was brought forward and, after a solemn parole of honor, was read. It proved to be a frame of government based on the national Constitution, but much simplified and adapted to a moving band of guerrillas. The first forty-five articles were accepted without debate. The next article was: "The foregoing articles shall not be so as in any way to encourage the overthrow of any state government, or the general government of the United States, and look to no dissolution of the Union, but simply to amendment and repeal, and our flag shall be the same that our fathers fought for under the Revolution."

To this Reynolds, the "coppersmith," one of the strongest men in the convention, objected. He felt no allegiance to the nation that had robbed and humiliated him. Brown, Delaney, Kagi and others, however, earnestly advocated the article and it passed. Saturday afternoon the constitution was finally adopted and signed. Brown induced James M. Jones, who had not attended all the sittings, to come to this one, as the constitution must be signed, and he wished his name to be on the roll of honor. As the paper was presented for signature, Brown said, "Now, friend Jones, give us John Hancock bold and strong."

The account continues:

"During one of the sittings, Mr. Jones had the floor, and discussed the chances of the success or failure of the slaves rising to support the plan proposed. Mr. Brown's scheme was to fortify some place in the mountains, and call the slaves to rally under his colors. Jones expressed fear that he would be disappointed, because the slaves did not know enough to rally to his support. The American slaves, Jones argued, were different from those of the West India Island of San Domingo, whose successful uprising is a matter of history, as they had there imbibed some of the impetuous character of their French masters, and were not so overawed by white men. 'Mr. Brown, no doubt thought,' says Mr. Jones, 'that I was making an impression on some of the members, if not on him, for he arose suddenly and remarked, "Friend Jones, you will please say no more on that side. There will be a plenty to defend that side of the question." A general laugh took place.'

"A question as to the time for making the attack came up in the convention. Some advocated that we should wait until the United States became involved in war with some first-class power; that it would be next to madness to plunge into a strife for the abolition of slavery while the government was at peace with other nations. Mr. Brown listened to the argument for some time, then slowly arose to his full height, and said: 'I would be the last one to take the advantage of my country in the face of a foreign foe.' He seemed to regard it as a great insult. That settled the matter in my mind that John Brown was not insane."*

At 6 p. m. the election of officers under the constitution took place, and was finished Monday, the tenth. John Brown was elected commander-in-chief; Kagi, secretary of war; Realf, secretary of state; Owen Brown, treasurer; and George B. Gill, secretary of the treasury. Members of congress chosen were Alfred Ellisworth and Osborne P. Anderson, colored.

After appointing a committee to fill other offices, the convention adjourned. Another and a larger body was also organized, as Delaney says: "This organization was an extensive body, holding the same relation to his movements as a state or national executive committee holds to its party principles, directing their adherence to fundamental principles."**

This committee still existed at the time of the Harper's Ferry raid. With characteristic reticence Brown revealed his whole plan to no one, and many of those close to him re-

* Reminiscences of J. M. Jones, in Hamilton, *John Brown in Canada*, pp. 14 and 16.
** Rollins, *Life and Public Services of Martin R. Delaney*, pp. 85–90.

ceived quite different impressions, or rather read their own ideas into Brown's careful speech. One of his Kansas band says: "I am sure that Brown did not communicate the details of his plans to the members of the convention, more than in a very general way. Indeed, I do not now remember that he gave them any more than the impressions which they could gather from the methods of organization. From those who were directly connected with his movements he solicited plans and methods — including localities — of operations in writing. Of course, we had almost precise knowledge of his methods, but all of us perhaps did not know just the locality selected by him, or, if knowing, did not comprehend the resources and surroundings."*

"John Brown, never, I think," said Mr. Jones, "communicated his whole plan, even to his immediate followers. In his conversations with me he led me to think that he intended to sacrifice himself and a few of his followers for the purpose of arousing the people of the North from the stupor they were in on this subject. He seemed to think such sacrifice necessary to awaken the people from the deep sleep that had settled upon the minds of the whites of the North. He well knew that the sacrifice of any number of Negroes would have no effect. What he intended to do, so far as I could gather from his conversation, from time to time, was to emulate Arnold Winkelried, the Swiss chieftain, when he threw himself upon the Austrian spearmen, crying, 'Make way for Liberty.' "** Delaney in his own bold, original way assumed that Brown intended another Underground Railway terminating in Kansas. Delaney himself was on his way to Africa and could take no active part in the movement.

The constitution adopted by the convention was an instrument designed for the government of a band of isolated people fighting for liberty. The preamble said:

* Reminiscences of George B. Gill, in Hinton, p. 185.
** Reminiscences of J. M. Jones, in Hamilton, *John Brown in Canada*, p. 16.

"Whereas slavery, throughout its entire existence in the United States, is none other than a most barbarous, unprovoked and unjustifiable war of one portion of its citizens upon another portion — the only conditions of which are perpetual imprisonment and hopeless servitude or absolute extermination — in utter disregard and violation of those eternal and self-evident truths set forth in our Declaration of Independence:

"Therefore, we, citizens of the United States, and the oppressed people who, by a recent decision of the Supreme Court, are declared to have no rights which the white man is bound to respect, together with all other people degraded by the laws thereof, do, for the time being, ordain and establish ourselves the following provisional constitution and ordinances, the better to protect our persons, property, lives, and liberties, and to govern our actions."*

The Declaration of Independence referred to was probably designed to be adopted July 4, 1858, when, as originally planned, the blow was to be actually struck. It was a paraphrase of the original declaration and ended by saying:

"Declaring that we will serve them no longer as slaves, knowing that the 'Laborer is worthy of his hire,' We therefore, the Representatives of the circumscribed citizens of the United States of America, in General Congress assembled, appealing to the supreme Judge of the World, for the rectitude of our intentions, Do in the name, & by authority of the oppressed Citizens of the Slave States, Solemnly publish and Declare: that the Slaves are, & of right ought to be as free & as independent as the unchangeable Law of God requires that All Men Shall be. That they are absolved from all allegiance to those Tyrants, who still persist in forcibly subjecting them to perpetual 'Bondage,' and that all friendly connection between them and such Tyrants, is & ought to be totally desolved, And that as free and independent citizens

* Hinton, pp. 619–633.

197

of these states, they have a perfect right, a sufficient and just cause, to defend themselves against the Tyranny of their oppressors. To solicit aid from & ask the protection of all true friends of humanity and reform, of whatever nation, & wherever found; A right to contract all Alliances, & to do all other acts and things which free independent Citizens may of right do. And for the support of the Declaration, with a firm reliance on the protection of divine Providence: We mutually pledge to each other, Our Lives, and Our sacred Honor."*

The constitution consisted of forty-eight articles. All persons of mature age were admitted to membership and there was established a congress with one house of five to ten members, a president and vice-president and a court of five members, each one of whom held circuit courts. All these officials were to unite in selecting a commander-in-chief, treasurer, secretaries, and other officials. All property was to be in common and no salaries were to be paid. All persons were to labor. All indecent behavior was forbidden: "The marriage relation shall be at all times respected, and families kept together, as far as possible; and broken families encouraged to reunite, and intelligence offices established for that purpose. Schools and churches established, as soon as may be, for the purpose of religious and other instructions; and the first day of the week regarded as a day of rest, and appropriated to moral and religious instruction and improvement, relief of the suffering, instruction of the young and ignorant, and the encouragement of personal cleanliness; nor shall any person be required on that day to perform ordinary manual labor, unless in extremely urgent cases."** All persons were to carry arms but not concealed. There were special provisions for the capture of prisoners, and protection of their persons and property.

John Brown was well pleased with his work and wrote

* Hinton, pp. 642–643.
** Provisional Constitution, Art. 42.

home: "Had a good Abolition convention here, from different parts, on the 8th and 10th inst. Constitution slightly amended and adopted, and society organized."*

Just now as everything seemed well started, came disquieting news from the East. Forbes had been there since November, growing more and more poverty-stricken and angry, and his threats, hints and visits were becoming frequent and annoying. He complained to Senator Wilson, to Charles Sumner, to Hale, Seward and Horace Greeley, and to the Boston coterie. He could not understand why these leaders of the movement against slavery, as he supposed, should leave the real power in the hands of John Brown, and neglect an experienced soldier like himself after raising false expectations. John Brown had dealt with Forbes gently but firmly, and had sought to conciliate him, but in vain. Brown was apparently determined to outwit him by haste; he had written his Massachusetts friends to join him at the Chatham Convention, but Sanborn and Howe had already received threatening letters from Forbes which alarmed them. He evidently had careful information of Brown's movements and was bent on making trouble. He probably was at this time in the confidence of McCune Smith and the able Negro group of New York who had developed a not unnatural distrust of whites, and a desire to foster race pride. Using information thus obtained, Forbes sought to put pressure on Republican leaders to organize more effective warfare on slavery, and to discredit John Brown. Sanborn wrote hastily: "It looks as if the project must, for the present, be deferred, for I find by reading Forbes's epistles to the doctor that he knows the details of the plan, and even knows (what very few do) that the doctor, Mr. Stearns, and myself are informed of it. How he got this knowledge is a mystery. He demands that Hawkins [John Brown] be dismissed as agent, and himself or some other be put in his place, threatening otherwise to make the busi-

* Letter to his family, 1858, in Sanborn, pp. 455–456.

ness public.' * Gerrit Smith concluded, "Brown must go no further." But Higginson wisely demurred. "I regard any postponement," he said, "as simply abandoning the project; for if we give it up now, at the command or threat of H. F., it will be the same next year. The only way is to circumvent the man somehow (if he cannot be restrained in his malice). When the thing is well started, who cares what he says?"**

Further efforts were made to conciliate Forbes but he wrote wildly: "I have been grossly defrauded in the name of humanity and anti-slavery. . . . I have for years labored in the anti-slavery cause, without wanting or thinking of a recompense. Though I have made the least possible parade of my work, it has nevertheless not been entirely without fruit. . . . Patience and mild measures having failed, I reluctantly have recourse to harshness. Let them not flatter themselves that I shall eventually become weary and shall drop the subject; it is as yet quite at its beginning."***

"To go on in face of this is madness," wrote Sanborn, and John Brown was urged to come to New York to meet Stearns and Howe. Brown had already been delayed nearly a month at Chatham by this trouble, but he obeyed the summons. Sanborn says: "When, about May 20th, Mr. Stearns met Brown in New York, it was arranged that hereafter the custody of the Kansas rifles should be in Brown's hands as the agent, not of this committee, but of Mr. Stearns alone. It so happened that Gerrit Smith, who seldom visited Boston, was coming there late in May. . . . He arrived and took rooms at the Revere House, where, on the 24th of May, 1858, the secret committee (organized in March, and consisting of Smith, Parker, Howe, Higginson, Stearns, and Sanborn) held a meeting to consider the situation. It had already been decided to postpone the attack, and the arms

* Letter from Sanborn to Higginson, 1858, in Sanborn, p. 458.
** Letter from Higginson to Theodore Parker, in Sanborn, p. 459.
*** Letter from Forbes to Higginson, 1858, in Sanborn, pp. 460 to 461.

had been placed under a temporary interdict, so that they could only be used, for the present, in Kansas. The questions remaining were whether Brown should be required to go to Kansas at once, and what amount of money should be raised for him in the future. Of the six members of the committee only one (Higginson) was absent.... It was unanimously resolved that Brown ought to go to Kansas at once."

As soon as possible after this, on May 21st, Brown visited Boston, and while there held a conversation with Higginson, who made a record of it at the time. He states that Brown was full of regret at the decision of the Revere House council to postpone the attack till the winter or spring of 1859, when the secret committee would raise for Brown two or three thousand dollars; he meantime was to blind Forbes by going to Kansas, and to transfer the property so as to relieve the Kansas committee of responsibility, they in future not to know his plans.

"On probing Brown," Higginson goes on, "I found that he ... considered delay very discouraging to his thirteen men, and to those in Canada. Impossible to begin in autumn; and he would not lose a day (he finally said) if he had three hundred dollars; it would not cost twenty-five dollars apiece to get his men from Ohio, and that was all he needed. The knowledge that Forbes could give of his plan would be injurious, for he wished his opponents to underrate him; but still ... the increased terror produced would perhaps counterbalance this, and it would not make much difference. If he had the means he would not lose a day. He complained that some of his Eastern friends were not men of action; that they were intimidated by Wilson's letter, and magnified the obstacles. Still, it was essential that they should not think him reckless, he said; and as they held the purse, he was powerless without them, having spent nearly everything received this campaign, on account of delay, — a month at Chatham, etc."*

* Sanborn, pp. 463–464.

There was nothing now for Brown but to conceal his arms, scatter his men and hide a year in Kansas. It was a bitter necessity and it undoubtedly helped ruin the success of the foray. The Negroes in Canada fell away from the plan when it did not materialize and doubted Brown's determination and wisdom. His son hid the arms in northern Ohio in a haymow.

Meantime, a part of the company — Stevens, Cook, Tidd, Gill, Taylor and Owen Brown — immediately after the adjournment of the convention, had gone to Cleveland, O., and had found work in the surrounding country. Brown wrote from Canada at the time:

"It seems that all but three have managed to stop their board bills, and I do hope the balance will follow the manlike and noble example of patience and perseverance set them by the others, instead of being either discouraged or out of humor. The weather is so wet here that no work can be obtained. I have only received $15 from the East, and such has been the effect of the course taken by F. [Col. Forbes], on our Eastern friends, that I have some fears that we shall be compelled to delay further action for the present. They [his Eastern friends] urge us to do so, promising us liberal assistance after a while. I am in hourly expectation of help sufficient to pay off our bills here, and to take us on to Cleveland, to see and advise with you, which we shall do at once when we shall get the means. Suppose we do have to defer our direct efforts; shall great and noble minds either indulge in useless complaint, or fold their arms in discouragement, or sit in idleness, when we may at least avoid losing ground? It is in times of difficulty that men show what they are; it is in such times that men mark themselves. Are our difficulties such as to make us give up one of the noblest enterprises in which men ever were engaged?"*

Two weeks later the rest of the party, except Kagi, fol-

* Letter to Owen Brown, 1858, in Richman, *John Brown Among the Quakers*, pp. 40–41.

lowed to Cleveland, John Brown going East to meet Stearns. Kagi, who was an expert printer, went to Hamilton, Canada, where he set up and printed the constitution, arriving in Cleveland about the middle of June when Brown returned from the East. Realf says that Brown did not have much money, but sent him to New York and Washington to watch Forbes and possibly regain his confidence. Realf, however, had become timid and lukewarm in the cause and sailed away to England. The rest of the men scattered. Owen Brown went to Akron, O. Cook left Cleveland for the neighborhood of Harper's Ferry; Gill secured work in a Shaker settlement, probably Lebanon, O., where Tidd was already employed; Steward Taylor went to Illinois; Stevens awaited Brown at Cleveland; while Leeman got some work in Ashtabula County. John Brown left Boston, on the 3rd of June, proceeding to the North Elba home for a short visit. Then he, Kagi, Stevens, Leeman, Gill, Parsons, Moffett, and Owen were gathered together and the party went to Kansas, arriving late in June.

Thus suddenly ended John Brown's attempt to organize the Black Phalanx. His intimate friends understood that the great plan was only postponed, but the postponement had, as Higginson predicted, a dampening effect, and Brown's chances of enlisting a large Canadian contingent were materially lessened. Nevertheless, seed had been sown. And there were millions of human beings to whom the last word of the Chatham Declaration of Independence was more than mere rhetoric: "Nature is mourning for its murdered and afflicted children. Hung be the Heavens in scarlet!"

X

The Great Black Way

"The Spirit of the Lord God is upon me; because the Lord hath anointed me to preach good tidings unto the meek; He hath sent me to bind up the broken-hearted, to proclaim liberty to the captives, and the opening of the prison to them that are bound."

Half-way between Maine and Florida, in the heart of the Alleghanies, a mighty gateway lifts its head and discloses a scene which, a century and a quarter ago, Thomas Jefferson said was "worth a voyage across the Atlantic." He continues: "You stand on a very high point of land; on your right comes up the Shenandoah, having ranged along the foot of the mountain a hundred miles to find a vent; on your left approaches the Potomac, in quest of a passage also. In the moment of their junction they rush together against the mountain, rend it asunder, and pass off to the sea."*

This is Harper's Ferry and this was the point which John Brown chose for his attack on American slavery. He chose it for many reasons. He loved beauty: "When I met Brown at Peterboro in 1858," writes Sanborn, "Morton played some fine music to us in the parlor, — among other things Schubert's *Serenade,* then a favorite piece, — and the old Puritan, who loved music and sang a good part himself, sat weeping at the air."** He chose Harper's Ferry because a United States arsenal was there and the capture of this would give that dramatic climax to the inception of his plan which was so necessary to its success. But both these were minor reasons. The foremost and decisive reason was that Harper's Ferry was the safest natural entrance to the Great Black Way. Look at the map (page 205). The shaded portion is "the black belt" of slavery where there were massed in 1859 at least three of the four million slaves. Two paths led

* Jefferson, *Notes on Virginia.*
** Sanborn, p. 467.

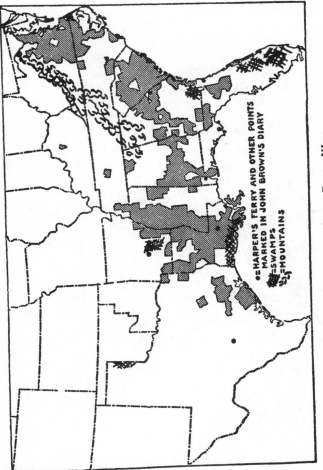

● = HARPER'S FERRY AND OTHER POINTS
    MARKED IN JOHN BROWN'S DIARY
    = SWAMPS
    = MOUNTAINS

MAP SHOWING THE GREAT BLACK WAY

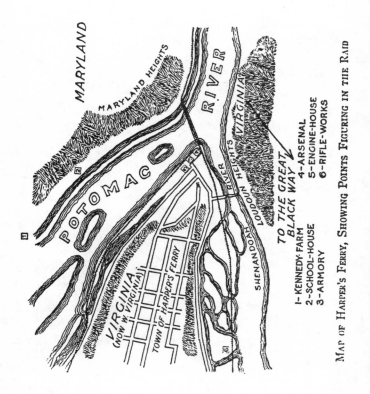

MARYLAND

MARYLAND HEIGHTS

POTOMAC

RIVER

VIRGINIA
(NOW W. VIRGINIA)

TOWN OF HARPER'S FERRY

RIVER

SHENANDOAH

LOUDOUN HEIGHTS

VIRGINIA

TO THE GREAT
BLACK WAY

1—KENNEDY FARM
2—SCHOOL-HOUSE
3—ARMORY
4—ARSENAL
5—ENGINE-HOUSE
6—RIFLE-WORKS

MAP OF HARPER'S FERRY, SHOWING POINTS FIGURING IN THE RAID

206

southward toward it in the East: — the way by Washington, physically broad and easy, but legally and socially barred to bondsmen; the other way, known to Harriet Tubman and all fugitives, which led to the left toward the crests of the Alleghanies and the gateway of Harper's Ferry. One has but to glance at the mountains and swamps of the South to see the Great Black Way. Here, amid the mighty protection of overwhelming numbers, lay a path from slavery to freedom, and along that path were fastnesses and hiding-places easily capable of becoming permanent fortified refuges for organized bands of determined armed men.

The exact details of Brown's plan will never be fully known. As Realf said: "John Brown was a man who would never state more than it was absolutely necessary for him to do. No one of his most intimate associates, and I was one of the most intimate, was possessed of more than barely sufficient information to enable Brown to attach such companion to him."*

A glance at the map shows clearly that John Brown intended to operate in the Blue Ridge mountains rising east of the Shenandoah and known at Harper's Ferry as Loudoun Heights. The Loudoun Heights rise boldly 500 to 700 feet above the village of Harper's Ferry and 1,000 feet above the sea. They run due south and then southwest, dipping down a little the first three miles, then rising to 1,500 feet, which level is practically maintained until twenty-five miles below Harper's Ferry where the mountains broaden to a dense and labyrinthical wilderness, and rise to a height of 2,000 or more feet. Right at this high point and in sight of High Knob (a peak of 2,400 feet) began, in Fauquier County, the Great Black Way. In this county in 1850 were over 10,000 slaves, and 650 free Negroes, as compared with 9,875 whites. From this county to the southern boundary of Virginia were a series of black counties with a majority of

* Reports of Senate Committees, 36th Congress, 1st Session, No. 278; Testimony of Richard Realf, p. 100.

slaves, containing in 1850 at least 260,000 Negroes. From here the Great Black Way went south as John Brown indicated in his diary and undoubtedly in the marked maps, which Virginia afterward hastily destroyed.

The easiest way to get to these heights was from Harper's Ferry. An hour's climb from the arsenal grounds would easily have hidden a hundred men in inaccessible fastnesses, provided they were not overburdened; and even with arms, ammunition and supplies, they could have repelled, without difficulty, attacks on the retreat. Forts and defenses could be prepared in these mountains, and before the raid they had been pretty thoroughly explored and paths marked. In Harper's Ferry just at the crossing of the main road from Maryland lay the arsenal. The plan without doubt was, first, to collect men and arms on the Maryland side of the Potomac; second, to attack the arsenal suddenly and capture it; third, to bring up the arms and ammunition and, together with those captured, to cross the Shenandoah to Loudoun Heights and hide in the mountain wilderness; fourth, thence to descend at intervals to release slaves and get food, and so retreat southward. Most writers have apparently supposed that Brown intended to retreat from the arsenal across the Potomac. A moment's thought will show the utter absurdity of this plan. Brown knew guerrilla warfare, and the failure of the Harper's Ferry raid does not prove it a blunder from the start. The raid was not a foray *from* the mountains, which failed because its retreat was cut off; but it was a foray *to* the mountains with the village and arsenal on the way, which was defeated apparently because the arms and ammunition train failed to join the advance-guard.

This then was the great plan which John Brown had been slowly elaborating and formulating for twenty years — since the day when kneeling beside a Negro minister he had sworn his sons to blood feud with slavery.

The money resources with which John Brown undertook his project are not exactly known. Sanborn says: "Brown's first request in 1858 was for a fund of a thousand dollars only; with this in hand he promised to take the field either in April or May. Mr. Stearns acted as treasurer of this fund, and before the 1st of May nearly the whole amount had been paid in or subscribed, — Stearns contributing three hundred dollars, and the rest of our committee smaller sums. It soon appeared, however, that the amount named would be too small, and Brown's movements were embarrassed from the lack of money before the disclosures of Forbes came to his knowledge."* From first to last George L. Stearns gave in cash and arms about $7,500, and Gerrit Smith contributed more than $1,000. Merriam brought with him $600 in gold in October. Between March 10th and October 16th, Brown expended at least $2,500. In all Sanborn raised $4,000 for Brown. Hinton says: "As near as can be estimated, the money received by Brown could not have exceeded $12,000, while the supplies, arms, etc., furnished may have cost $10,000 more. Of course, there were smaller contributions and support coming in, but if the total estimate be placed at $25,000, for the period between the 15th of September, 1856, when he left Lawrence, Kan., and the 16th of October, 1859, when he moved on Harper's Ferry, Va., with twenty-one men, it will certainly cover all of the outlay except that of time, labor, and lives."**

This total, however, does not include a fund of $1,000 raised for his family.

The civic organization under which Brown intended to work has been spoken of. The military organization was based on his Kansas experience and his reading. In his diary is this entry:

> "Circassia has about 550,000
> Switzerland 2,037,030
> Guerrilla warfare See Life of Lord Wellington
> Page 71 to Page 75 (Mina)
> See also Page 102 some valuable hints

* Sanborn, p. 457.
** Hinton, pp. 130–131.

in Same Book. See also Page 196 some
most important instructions to officers.
See also same Book Page 235 these words
 deep, and
narrow defiles where 300 men would suffise
 to check an army.
See also Page 236 on top of Page   "

This life of Wellington, W. P. Garrison states,[*] was
Stocqueler's and the pages referred to tell of the Spanish
guerrillas under Mina in 1810, and of methods of cooking
and discipline. In one place the author says: "Here we have
a chaos of mountains, where we meet at every step huge
fallen masses of rock and earth, yawning fissures, deep and
narrow defiles, where 300 men would suffice to check an
army." The Alleghanies in Virginia and Carolina were similar in topography and, for operation here, Brown proposed
a skeleton army which could work together or in small units
of any size:

"A company will consist of fifty-six privates, twelve non-
commissioned officers, eight corporals, four sergeants and
three commissioned officers (two lieutenants, a captain),
and a surgeon.

"The privates shall be divided into bands or messes of
seven each, numbering from one to eight, with a corporal to
each, numbered like his band.

"Two bands will comprise a section. Sections will be numbered from one to four.

"A sergeant will be attached to each section, and numbered like it.

"Two sections will comprise a platoon. Platoons will be
numbered one and two, and each commanded by a lieutenant designed by like number."[**]

[*] W. P. Garrison in the *Andover Review*, Dec., 1890, and Jan.,
1891.
[**] General Orders, Oct. 10, 1859, Hinton, pp. 646–647.

Four companies composed a battalion, four battalions a regiment, and four regiments a brigade.

So much for his resources and plans. Now for the men whom he chose as co-workers. The number of those who took part in the Harper's Ferry raid is not known. Perhaps, including active slave helpers, there were about fifty. Seventeen Negroes, reported as probably killed, are wholly unknown, and those slaves who helped and escaped are also unknown. This leaves the twenty-two men usually regarded as making the raid. They fall, of course, into two main groups, the Negroes and the whites. Six or seven of the twenty-two were Negroes.

First in importance came Osborne Perry Anderson, a free-born Pennsylvania mulatto, twenty-four years of age. He was a printer by trade, "well educated, a man of natural dignity, modest, simple in character and manners." He met John Brown in Canada. He wrote the most interesting and reliable account of the raid, and afterward fought in the Civil War.

Next came Shields Green, a full-blooded Negro from South Carolina, whence he had escaped from slavery, after his wife had died, leaving a living boy still in bondage. He was about twenty-four years old, small and active, uneducated but with natural ability and absolutely fearless. He met Brown at the home of Frederick Douglass, who says: "While at my house, John Brown made the acquaintance of a colored man who called himself by different names — sometimes 'Emperor,' at other times, 'Shields Green.'... He was a fugitive slave, who had made his escape from Charleston, S. C.; a state from which a slave found it no easy matter to run away. But Shields Green was not one to shrink from hardships or dangers. He was a man of few words, and his speech was singularly broken; but his courage and self-respect made him quite a dignified character. John Brown saw at once what 'stuff' Green 'was made of,' and confided to him his plans and purposes. Green easily believed in

Brown, and promised to go with him whenever he should be ready to move."*

Dangerfield Newby was a free mulatto from the neighborhood of Harper's Ferry. He was thirty years of age, tall and well built, with a pleasant face and manner; he had a wife and seven children in slavery about thirty miles south of Harper's Ferry. The wife was about to be sold south at this time, and was sold immediately after the raid. Newby was the spy who gave general information to the party, and lived out in the community until the night of the attack.

John A. Copeland was born of free Negro parents in North Carolina, reared in Oberlin and educated at Oberlin College. He was a straight-haired mulatto, twenty-two years old, of medium size, and a carpenter by trade. Hunter, the prosecuting attorney of Virginia, says: "From my intercourse with him I regarded him as one of the most respectable prisoners that we had. . . . He was a copper-colored Negro, behaved himself with as much firmness as any of them, and with far more dignity. If it had been possible to recommend a pardon for any of them, it would have been for this man Copeland, as I regretted as much, if not more, at seeing him executed than any other one of the party."**

Lewis Sherrard Leary was born in slavery in North Carolina and also reared in Oberlin, where he worked as a harness-maker. An Oberlin friend testified: "He called again afterward, and told me he would like to keep to the amount I had given him, and would like a certain amount more for a certain purpose, and was very chary in his communications to me as to how he was to use it, except that he did inform me that he wished to use it in aiding slaves to escape. Circumstances just then transpired which had interested me contrary to any thought I ever had in my own mind before.

---

* Douglass, *Life and Times of Frederick Douglass*, p. 387.

** Hunter, *John Brown's Raid*, republished in the Publications of the Southern History Association, Vol. 1, No. 3, p. 188.

I had had exhibited to me a daguerreotype of a young lady, a beautiful appearing girl, who I was informed was about eighteen years of age...."* But here Senator Mason of the Inquisition scented danger, and we can only guess the reasons that sent Leary to his death. He was said to be Brown's first recruit outside the Kansas band.

John Anderson, a free Negro from Boston, was sent by Lewis Hayden and started for the front. Whether he arrived and was killed, or was too late has never been settled.

The seventh man of possible Negro blood was Jeremiah Anderson. He is listed with the Negroes in all the original reports of the Chatham Convention and was, as a white Virginian who saw him says, "of middle stature, very black hair and swarthy complexion. He was supposed by some to be a Canadian mulatto."** He was descended from Virginia slaveholders who had moved north and was born in Indiana. He was twenty-six years old.

Of the white men there were, first of all, John Brown and his family, consisting of three sons, and two brothers of his eldest daughter's husband, William and Dauphin Thompson.

Oliver Brown was a boy not yet twenty-one, though tall and muscular, and had just been married. Watson was a man of twenty-five, tall and athletic; while Owen was a large, red-haired prematurely aged man of thirty-five, partially crippled, good-tempered and cynical. The Thompsons were neighbors of John Brown and part of a brood of twenty children. The Brown family and theirs intermarried and Anne Brown says that William, who was twenty-six years of age, was "kind, generous-hearted, and helpful to others." Dauphin, a boy of twenty-two, was, she writes, "very quiet, with a fair, thoughtful face, curly blonde hair,

* Report: Reports of Senate Committees, 36th Congress, 1st Session, No. 278; Testimony of Ralph Plumb, p. 181.
** Barry, *The Strange Story of Harper's Ferry,* p. 93.

and baby-blue eyes. He always seemed like a very good girl."*

The three notable characters of the band were Kagi, Stevens and Cook, the reformer, the soldier and the poet. Kagi's family came from the Shenandoah Valley. He was twenty-four, had a good English education and was a newspaper reporter in Kansas, where he earnestly helped the free state cause. He had strong convictions on the subject of slavery and was willing to risk all for them. "You will all be killed," cried a friend who heard his plan. "Yes, I know it, Hinton, but the result will be worth the sacrifice." Hinton adds: "I recall my friend as a man of personal beauty, with a fine, well-shaped head, a voice of quiet, sweet tones, that could be penetrating and cutting, too, almost to sharpness."** Anderson writes that Kagi "left home when a youth, an enemy to slavery, and brought as his gift offering to freedom three slaves, whom he piloted to the North. His innate hatred of the institution made him a willing exile from the state of his birth, and his great abilities, natural and acquired, entitled him to the position he held in Captain Brown's confidence. Kagi was indifferent to personal appearance; he often went about with slouched hat, one leg of his pantaloons properly adjusted, and the other partly tucked into his high boot-top; unbrushed, unshaven, and in utter disregard of 'the latest style.' "***

Stevens was a handsome six-foot Connecticut soldier of twenty-eight years of age, who had thrashed his major for mistreating a fellow soldier and deserted from the United States army. He was active in Kansas and soon came under John Brown's discipline.

"Why did you come to Harper's Ferry?" asked a Virginian.

He replied: "It was to help my fellow men out of bond-

* Anne Brown in Hinton, pp. 529–530.
** Hinton, p. 453.
*** Anderson, *A Voice from Harper's Ferry,* p. 15.

age. You know nothing of slavery — I know a great deal. It is the crime of crimes. I hate it more and more the longer I live. Even since I have been lying in this cell, I have heard the crying of slave-children torn from their parents."*

Cook was also a Connecticut man of twenty-nine years, tall, blue-eyed, golden-haired and handsome, but a far different type from Stevens. He was talkative, impulsive and restless, eager for adventure but hardly steadfast. He followed John Brown as he would have followed any one else whom he liked, dreaming his dreams, rushing ahead in the face of danger and shrinking back appalled and pitiful before the grim face of death. He was the most thoroughly human figure in the band.

One other deserves mention, because it was probably his slowness or obstinacy that ruined the success of John Brown's raid. This was Charles P. Tidd. He was from Maine, twenty-seven years old, trained in Kansas warfare — a nervous, overbearing and quarrelsome man. He bitterly opposed the plan of capturing Harper's Ferry when it was finally revealed, and as Anne Brown said, "got so warm that he left the farm and went down to Cook's dwelling near Harper's Ferry to let his wrath cool off." A week passed before he sullenly gave in.

Beside these there were six other men of more or less indistinct personalities. Five were young Kansas settlers from Maine, the Middle West and Canada, trained in guerrilla warfare under Brown and Montgomery and thoroughly disliking the slave system which they had seen. They were personal admirers of Brown and lovers of adventure. The last recruit, Merriam, was a New England aristocrat turned crusader, fighting the world's ills blindly but devotedly. The Negro Lewis Hayden met him in Boston, "and, after a few words, said, 'I want five hundred dollars and must have it.' Merriam, startled at the manner of the request, replied, 'If you have a good cause, you shall have it.' Hayden then told

* Hinton, pp. 496–497.

215

Merriam briefly what he had learned from John Brown, Jr.: that Captain Brown was at Chambersburg, or could be heard of there; that he was preparing to lead a party of liberators into Virginia, and that he needed money; to which Merriam replied: 'If you tell me John Brown is there, you can have my money and me along with it.' "*

These were the men — idealists, dreamers, soldiers and avengers, varying from the silent and thoughtful to the quick and impulsive; from the cold and bitter to the ignorant and faithful. They believed in God, in spirits, in fate, in liberty. To them the world was a wild, young unregulated thing, and they were born to set it right. It was a veritable band of crusaders, and while it had much of weakness and extravagance, it had nothing nasty or unclean. On the whole, they were an unusual set of men. Anne Brown who lived with them said: "Taking them all together, I think they would compare well [she is speaking of manners, etc.] with the same number of men in any station of life I have ever met."**

They were not men of culture or great education, although Kagi had had a fair schooling. They were intellectually bold and inquiring — several had been attracted by the then rampant Spiritualism; nearly all were skeptical of the world's social conventions. They had been trained mostly in the rough school of frontier life, had faced death many times, and were eager, curious and restless. Some of them were musical, others dabbled in verse. Their broadest common ground of sympathy lay in the personality of John Brown — him they revered and loved. Through him they had come to hate slavery, and for him and for what he believed, they were willing to risk their lives. They themselves had convictions on slavery and other matters, but John Brown narrowed down their dreaming to one intense deed.

Finally there was John Brown himself. His personal appearance has been often described — several times in these

* Sanborn in the *Atlantic Monthly*, Hinton, p. 570.
** Anne Brown in Hinton, p. 450.

pages. In 1859 he was the same striking figure with whitening hair, burning eyes and the great white beard which hardly hid the pendulous side lips of Olympian Jove. One thing, however, must not be forgotten. John Brown was at this time a sick man. From 1856 to 1859, scarce a month passed without telling of illness. His health was "some improved" in May, 1857, but soon he lost a week "with ague and fever and left home feeble." In August he wrote of "ill health" and "repeated returns of fever and ague." In September and October his health was "poor." The spring and summer of 1858 found him "not very stout," and in July and August he was "down with ague" and "too sick" to write. In September he was "still weak," and, although "some improved" in December, the following spring found him "not very strong." In April, amid the feverish activity of his fatal year, he was "quite prostrated," with "the difficulty in my head and ear and with the ague in consequence." Late in July he was "delayed with sickness" and there can be little doubt that it was an ill and pain-racked body which his indomitable will forced into the raid of Harper's Ferry.

Having collected a part of the funds and organized the band, John Brown was about to strike his blow in the early summer of 1858, as we have seen, when the Forbes disclosures compelled him to hide in Kansas, where the last massacre on the Swamp of the Swan invited him. He left Canada for Kansas in June, 1858. Cook, somewhat against the wishes of Brown who feared his garrulity, went to Harper's Ferry, worked as book agent and canal keeper, made love to a maid and married her and then acted as advance agent awaiting the main band. Ten months after leaving Canada, and in mid-March, 1859, John Brown appeared again in Canada (as has been told in Chapter VII) with twelve rescued slaves as an earnest of the feasibility of his plan. He stayed long enough to spread the news and then went to northern Ohio where he spoke in public of Kansas and slavery. "He said that he had never lifted a finger toward any one whom he did not know was a violent persecutor of the free state men. He had never killed anybody; although, on some occasions, he had shown the young men with him how some things might be done as well as others; and they had done the business. He had never destroyed the value of an ear of corn, and had never set fire to any pro-slavery man's house or property. He had never by his own action driven out pro-slavery men from the Territory; but if occasion demanded it, he would drive them into the ground, like fence stakes, where they would remain permanent settlers.

"Brown remarked that he was an outlaw, the governor of Missouri having offered a reward of $3,000, and James Buchanan $250 more, for him. He quietly remarked, parenthetically, that John Brown would give two dollars and fifty cents for the safe delivery of the body of James Buchanan in any jail of the free states. He would never submit to an arrest, as he had nothing to gain from submission; but he should settle all questions on the spot if any attempt was made to take him. The liberation of those slaves was meant as a direct blow to slavery, and he laid down his platform that he had considered it his duty to break the fetters from any slave when he had an opportunity. He was a thorough Abolitionist."*

Then he went East to see his family and visit Douglass (where he met and persuaded Shields Green), and to consult with Gerrit Smith and Sanborn. Alcott at Concord wrote:

"This evening I heard Captain Brown speak at the town hall on Kansas affairs, and the part taken by them in the late troubles there. He tells his story with surpassing simplicity and sense, impressing us all deeply by his courage and religious earnestness. Our best people listen to his words, — Emerson, Thoreau, Judge Hoar, my wife; and some of them contribute something in aid of his plans without asking particulars, such confidence does he inspire in his integrity

* From the newspaper report of the speech at Cleveland, March 22d, Redpath, pp. 239–240.

and abilities. I have a few words with him after his speech, and find him superior to legal traditions, and a disciple of the Right in ideality and the affairs of the state. He is Sanborn's guest, and stays for a day only. A young man named Anderson accompanies him. They go armed, I am told, and will defend themselves, if necessary. I believe they are now on their way to Connecticut and farther south; but the captain leaves us much in the dark concerning his destination and designs for the coming months. Yet he does not conceal his hatred of slavery, nor his readiness to strike a blow for freedom at the proper moment. I infer it is his intention to run off as many slaves as he can, and so render that property insecure to the master. I think him equal to anything he dares, — the man to do the deed, if it must be done, and with the martyr's temper and purpose. Nature obviously was deeply intent in the making of him. He is of imposing appearance, personally, — tall, with square shoulders and standing; eyes of deep gray, and couchant, as if ready to spring at the least rustling, dauntless yet kindly; his hair shooting backward from low down on his forehead; nose trenchant and Romanesque; set lips, his voice suppressed yet metallic, suggesting deep reserves; decided mouth; the countenance and frame charged with power throughout. Since here last he has added a flowing beard, which gives the soldierly air and the port of an apostle. Though sixty years old he is agile and alert, and ready for any audacity, in any crisis. I think him about the manliest man I have ever seen, — the type and synonym of the Just."*

The month of May John Brown spent in Boston collecting funds, and in New York consulting his Negro friends, with a trip to Connecticut to hurry the making of his thousand pikes. Sickness intervened, but at last on June 20th, the advance-guard of five — Brown and two of his sons, Jerry Anderson and Kagi — started southward. They stayed several days at Chambersburg, where Kagi, coöperating

---

* Diary of A. Bronson Alcott, Sanborn, pp. 504–505.

with a faithful Negro barber, Watson, was established as general agent to forward men, mail and freight. Then passing through Hagerstown, they appeared at Harper's Ferry on July 4th. Here they met Cook, who had been selling maps, keeping the canal-lock near the arsenal, and sending regular information to Brown. Brown and his sons wandered about at first, and a local farmer greeted them cheerily: "Goodmorning, gentlemen, how do you do?" They returned the greeting pleasantly. The conversation is recounted as follows:

"I said, 'Well, gentlemen,' after saluting them in that form 'I suppose you are out hunting minerals, gold, and silver?' His answer was, 'No, we are not, we are out looking for land; we want to buy land; we have a little money, but we want to make it go as far as we can.' He asked me the price of the land. I told him that it ranged from fifteen dollars to thirty dollars in the neighborhood. He remarked, 'That is high; I thought I could buy land here for about a dollar or two dollars per acre.' I remarked to him, 'No, sir; if you expect to get land for that price, you will have to go further west, to Kansas, or some of those Territories where there is government land.' ... I then asked him where they came from. His answer was, 'From the northern part of the state of New York.' I asked him what he followed there. He said farming, and the frost had been so heavy lately, that it cut off their crops there; that he could not make anything, and sold out, and thought he would come further south and try it awhile."*

Through this easy-going, inquisitive farmer, Brown learned of a farm for rent, which he hired for nine months for thirty-five dollars. It was on the main road between Harper's Ferry, Chambersburg and the North, about five miles from the Ferry and in a quiet secluded place. The house stood about 300 yards back from the Boonesborough pike, in plain

* Report: Reports of Senate Committees, 36th Congress, 1st Session, No. 278; Testimony of John C. Unseld, pp. 1–2.

sight. About 600 yards away on the other side of the road was another cabin of one room and a garret, which was largely hidden from view by the shrubbery. Here Brown settled and gradually collected his men and material. The arms were especially slow in coming. Most of the guns arrived at Chambersburg from Connecticut about August, but the pikes did not come until a month later. Then too the men were gathered slowly. They were at the four ends of the country, in all sorts of employment and in different financial conditions, and they were not certain just when the raid would take place. All this delayed Brown from July until October and greatly increased the cost of maintenance. A daughter, Anne, and Oliver's girl wife came and kept house from July 16th to October 1st.

At this critical juncture Harriet Tubman fell sick — a grave loss to the cause — and there were other delays. By August 1st, there were at Harper's Ferry the two Brown daughters and three sons, and the two brothers of a son-in-law, besides the two Coppocs, Tidd, Jerry Anderson and Stevens. Hazlett, Leeman and Taylor came soon after. Kagi was still at Chambersburg and John Brown himself "labored and traveled night and day, sometimes on old Dolly, his brown mule, and sometimes in the wagon. He would start directly after night, and travel the fifty miles between the farm and Chambersburg by daylight next morning; and he otherwise kept open communication between headquarters and the latter place, in order that matters might be arranged in due season."*

In the North John Brown, Jr., was shipping the arms and gathering men and money. He was in Boston August 10th, at Douglass's home soon after, and later in Canada with Loguen. All the chief branches of the League were visited and then northern Ohio. The result was meagre; not because of lack of men but lack of the kind of men wanted at this time. There were thousands of Negroes ready to fight

* Anderson, *A Voice from Harper's Ferry*, p. 19.

for liberty in the ranks. But most of these John Brown could not use at present. No considerable band of armed black men could have been introduced into the South without immediate discovery and civil war. It was therefore picked leaders like Douglass, Reynolds, Holden and Delaney that Brown wanted at first — discreet and careful men of influence, who, as he said to Douglass, could hive the swarming bees both North and South. To get these picked men interested was, however, difficult. Each had his work and his theory of racial salvation; they were widely scattered. A number of them had been convinced in 1858, but the postponement had given time for reflection and doubt. In many ways the original enthusiasm had waned, but it was not dead. The cause was just as great and all that was needed was to convince men that this was a real chance to strike an effective blow. They required the magic of Brown's own presence to impress this fact upon them. They were not sure of his agents. Men continued to come, however, others began to prepare and still others were almost persuaded. An urgent summons went to Kansas to white fellow workers, and the response there was similarly small. Brown knew that his ability to command the services of a large number of Northern Negroes depended in some degree on Frederick Douglass's attitude. He was the first great national Negro leader — a man of ability, *finesse* and courage. If he followed John Brown, who could hesitate? If he refused, was it not for the best of reasons? Thus John Brown continually urged Douglass and as a last appeal arranged for a final conference on August 19th at Chambersburg in an abandoned stone quarry. Douglass says:

"As I came near, he regarded me rather suspiciously, but soon recognized me, and received me cordially. He had in his hand when I met him a fishing-tackle, with which he had apparently been fishing in a stream hard by; but I saw no fish and did not suppose he cared much for his 'fisherman's luck.' The fishing was simply a disguise, and was certainly a good one. He looked every way like a man of the neighborhood, and as much at home as any of the farmers around there. His hat was old and storm-beaten, and his clothing was about the color of the stone quarry itself — his then present dwelling place.

"His face wore an anxious expression, and he was much worn by thought and exposure. I felt that I was on a dangerous mission, and was as little desirous of discovery as himself, though no reward had been offered for me. We — Mr. Kagi, Captain Brown, Shields Green, and myself — sat down among the rocks and talked over the enterprise which was about to be undertaken. The taking of Harper's Ferry, of which Captain Brown had merely hinted before, was now declared as his settled purpose, and he wanted to know what I thought of it. I at once opposed the measure with all the arguments at my command. To me such a measure would be fatal to running off slaves (as was the original plan), and fatal to all engaged in doing so. It would be an attack upon the Federal government, and would array the whole country against us. Captain Brown did most of the talking on the other side of the question. He did not at all object to rousing the nation; it seemed to him that something startling was just what the nation needed. . . . Our talk was long and earnest; we spent the most of Saturday and a part of Sunday in this debate — Brown for Harper's Ferry, and I against it; he for striking a blow which should instantly rouse the country, and I for the policy of gradually and unaccountably drawing off the slaves to the mountains, as at first suggested and proposed by him. When I found that he had fully made up his mind and could not be dissuaded, I turned to Shields Green and told him he heard what Captain Brown had said; his old plan was changed, and that I should return home, and if he wished to go with me he could do so. Captain Brown urged us both to go with him, but I could not do so, and could but feel that he was about to rivet the fetters more firmly than ever on the limbs of the enslaved. In parting he put his arms around me in a manner more than friendly, and said: 'Come with me, Douglass; I will defend you with my life. I want you for a special purpose. When I strike, the bees will begin to swarm, and I shall want you to help hive them.' But my discretion or my cowardice made me proof against the dear old man's eloquence — perhaps it was something of both which determined my course. When about to leave, I asked Green what he had decided to do, and was surprised by his coolly saying, in his broken way, 'I b'lieve I'll go wid de ole man.' Here we separated; they to go to Harper's Ferry, I to Rochester."*

Douglass's decision undoubtedly kept many Negroes from joining Brown. Shields Green, however, started south. The slave-catchers followed him and made him and Owen Brown swim a river. Only their journeying southward instead of northward saved them from capture.

The life at the farm during this time was curious. Anderson says:

"There was no milk and water sentimentality — no offensive contempt for the Negro, while working in his cause; the pulsations of each and every heart beat in harmony for the suffering and pleading slave. I thank God that I have been permitted to realize to its furthest, fullest extent, the moral, mental, physical, social harmony of an anti-slavery family, carrying out to the letter the principles of its antitype, the anti-slavery cause. In John Brown's house, and in John Brown's presence, men from widely different parts of the continent met and united into one company, wherein no hateful prejudice dared intrude its ugly self — no ghost of distinction found space to enter. . . .

"To a passer-by, the house and its surroundings presented but indifferent attractions. Any log tenement of equal dimensions would be as likely to arrest a stray glance. Rough, unsightly, and aged, it was only for those privileged to enter and tarry for a long time, and to penetrate the mysteries of the two rooms it contained — kitchen, parlor, dining-room below, and the spacious chamber, attic, store-room, prison,

* Douglass, *Life and Times of Frederick Douglass*, pp. 388–391.

drilling-room, comprised in the loft above — who could tell how we lived at Kennedy Farm.

"Every morning, when the noble old man was at home, he called the family around, read from his Bible, and offered to God most fervent and touching supplications for all flesh; and especially pathetic were his petitions in behalf of the oppressed. I never heard John Brown pray, that he did not make strong appeals to God for the deliverance of the slave. This duty over, the men went to the loft, there to remain all day long; few only could be seen about, as the neighbors were watchful and suspicious. It was also important to talk but little among ourselves, as visitors to the house might be curious. Besides the daughter and daughter-in-law, who superintended the work, some one or other of the men was regularly detailed to assist in the cooking, washing, and other domestic work. After the ladies left, we did all the work, no one being exempt, because of age or official grade in the organization.

"The principal employment of the prisoners, as we severally were when compelled to stay in the loft, was to study Forbes's Manual, and to go through a quiet, though rigid drill, under the training of Captain Stevens, at some times. At other times we applied a preparation for bronzing our gun-barrels — discussed subjects of reform — related our personal history; but when our resources became pretty well exhausted, the *ennui* from confinement, imposed silence, etc., would make the men almost desperate. At such times, neither slavery nor slaveholders were discussed mincingly. We were, while the ladies remained, often relieved of much of the dullness growing out of restraint by their kindness. As we could not circulate freely, they would bring in wild fruit and flowers from the woods and fields."*

Anne, the young daughter, says: "One day, a short time after I went down there, father was sitting at the table writing. I was near by sewing (he and I being alone in the room),

* Anderson, *A Voice from Harper's Ferry*, pp. 23–25.

when two little wrens that had a nest under the porch came flying in at the door, fluttering and twittering; then they flew back to their nest and again to us several times, seemingly trying to attract our attention. They appeared to be in great distress. I asked father what he thought was the matter with the little birds. He asked if I had ever seen them act so before; I told him no. 'Then let us go and see,' he said. We went out and found that a snake had crawled up the post and was just ready to devour the little ones in the nest. Father killed the snake; and then the old birds sat on the railing and sang as if they would burst. It seemed as if they were trying to express their joy and gratitude to him for saving their little ones. After we went back into the room, he said he thought it very strange the way the birds asked him to help them, and asked if I thought it an omen of his success. He seemed very much impressed with that idea. I do not think he was superstitious; but you know he always thought and felt that God called him to that work; and seemed to place himself, or rather to imagine himself, in the position of the figure in the old seal of Virginia, with the tyrant under her foot."*

The men discussed religion and slavery freely, read Paine's *Age of Reason* and the Baltimore *Sun*. John Brown himself was careful to cultivate the good-will of his neighbors, attending with skill the sick among animals and men, so much so that he and his sons became prime favorites. Owen had long conversations with the people, while Cook was also moving about the country selling maps. A little Dunker chapel was near with non-resistant, anti-slavery principles; here John Brown often worshiped and preached. Yet with all this caution and care, suspicion lurked about them and discovery was always imminent.

Brown's daughter relates that "there was a family of poor people who lived near by and who had rented the garden on the Kennedy place, directly back of the house. The little

* Anne Brown in Sanborn, p. 531.

barefooted woman and four small children (she carried the youngest in her arms) would all come trooping over to the garden at all hours of the day, and, at times, several times during the day. Nearly always they would come up the steps and into the house and stay a short time. This made it very troublesome for us, compelling the men, when she came in sight at meal-times, to gather up the victuals and table-cloth and quietly disappear up-stairs.

"One Saturday father and I went to a religious (Dunker) meeting that was held in a grove near the schoolhouse, and the folks left at home forgot to keep a sharp lookout for Mrs. Heiffmaster, and she stole into the house before they saw her, and saw Shields Green (that must have been in September), Barclay Coppoc, and Will Leeman. And another time after that she saw C. P. Tidd standing on the porch. She thought these strangers were running off Negroes to the North. I used to give her everything she wanted or asked for to keep her on good terms, but we were in constant fear that she was either a spy or would betray us. It was like standing on a powder magazine, after a slow match had been lighted."*

Despite all precautions, rumor began to get in the air. A Prussian Pole was among the Kansas cooperators invited. He had been in Kansas in 1856 and was known to Brown and Kagi. After hearing from Brown in August, 1859, the Pole disclosed their plans to Edmund Babb, a correspondent of the Cincinnati *Gazette*. It was probably Babb who thereupon wrote to the United States Secretary of War: "I have discovered the existence of a secret association, having for its object the liberation of the slaves at the South and by a general insurrection. The leader of the movement is 'old John Brown,' late of Kansas." Approximately correct details of the plot followed; but Secretary Floyd was lolling at a summer resort and had some little conspiracies of his own in hand not unconnected with United States arsenals.

* Anne Brown in Hinton, p. 265.

Being, therefore, as he said magniloquently, "satisfied in my own mind that a scheme of such wickedness and outrage could not be entertained by any citizens of the United States, I put the letter away, and thought no more of it until the raid broke out."*

Gerrit Smith, too, with little discretion, addressed to a Negro audience words which plainly showed he shortly expected a slave insurrection. Even among the Harper's Ferry party forced inaction led to dispute and disaffection. John Brown sharply rebuked the letter-writing and gossiping of his own men. "Any person is a stupid fool," he told Kagi, "who expects his friends to keep for him that which he cannot keep himself. All our friends have each got their special friends; and they again have theirs; and it would not be right to lay the burden of keeping a secret on any one at the end of a long string. I could tell you of reasons I have for feeling rather keenly on this point."**

The men, on the other hand, were dissatisfied with Brown's plans as they were finally disclosed. Anne Brown writes that they generally "did not know that the raid on the government works was a part of the 'plan' until after they arrived at the farm in the beginning of August."*** They wanted simply to repeat the Missouri raid on a larger scale and not try to capture the arsenal. Tidd was especially stubborn and irreconcilable. The discussion became so warm that John Brown at one time resigned, but he was immediately reëlected and this formal letter was sent him:

"*Dear Sir* — We have all agreed to sustain your decisions, until you have proved incompetent, and many of us will adhere to your decisions so long as you will."****

* Report: Reports of Senate Committees, 36th Congress, 1st Session, No. 278; Testimony of John B. Floyd, pp. 250–252.
** Letter to Kagi, 1859, in Hinton, pp. 257–258.
*** Anne Brown in Hinton, p. 260.
**** Letter of Owen to John Brown, 1850, in Hinton, p. 259.

In these ways Brown was compelled to hurry and accordingly he urged his eldest son, who replied: "Through those associations which I formed in Canada, I am able to reach each individual member at the shortest notice by letter. I am devoting my whole time to our company business. Shall immediately go out organizing and raising funds. From what I even had understood, I had supposed you would not think it best to commence opening the coal banks before spring, unless circumstances should make it imperative. However, I suppose the reasons are satisfactory to you, and if so, those who own smaller shares ought not to object. I hope we shall be able to get on in season some of those old miners of whom I wrote you. Shall strain every nerve to accomplish this. You may be assured that what you say to me will reach those who may be benefited thereby, and those who would take stock, in the shortest possible time; so don't fail to keep me posted."*

As late as October 6th Brown expected to "move about the end of the month" and made a hurried trip to Philadelphia. There he met a large group of Negroes, and Dorsey the caterer with whom he stayed, at 1221 Locust Street, is said to have given him $300. In some way he was disappointed with the visit. Anderson says he went "on business of great importance. How important, men there and elsewhere now know. How affected by, and affecting the main features of the enterprise, we at the farm knew full after their return, as the old captain, in the fullness of his overflowing, saddened heart, detailed point after point of interest."** Perhaps he was still trying to persuade Douglass and the leaders of the Philadelphia and New York groups.

The women left the farm late in September and O. P. Anderson, Copeland and Leary arrived. Merriam joined Brown while he was on the Philadelphia trip and was sent to Baltimore to buy caps for the guns. Others were coming

* John Brown, Jr., to Kagi, 1859, in Sanborn, pp. 547–548.
** Anderson, *A Voice from Harper's Ferry*, p. 26.

when suddenly Brown fixed on October 17th as the date of the raid. This hurried change was probably because officials and neighbors were getting inquisitive, and arms were being removed from the arsenal to man Southern stations. Yet it was unfortunate, as Anderson says: "Could other parties, waiting for the word, have reached the headquarters in time for the outbreak when it took place, the taking of the armory, engine-house, and rifle factory, would have been quite different. But the men at the farm had been so closely confined, that they went out about the house and farm in the daytime during that week, and so indiscreetly exposed their numbers to the prying neighbors, who thereupon took steps to have a search instituted in the early part of the coming week. Captain Brown was not seconded in another quarter, as he expected, at the time of the action, but could the fears of the neighbors have been allayed for a few days, the disappointment in the former respect would not have been of much weight."*

Only the nearest of the slaves round about who awaited the word could be communicated with and several recruits like Hinton were left stranded on the way, unable to get through in time. So the great day dawned: "On Sunday morning, October 16th, Captain Brown arose earlier than usual, and called his men down to worship. He read a chapter from the Bible, applicable to the condition of the slaves, and our duty as their brethren, and then offered up a fervent prayer to God to assist in the liberation of the bondmen in that slaveholding land. The services were impressive."**

A council was held, over which O. P. Anderson, the colored man, presided. In the afternoon the final orders were given and at night just before setting out, John Brown said: "And now, gentlemen, let me impress this one thing upon your minds. You all know how dear life is to you, and how

* Anderson, *A Voice from Harper's Ferry*, p. 27.
** *Ibid.*, p. 28.

dear life is to your friends. And in remembering that, consider that the lives of others are as dear to them as yours are to you. Do not, therefore, take the life of any one, if you can possibly avoid it; but if it is necessary to take life in order to save your own, then make sure work of it."*

* Anderson, *A Voice from Harper's Ferry*, p. 29.

XI

The Blow

"Woe unto them that call evil, good; and good, evil."

"At eight o'clock on Sunday evening, Captain Brown said: 'Men, get on your arms; we will proceed to the Ferry.' His horse and wagon were brought out before the door, and some pikes, a sledge-hammer and a crowbar were placed in it. The captain then put on his old Kansas cap, and said: 'Come, boys!' when we marched out of the camp behind him, into the lane leading down the hill to the main road."*

The orders given commanded Owen Brown, Merriam and Barclay Coppoc to watch the house and arms until ordered to bring them toward the Ferry. Tidd and Cook were to cut the telegraph lines and Kagi and Stephens to detain the bridge guard. Watson Brown and Taylor were to hold the bridge over the Potomac, and Oliver Brown and William Thompson the bridge over the Shenandoah. Jerry Anderson and Dauphin Thompson were to occupy the engine-house in the arsenal yard, while Hazlett and Edwin Coppoc were to hold the armory.

During the night Kagi and Copeland were to seize and guard the rifle factory, and others were to go out in the country and bring in certain masters and their slaves.

It was a cold dark night when the band started. Ahead was John Brown in his one-horse farm-wagon, with pikes, a sledge-hammer and a crowbar. Behind him marched the men silently and at intervals, Cook and Tidd leading. They had five miles to go, over rolling hills and through woods and then down to a narrow road between the cliffs and the Cincinnati and Ohio canal. As they approached the railroad, Cook and Tidd cut the telegraph wires which led to Baltimore and Washington. At the bridge they halted and made ready their arms. At ten o'clock William Williams, one of

* Anderson, *A Voice from Harper's Ferry*, pp. 31–32.

232

the watchmen there, was surprised to find himself a prisoner in the hands of Kagi and Stevens, who took him through the covered structure to the town, leaving Watson Brown and Steward Taylor to guard the bridge. The rest of the company entered Harper's Ferry.

The land between the rivers is itself high, though dwarfed by the mountains and running down to a low point where the rivers join. At this place the bridge leads to Maryland. After crossing the bridge to Virginia, about sixty yards up the street, running parallel to the Potomac, was the gate of the armory where the arms were made. On the Shenandoah side about sixty yards from the armory gate is the arsenal, where the arms were stored. The company proceeded to the armory gate. The watchman tells how the place was captured:

"'Open the gate,' said they; I said, 'I could not if I was stuck,' and one of them jumped up on the pier of the gate over my head, and another fellow ran and put his hand on me and caught me by the coat and held me; I was inside and they were outside, and the fellow standing over my head upon the pier, and then when I would not open the gate for them, five or six ran in from the wagon, clapped their guns against my breast, and told me I should deliver up the key; I told them I could not; and another fellow made an answer and said they had not time now to be waiting for the key, but to go to the wagon and bring out the crowbar and large hammer, and they would soon get in; they went to the little wagon and brought a large crowbar out of it; there is a large chain around the two sides of the wagon-gate going in; they twisted the crowbar in the chain and they opened it, and in they ran and got in the wagon; one fellow took me; they all gathered about me and looked in my face; I was nearly scared to death with so many guns about me."*

* Report: Reports of Senate Committees, 36th Congress, 1st Session, No. 278; Testimony of Daniel Wheeler, pp. 21–22.

The two captured watchmen, Anderson says, "were left in the custody of Jerry Anderson and Dauphin Thompson, and A. D. Stevens arranged the men to take possession of the armory and rifle factory. About this time, there was apparently much excitement. People were passing back and forth in the town, and before we could do much, we had to take several prisoners. After the prisoners were secured, we passed to the opposite side of the street and took the armory, and Albert Hazlett and Edwin Coppoc were ordered to hold it for the time being."*

The other fourteen men quickly dispersed through the village. Oliver Brown and William Thompson seized and guarded the bridge across the Shenandoah. This bridge was sixty rods from the railway bridge up the river and was the direct route to Loudoun Heights, the slave-filled lower valley, and the Great Black Way. It was, however, not the only way across the Shenandoah: a little more than half a mile farther up were the rifle works, where the stream could be easily forded. Kagi and Copeland went there, captured the watchman and took possession.

"These places were all taken, and the prisoners secured, without the snap of a gun, or any violence whatever," says Anderson, and he continues: "The town being taken, Brown, Stevens, and the men who had no post in charge, returned to the engine-house, where council was held, after which Captain Stevens, Tidd, Cook, Shields Green, Leary and myself went to the country. On the road we met some colored men, to whom we made known our purpose, when they immediately agreed to join us. They said they had been long waiting for an opportunity of the kind. Stevens then asked them to go around among the colored people and circulate the news, when each started off in a different direction. The result was that many colored men gathered to the scene of action. The first prisoner taken by us was Colonel Lewis Washington (a relative of George Washington). When we

* Anderson, *A Voice from Harper's Ferry*, p. 33.

234

neared his house, Captain Stevens placed Leary and Shields Green to guard the approaches to the house, the one at the side, and the other in front. We then knocked, but no one answering, although females were looking from upper windows, we entered the building and commenced a search for the proprietor. Colonel Washington opened his room door, and begged us not to kill him. Captain Stevens replied, 'You are our prisoner,' when he stood as if speechless or petrified. Stevens further told him to get ready to go to the Ferry; that he had come to abolish slavery, not to take life but in self-defense, but that he must go along. The colonel replied: 'You can have my slaves, if you will let me remain.' 'No,' said the captain, 'you must go along too; so get ready.'"*

He and his male slaves were thus taken, together with a large four horse wagon and some arms, including the Lafayette sword. Away the party went and after capturing another planter and his slaves, arrived at the Ferry before daybreak.

Meantime the citizens of the Ferry, returning late from protracted Methodist meeting, were being taken prisoners and about one o'clock in the morning the east-bound Baltimore and Ohio train arrived. This was detained and the local colored porter shot dead by Brown's guards on the bridge. The passengers were greatly excited, but at first thought it was a strike of some kind. After sunrise the train was allowed to proceed, John Brown himself walking ahead across the bridge to reassure the conductor. So Monday, October 17th, began and Anderson says it "was a time of stirring and exciting events. In consequence of the movements of the night before we were prepared for commotion and tumult, but certainly not for more than we beheld around us. Gray dawn and yet brighter daylight revealed great confusion, and as the sun arose, the panic spread like wild-fire. Men, women and children could be seen leaving their homes

* Anderson, *A Voice from Harper's Ferry*, pp. 33–34.

in every direction; some seeking refuge among residents, and in quarters further away; others climbing up the hillsides, and hurrying off in various directions, evidently impelled by a sudden fear, which was plainly visible in their countenances or in their movements.

"Captain Brown was all activity, though I could not help thinking that at times he appeared somewhat puzzled. He ordered Lewis Sherrard Leary and four slaves, and a free man belonging in the neighborhood, to join John Henry Kagi and John Copeland at the rifle factory, which they immediately did.... After the departure of the train, quietness prevailed for a short time; a number of prisoners were already in the engine-house, and of the many colored men living in the neighborhood, who had assembled in the town, a number were armed."*

Up to this point everything in John Brown's plan had worked like clockwork, and there had been but one death. The armory was captured, from twenty-five to fifty slaves had been armed, several masters were in custody and the next move was to get the arms and ammunition from the farm. Cook says that when the party returned from the country at dawn, "I stayed a short while in the engine-house to get warm, as I was chilled through. After I got warm, Captain Brown ordered me to go with C. P. Tidd, who was to take William H. Leeman, and I think, four slaves [Anderson says fourteen slaves] with him, in Colonel Washington's large wagon, across the river, and to take Terrence Burns and his brother and their slaves prisoners. My orders were to hold Burns and brother as prisoners at their own house, while Tidd and the slaves who accompanied him were to go to Captain Brown's house and to load in arms and bring them down to the schoolhouse, stopping for the Burnses and their guard. William H. Leeman remained with me to guard the prisoners. On return of the wagon, in compliance with orders, we all started for the schoolhouse.

* Anderson, *A Voice from Harper's Ferry*, pp. 36–37.

When we got there, I was to remain, by Captain Brown's orders, with one of the slaves to guard the arms, while C. P. Tidd, with the other Negroes, was to go back for the rest of the arms, and Burns was to be sent with William H. Leeman to Captain Brown at the armory. It was at this time that William Thompson came up from the Ferry and reported that everything was all right, and then hurried on to overtake William H. Leeman. A short time after the departure of Tidd, I heard a good deal of firing and became anxious to know the cause, but my orders were strict to remain in the schoolhouse and guard the arms, and I obeyed the orders to the letter. About four o'clock in the evening C. P. Tidd came with the second load."*

Here, in all probability, was the fatal hitch. The farm was not over three miles from the schoolhouse, and there was a heavy farm-wagon with four large strong horses and a dozen men or more to help. The fact that it took these men eleven hours to move two wagon-loads of material less than three miles is the secret of the extraordinary failure of Brown's foray at a time when victory was in his grasp. That Cook was needlessly dilatory in the moving is certain. He sat down in Byrnes's house and made a speech on human equality. Then Tidd went on to the farm with the wagon and brought a load of arms, which he deposited at the point where the Kennedy farm road meets the Potomac almost at right angles, about three miles or less from the Ferry. The schoolhouse stood here and the children were frightened half to death. Cook stopped at this place and unloaded the wagon, and then Leeman went with Byrnes to the guard-house, lingering and actually sitting beside the road. Even then they arrived before ten o'clock. With haste it is certain that, despite the muddy road, the first load of arms could have been at the schoolhouse before eight o'clock in the morning, and the whole of the stores by ten o'clock. That Brown expected this is shown by his sending William

* Statement by John Edwin Cook in Hinton, pp. 700–718.

Thompson to reassure the men at the farm of his safety and probably to urge haste; yet when the second load of arms appeared, it was four o'clock in the afternoon, at least three hours after Brown had been completely surrounded. Judging from Cook's narrative, it is likely that Thompson did not see Tidd at all. It was this inexcusable delay on the part of Tidd and Cook and, possibly, William Thompson that undoubtedly made the raid a failure. To be sure, John Brown never said so — never hinted that any one was to blame but himself. But that was John Brown's way.

Events in the town had moved quickly. After Cook had departed, Brown ordered O. P. Anderson "to take the pikes out of the wagon in which he rode to the Ferry, and to place them in the hands of the colored men who had come with us from the plantations, and others who had come forward without having had communication with any of our party."*

The citizens were "wild with fright and excitement.... The prisoners were also terror-stricken. Some wanted to go home to see their families, as if for the last time. The privilege was granted them, under escort, and they were brought back again. Edwin Coppoc, one of the sentinels at the armory gate, was fired at by one of the citizens, but the ball did not reach him, when one of the insurgents close by put up his rifle, and made the enemy bite the dust. Among the arms taken from Colonel Washington was one double barreled gun. This weapon was loaded by Leeman with buckshot, and placed in the hands of an elderly slave man, early in the morning. After the cowardly charge upon Coppoc, this old man was ordered by Captain Stevens to arrest a citizen. The old man ordered him to halt, which he refused to do, when instantly the terrible load was discharged into him, and he fell, and expired without a struggle."**

The next step which John Brown had in mind is unknown,

* Anderson, *A Voice from Harper's Ferry*, p. 37.
** *Ibid.*, pp. 37–38.

but there were two safe movements at 9 a. m. Monday morning:

(a) The arms could have been brought across the Potomac bridge and then across the Shenandoah, and so up Loudoun Heights. The men from the Maryland side could have joined, and Brown and his men covered their retreat by compelling the hostages to march with them. Kagi and his men, by wading the Shenandoah, could have supported them.

(b) The arms could have been taken down to the Potomac from the schoolhouse, ferried across and moved over to Kagi. Brown and his men could have joined the party there and all retreated up Loudoun Heights. From the fact that Brown had the arms stopped at the schoolhouse, this seems probably to have been the thought in his mind.

On the other hand, the plan usually attributed to Brown is unthinkable; viz., that he intended retreating across the Potomac into the Maryland mountains. First, he had just come out of the Maryland mountains and had moved down his arms and ammunition; and second, this manœuvre would have cut his band off from the Great Black Way to the South unless he captured the Ferry a second time. Manifestly this, then, was not Brown's idea. It has, however, been suggested that the arms had been moved down to the schoolhouse to be placed in the hands of slaves there. But why were they left on the Maryland side? In the whole Maryland country west of the mountains were less than a thousand able-bodied Negroes, of whom not a tenth could have been cognizant of the uprising, while Brown had arms for 1,200 men or more. No, Brown intended to move the arms in bulk. He had perhaps a ton, or a ton and a half of baggage. He wished it moved first to the schoolhouse, and then if all was well to the Ferry, or straight across to the mountains. Cook started before five o'clock in the morning, and Brown no doubt expected to hear that the arms were at the schoolhouse by ten. At eleven o'clock he dispatched William Thompson to Kennedy farm. Anderson thinks that Thompson's message made the farm party even more leisurely because it told of success so far. This is surely impossible. The veriest tyro must have known that minutes were golden despite the tremendous fortune of the expedition. Did Thompson misapprehend his message? Was the delay Tidd's and what was Owen Brown thinking and doing? It is a curious puzzle, but it is the puzzle of the foray. If the party with the arms had arrived at the bridge any time before noon, the raid would have been successful. Even as it was, Brown still had three courses open to him, all of which promised a measure of success:

(a) He could have gotten his band and crossed back to Maryland, — although this meant the abandonment of the main features of his whole plan. As time waned Stevens and Kagi urged this but Brown refused.

(b) He could have gone to Loudoun Heights, but this would have involved abandoning his arms and stores and above all, one of his sons, Cook, Tidd, Merriam, Coppoc and the slaves. This was unthinkable.

(c) He could have used his hostages to force terms. For not doing this he afterward repeatedly blamed himself, but characteristically blamed no one else for anything.

Meantime every minute of delay aroused the country and brought the citizens to their senses. "The train that left Harper's Ferry carried a panic to Virginia, Maryland and Washington with it. The passengers, taking all the paper they could find, wrote accounts of the insurrection, which they threw from the windows as the train rushed onward."*

A local physician says: " I went back to the hillside then, and tried to get the citizens together, to see what we could do to get rid of these fellows. They seemed to be very troublesome. When I got on the hill I learned that they had shot Boerly. That was probably about seven o'clock.... I had ordered the Lutheran church bell to be rung to get the citizens together to see what sort of arms they had. I found one or two squirrel rifles and a few shotguns. I had sent a

* Redpath, p. 249.

messenger to Charlestown in the meantime for Captain Rowan, commander of a volunteer company there. I also sent messengers to the Baltimore and Ohio Railroad to stop the trains coming east, and not let them approach the Ferry, and also a messenger to Shepherdstown."*

Another eye-witness adds: "There was unavoidable delay in the preparations for a fight, because of the scarcity of weapons; for only a few squirrel guns and fowling-pieces could be found. There were then at Harper's Ferry thousands and tens of thousands of muskets and rifles of the most approved patterns, but they were all boxed up in the arsenal, and the arsenal was in the hands of the enemy. And such, too, was the scarcity of the ammunition that, after using up the limited supply of lead found in the village stores, pewter plates and spoons had to be melted and molded into bullets for the occasion.

"By nine o'clock a number of indifferently armed citizens assembled on Camp Hill and decided that the party, consisting of half a dozen men, should cross the Potomac a short distance above the Ferry, and, going down the tow-path of the Chesapeake and Ohio Canal as far as the railway bridge, should attack the two sentinels stationed there, who, by the way, had been reinforced by four more of Brown's party. Another small party under Captain Medler was to cross the Shenandoah and take position opposite the rifle works, while Captain Avis, with a sufficient force, should take possession of the Shenandoah bridge, and Captain Roderick, with some of the armorers, should post themselves on the Baltimore and Ohio Railway west of the Ferry just above the armories."**

At last the militia commenced to arrive and the movements to cut off Brown's men began. The Jefferson Guards crossed the Potomac, came down to the Maryland side and

* Report: Reports of Senate Committees, 36th Congress, 1st Session, No. 278; Testimony of John D. Starry, p. 25.

** Boteler, "Recollections of the John Brown Raid" in the *Century Magazine*, July, 1883, p. 405.

seized the Potomac bridge. The local company was sent to take the Shenandoah bridge, leave a guard and march to the rear of the arsenal, while another local company was to seize the houses in front of the arsenal.

"As strangers poured in," says Anderson, "the enemy took positions round about, so as to prevent any escape, within shooting distance of the engine-house and arsenal. Captain Brown, seeing their manœuvres, said, 'We will hold on to our three positions, if they are unwilling to come to terms, and die like men.'"*

The attack came at noon from the Jefferson Guards, who started across the Potomac bridge from Maryland. This is Anderson's story:

"It was about twelve o'clock in the day when we were first attacked by the troops. Prior to that, Captain Brown, in anticipation of further trouble, had girded to his side the famous sword taken from Colonel Lewis Washington the night before, and with that memorable weapon, he commanded his men against General Washington's own state. When the captain received the news that the troops had entered the bridge from the Maryland side, he, with some of his men, went into the street, and sent a message to the arsenal for us to come forth also. We hastened to the street as ordered, when he said — 'The troops are on the bridge, coming into town; we will give them a warm reception.' He then walked around amongst us, giving us words of encouragement, in this wise: — 'Men! be cool! Don't waste your powder and shot! Take aim, and make every shot count!' 'The troops will look for us to retreat on their first appearance; be careful to shoot first.' Our men were well supplied with firearms, but Captain Brown had no rifle at that time; his only weapon was the sword before mentioned.

"The troops soon came out of the bridge, and up the street facing us, we occupying an irregular position. When they got within sixty or seventy yards, Captain Brown said, 'Let go

* Anderson, *A Voice from Harper's Ferry*, p. 42.

242

upon them!' which we did, when several of them fell. Again and again the dose was repeated. There was now consternation among the troops. From marching in solid martial columns, they became scattered. Some hastened to seize upon and bear up the wounded and dying, — several lay dead upon the ground. They seemed not to realize, at first, that we would fire upon them, but evidently expected that we would be driven out by them without firing. Captain Brown seemed fully to understand the matter, and hence, very properly and in our defense, undertook to forestall their movements. The consequence of their unexpected reception was, after leaving several of their dead on the field, they beat a confused retreat into the bridge, and there stayed under cover until reinforcements came to the Ferry. On the retreat of the troops, we were ordered back to our former posts."*

At this time the Negro, Newby, was killed and his assailant shot in turn by Green. Two slaves also died fighting. Now "there was comparative quiet for a time, except that the citizens seemed to be wild with terror. Men, women and children forsook the place in great haste, climbing up hillsides, and scaling the mountains. The latter seemed to be alive with white fugitives, fleeing from their doomed city. During this time, William Thompson, who was returning from his errand to the Kennedy farm, was surrounded on the bridge by railroad men, who next came up, and taken a prisoner to the Wager house."**

It was now one o'clock in the day and while things were going against Brown, his cause was not desperate. His Maryland men might yet attack the disorganized Jefferson Guards in the rear and the arsenal was full of hostages. But militia and citizens kept pouring into the town and by three o'clock "could be seen coming from every direction." Kagi sent word to Brown, urging retreat; but Brown faced a difficult

* Anderson, A Voice from Harper's Ferry, pp. 39–40.
** Ibid., p. 40.

dilemma: Should he go to Loudoun Heights and lose half his men and all his munitions? or should he retreat to Maryland? This latter path lay open, he was sure, by means of his hostages. Meantime the Maryland party might appear at any moment. Indeed, the Jefferson Guards had once been mistaken for them. On this account the message was sent back to Kagi "to hold out for a few minutes, when we would all evacuate the place." Still the Maryland party lingered with the stubborn Tidd somewhere up the road, and Cook idly kicking his heels at the schoolhouse.

The messenger, Jerry Anderson, was fired on and mortally wounded before he reached Kagi, and the latter's party was attacked by a large force and driven into the river.

"The river at that point runs rippling over a rocky bed," writes a Virginian, "and at ordinary stages of the water is easily forded. The raiders, finding their retreat to the opposite shore intercepted by Medler's men, made for a large flat rock near the middle of the stream. Before reaching it, however, Kagi fell and died in the water, apparently without a struggle. Four others reached the rock, where, for a while, they made an ineffectual stand, returning the fire of the citizens. But it was not long before two of them were killed outright and another prostrated by a mortal wound, leaving Copeland, a mulatto, standing alone unharmed upon their rock of refuge.

"Thereupon, a Harper's Ferry man, James H. Holt, dashed into the river, gun in hand, to capture Copeland, who, as he approached him, made a show of fight by pointing his gun at Holt, who halted and leveled his; but, to the surprise of the lookers-on, neither of their weapons were discharged, both having been rendered temporarily useless, as I afterward learned, from being wet. Holt, however, as he again advanced, continued to snap his gun, while Copeland did the same."*

* Boteler, "Recollections of the John Brown Raid" in the *Century Magazine*, July, 1883, p. 407.

Copeland was taken alive and Leeman, with a second message from Kagi to Brown, was killed. Matters were now getting desperate, but the armory was full of prisoners and therein lay John Brown's final hope. Easily as a last resort he could use these citizens as a screen and so escape to the mountains. In attempting this, however, some of the prisoners were bound to be killed and Brown hesitated at sacrificing innocent blood to save himself. He thought that the same end might be accomplished by negotiation. His first move, therefore, was to withdraw all his force and the important prisoners to a small brick building near the armory gate called the "engine-house." Captain Daingerfield, one of the prisoners, says: "He entered the engine-house, carrying his prisoners along, or rather part of them, for he made selections. After getting into the engine-house he made this speech: 'Gentlemen, perhaps you wonder why I have selected you from the others. It is because I believe you to be the most influential; and I have only to say now, that you will have to share precisely the same fate that your friends extend to my men.' He began at once to bar the doors and windows, and to cut port-holes through the brick wall."*

This evident weakening of the raiders let pandemonium loose. The citizens realized how small a force Brown had and were filled with fury at his presumption. His men began to fight desperately for their lives.

"About the time when Brown immured himself," a narrator reports, "a company of Berkeley County militia arrived from Martinsburg who, with some citizens of Harper's Ferry and the surrounding country, made a rush on the armory and released the great mass of the prisoners outside of the engine-house, not, however, without suffering some loss from a galling fire kept up by the enemy from 'the fort.'"**

This released the arms and one of the Virginia watchmen

* Daingerfield in the *Century Magazine*, June, 1885.
** Barry, *Strange Story of Harper's Ferry*, p. 67.

says: "The people, who came pouring into town, broke into liquor saloons, filled up, and then got into the arsenal, arming themselves with United States guns and ammunition. They kept shooting at random and howling."*

The prisoners within the engine-house heard "a terrible firing from without, at every point from which the windows could be seen, and in a few minutes every window was shattered, and hundreds of balls came through the doors. These shots were answered from within whenever the attacking party could be seen. This was kept up most of the day, and, strange to say, not a prisoner was hurt, though thousands of balls were imbedded in the walls, and holes shot in the doors almost large enough for a man to creep through."**

The doomed raiders saw "volley upon volley" discharged, while "the echoes from the hills, the shrieks of the townspeople, and the groans of their wounded and dying, all of which filled the air, were truly frightful." Yet "no powder and ball were wasted. We shot from under cover, and took deadly aim. For an hour before the flag of truce was sent out, the firing was uninterrupted, and one and another of the enemy were constantly dropping to the earth."***

Oliver Brown was shot and died without a word and Taylor was mortally wounded. The mayor of the city ventured out, unarmed, to reconnoitre and was killed. Immediately the son of Andrew Hunter, who afterward was state's attorney against Brown, rushed into the hotel after the prisoner William Thompson:

"We burst into the room where he was, and found several around him, but they offered only a feeble resistance; we brought our guns down to his head repeatedly, — myself and another person, — for the purpose of shooting him in the room.

* Patrick Higgins in Hinton, p. 290.
** Daingerfield in the *Century Magazine*, June, 1885.
*** Anderson, *A Voice from Harper's Ferry*, p. 42.

"There was a young lady there, the sister of Mr. Fouke, the hotel-keeper, who sat in this man's lap, covered his face with her arms, and shielded him with her person whenever we brought our guns to bear. She said to us, 'For God's sake, wait and let the law take its course.' My associate shouted to kill him. 'Let us shed his blood,' were his words. All round were shouting, 'Mr. Beckham's life was worth ten thousand of these vile Abolitionists.' I was cool about it, and deliberate. My gun was pushed by some one who seized the barrel, and I then moved to the back part of the room, still with purpose unchanged, but with a view to divert attention from me, in order to get an opportunity, at some moment when the crowd would be less dense, to shoot him. After a moment's thought it occurred to me that that was not the proper place to kill him. We then proposed to take him out and hang him. Some portion of our band then opened a way to him, and first pushing Miss Fouke aside, we slung him out-of-doors. I gave him a push, and many others did the same. We then shoved him along the platform and down to the trestle work of the bridge; he begged for his life all the time, very piteously at first."*

Thus he was shot to death as he crawled in the trestle work. The prisoners in the engine-house now urged Brown to make terms with the citizens, representing that this was possible and that he and his men could escape. Brown sent out his son Watson with a white flag, but the maddened citizens paid no attention to it and shot him down. A lull in the fighting came a little later, and Stevens took a second flag of truce, but was captured and held prisoner. Daingerfield says:

"At night the firing ceased, for we were in total darkness, and nothing could be seen in the engine-house. During the day and night I talked much with Brown. I found him as brave as a man could be, and sensible upon all subjects except slavery. He believed it was his duty to free the slaves,

---

* Testimony of Henry Hunter in Redpath, pp. 320-321.

even if in doing so he lost his own life. During a sharp fight one of Brown's sons was killed. He fell; then trying to raise himself, he said, 'It is all over with me,' and died instantly. Brown did not leave his post at the port-hole; but when the fighting was over he walked to his son's body, straightened out his limbs, took off his trappings, and then, turning to me, said, 'This is the third son I have lost in this cause.' Another son had been shot in the morning, and was then dying, having been brought in from the street. Often during the affair at the engine-house, when his men would want to fire upon some one who might be seen passing, Brown would stop them, saying, 'Don't shoot; that man is unarmed.' The firing was kept up by our men all day and until late at night, and during this time several of his men were killed, but none of the prisoners were hurt, though in great danger. During the day and night many propositions, pro and con, were made, looking to Brown's surrender and the release of the prisoners, but without result."*

Another eye-witness says:

"A little before night Brown asked if any of his captives would volunteer to go out among the citizens and induce them to cease firing on the fort, as they were endangering the lives of their friends — the prisoners. He promised on his part that, if there was no more firing on his men, there should be none by them on the besiegers. Mr. Israel Russel undertook the dangerous duty; the risk arose from the excited state of the people who would be likely to fire on anything seen stirring around the prison-house, and the citizens were persuaded to stop firing in consideration of the danger incurred of injuring the prisoners. . . .

"It was now dark and the wildest excitement existed in the town, especially among the friends of the killed, wounded and prisoners of the citizens' party. It had rained some little all day and the atmosphere was raw and cold. Now, a cloudy and moonless sky hung like a pall over the scene of

* Daingerfield in the *Century Magazine*, June, 1885.

war, and, on the whole, a more dismal night cannot be imagined. Guards were stationed round the engine-house to prevent Brown's escape and, as forces were constantly arriving from Winchester, Frederick City, Baltimore and other places to help the Harper's Ferry people, the town soon assumed quite a military appearance. The United States authorities in Washington had been notified in the meantime, and, in the course of the night, Colonel Robert E. Lee, afterward the famous General Lee of the Southern Confederacy, arrived with a force of United States marines, to protect the interests of the government, and kill or capture the invaders."[*]

Meantime Cook had awakened to the fact that something was wrong. He left Tidd at the schoolhouse and started toward the Ferry; finding it surrounded, he fired one volley from a tree and fled. He found no one at the schoolhouse, but met Tidd, and the whole farm guard, and one Negro on the road beyond. They all turned and fled north, Tidd and Cook quarreling. They wandered fourteen days in rain and snow, and finally all escaped except Cook who went into a town for food and was arrested.

Robert E. Lee, with 100 marines, arrived just before midnight on Monday and one of the prisoners tells the story of the last stand:

"When Colonel Lee came with the government troops in the night, he at once sent a flag of truce by his aid, J. E. B. Stuart, to notify Brown of his arrival, and in the name of the United States to demand his surrender, advising him to throw himself on the clemency of the government. Brown declined to accept Colonel Lee's terms, and determined to await the attack. When Stuart was admitted and a light brought, he exclaimed, 'Why, aren't you old Osawatomie Brown of Kansas, whom I once had there as my prisoner?' 'Yes,' was the answer, 'but you did not keep me.' This was the first intimation we had of Brown's real name. When

* Barry, *Strange Story of Harper's Ferry*, pp. 70–71.

Colonel Lee advised Brown to trust to the clemency of the government, Brown responded that he knew what that meant, — a rope for his men and himself; adding, 'I prefer to die just here.' Stuart told him he would return at early morning for his final reply, and left him. When he had gone, Brown at once proceeded to barricade the doors, windows, etc., endeavoring to make the place as strong as possible. All this time no one of Brown's men showed the slightest fear, but calmly awaited the attack, selecting the best situations to fire from, and arranging their guns and pistols so that a fresh one could be taken up as soon as one was discharged. . . .

"When Lieutenant Stuart came in the morning for the final reply to the demand to surrender, I got up and went to Brown's side to hear his answer. Stuart asked, 'Are you ready to surrender, and trust to the mercy of the government?' Brown answered, 'No, I prefer to die here.' His manner did not betray the least alarm. Stuart stepped aside and made a signal for the attack, which was instantly begun with sledge-hammers to break down the door. Finding it would not yield, the soldiers seized a long ladder for a battering-ram, and commenced beating the door with that, the party within firing incessantly. I had assisted in the barricading, fixing the fastenings so that I could remove them on the first effort to get in. But I was not at the door when the battering began, and could not get to the fastenings till the ladder was used. I then quickly removed the fastenings; and, after two or three strokes of the ladder, the engine rolled partially back, making a small aperture, through which Lieutenant Green of the marines forced his way, jumped on top of the engine, and stood a second, amidst a shower of balls, looking for John Brown. When he saw Brown, he sprang about twelve feet at him, giving an under-thrust of his sword, striking Brown about midway the body, and raising him completely from the ground. Brown fell forward, with his head between his knees, while Green struck him several times over the head, and, as I then supposed, split his skull at every stroke. I was not two feet from Brown at that time. Of course, I got out of the building as soon as possible, and did not know till some time later that Brown was not killed. It seems that Green's sword, in making the thrust, struck Brown's belt and did not penetrate the body. The sword was bent double. The reason that Brown was not killed when struck on the head was, that Green was holding his sword in the middle, striking with the hilt, and making only scalp wounds."*

After the attack on the troops at the bridge, Brown had ordered O. P. Anderson, Hazlett and Green back to the arsenal. But Green saw the desperate strait of Brown and chose voluntarily to go into the engine-house and fight until the last. Anderson and Hazlett, when they saw the door battered in, went to the back of the arsenal, climbed the wall and fled along the railway that goes up the Shenandoah. Here in the cliffs they had a skirmish with the troops but finally escaped in the night, crossed the town and the Potomac and so got into Maryland and went to the farm. It was deserted and pillaged. Then they came back to the schoolhouse and found that empty. In the morning they heard firing and Anderson's narrative continues:

"Hazlett thought it must be Owen Brown and his men trying to force their way into the town, as they had been informed that a number of us had been taken prisoners, and we started down along the ridge to join them. When we got in sight of the Ferry, we saw the troops firing across the river to the Maryland side with considerable spirit. Looking closely, we saw, to our surprise, that they were firing upon a few of the colored men, who had been armed the day before by our men, at the Kennedy farm, and stationed down at the schoolhouse by C. P. Tidd. They were in the bushes on the edge of the mountains, dodging about, occasionally exposing themselves to the enemy. The troops crossed the bridge in pursuit of them, but they retreated in dif-

* Daingerfield in the *Century Magazine*, June, 1885.

ferent directions. Being further in the mountains, and more secure, we could see without personal harm befalling us. One of the colored men came toward where we were, when we hailed him, and inquired the particulars. He said that one of his comrades had been shot, and was lying on the side of the mountains; that they thought the men who had armed them the day before must be in the Ferry. That opinion, we told him, was not correct. We asked him to join with us in hunting up the rest of the party, but he declined, and went his way.

"While we were in this part of the mountains, some of the troops went to the schoolhouse, and took possession of it. On our return along up the ridge, from our position, screened by the bushes, we could see them as they invested it. Our last hope of shelter or of meeting our companions, now being destroyed, we concluded to make our escape north."*

Anderson managed to get away, but Hazlett was captured in Pennsylvania and was returned to Virginia. Thus John Brown's raid ended. Seven of the men — John Brown himself, Shields Green, Edwin Coppoc, Stevens and Copeland and eventually Cook and Hazlett — were captured and hanged. Watson and Oliver Brown, the two Thompsons, Kagi, Jerry Anderson, Taylor, Newby, Leary, and John Anderson, ten in all, were killed in the fight, and six others — Owen Brown, Tidd, Leeman, Barclay Coppoc, Merriam and O. Anderson escaped.

At high noon on Tuesday, October 18th, the raid was over. John Brown lay wounded and blood-stained on the floor and the governor of Virginia bent over him.

"Who are you?" he asked.

"My name is John Brown; I have been well known as old John Brown of Kansas. Two of my sons were killed here today, and I'm dying too. I came here to liberate slaves, and was to receive no reward. I have acted from a sense of duty,

* Anderson, *A Voice from Harper's Ferry*, p. 52.

and am content to await my fate; but I think the crowd have treated me badly. I am an old man. Yesterday I could have killed whom I chose; but I had no desire to kill any person, and would not have killed a man had they not tried to kill me and my men. I could have sacked and burned the town, but did not; I have treated the persons whom I took as hostages kindly, and I appeal to them for the truth of what I say. If I had succeeded in running off slaves this time, I could have raised twenty times as many men as I have now, for a similar expedition. But I have failed."*

* John Brown in Sanborn, pp. 560–561.

XII

The Riddle of the Sphinx

"Surely He hath borne our griefs, and carried our sorrows; yet we did esteem Him stricken, smitten of God, and afflicted.

"But He was wounded for our transgressions, He was bruised for our iniquities: the chastisement of our peace was upon Him; and with His stripes we are healed."

The deed was done. The next day the world knew and the world sat in puzzled amazement. It was ever so and ever will be. When a prophet like John Brown appears, how must we of the world receive him? Must we follow out the dreat, dread logic of surrounding facts, as did the South, even if they crucify a clean and pure soul, simply because consistent allegiance to our cherished, chosen ideal demands it? If we do, the shame will brand our latest history. Shall we hesitate and waver before his clear white logic, now helping, now fearing to help, now believing, now doubting? Yes, this we must do so long as the doubt and hesitation are genuine; but we must not lie. If we are human, we must thus hesitate until we know the right. How shall we know it? That is the Riddle of the Sphinx. We are but darkened groping souls, that know not light often because of its very blinding radiance. Only in time is truth revealed. To-day at last we know: John Brown was right.

Yet there are some great principles to guide us. That there are in this world matters of vast human import which are eternally right or eternally wrong, all men believe. Whether that great right comes, as the simpler, clearer minded think, from the spoken word of God, or whether it is simply another way of saying: this deed makes for the good of mankind, or that, for the ill — however it may be, all men know that there are in this world here and there and again and again great partings of the ways — the one way wrong, the other right, in some vast and eternal sense. This certainly is true at times — in the mighty crises of lives and nations.

On the other hand, it is also true, as human experience again and again shows, that the usual matters of human debate and difference of opinion are not so vitally important, or so easily classified; that in most cases there is much of right and wrong on both sides and, so usual is it to find this true, that men tend to argue it always so. Their life morality becomes always a wavering path of expediency, not necessarily the best or the worst path, as they freely even smilingly admit, but a good path, a safe path, a path of little resistance and one that leads to the good if not to the theoretical (but usually impracticable) best. Such philosophy of the world's ways is common, and probably it is well that thus it is. And yet we all feel its temporary, tentative character; we instinctively distrust its comfortable tone, and listen almost fearfully for the greater voice; its better is often so far below that which we feel is a possible best, that its present temporizing seems evil to us, and ever and again after the world has complacently dodged and compromised with, and skilfully evaded a great evil, there shines, suddenly, a great white light — an unwavering, unflickering brightness, blinding by its all-seeing brilliance, making the whole world simply a light and a darkness — a right and a wrong. Then men tremble and writhe and waver. They whisper, "But — but — of course"; "the thing is plain, but it is too plain to be true — it is true but truth is not the only thing in the world." Thus they hide from the light, they burrow and grovel, and yet ever in, and through, and on them blazes that mighty light with its horror of darkness and behind it peals the voice — the Riddle of the Sphinx, that must be answered.

Such a light was the soul of John Brown. He was simple, exasperatingly simple; unlettered, plain, and homely. No casuistry of culture or of learning, of well-being or tradition moved him in the slightest degree: "Slavery is wrong," he said, — "kill it." Destroy it — uproot it, stem, blossom, and branch; give it no quarter, exterminate it and do it now. Was he wrong? No. The forcible staying of human uplift by barriers of law, and might, and tradition is the most wicked thing on earth. It is wrong, eternally wrong. It is wrong by whatever name it is called, or in whatever guise it lurks, and whenever it appears. But it is especially heinous, black, and cruel when it masquerades in the robes of law and justice and patriotism. So was American slavery clothed in 1859, and it had to die by revolution, not by milder means. And this men knew. They had known it a hundred years. Yet they shrank and trembled. From round about the white and blinding path of this soul flew equivocations, lies, thievings and red murders. And yet all men instinctively felt that these things were not of the light but of the surrounding darkness. It is at once surprising, baffling and pitiable to see the way in which men — honest American citizens — faced this light. Many types met and answered the argument, John Brown (for he did not use argument, he was himself an argument). First there was the Western American — the typical American, like Charles Robinson — one to whose imagination the empire of the vale of the Mississippi appealed with tremendous force. Then there was the Abolitionist — shading away from him who held slavery an incubus to him who saw its sin, of whom Gerrit Smith was a fair type. Then there was the lover of men, like Dr. Howe, and the merchant-errant like Stearns. Finally, there were the two great fateful types — the master and the slave.

To Robinson, Brown was simply a means to an end — beyond that he was whatever prevailing public opinion indicated. When the gratitude of Osawatomie swelled high, Brown was fit to be named with Jesus Christ; when the wave of Southern reaction subjugated the nation, he was something less than a fanatic. But whatever he was, he was the sword on which struggling Kansas and its leaders could depend, the untarnished doer of its darker deeds, when they that knew them necessary cowered and held their hands. Brown's was not the only hand that freed Kansas, but his hand was indispensable, and not the first time, nor the last, has a cool and skilful politician, like Robinson, climbed to power on the heads of those helpers of his, whose half-realized ideals he bartered for present possibilities — human freedom for statehood. For the Abolitionist of the Garrison type Brown had a contempt, as undeserved as it was natural to his genius. To recognize an evil and not strike it was to John Brown sinful. "Talk, talk, talk," he said derisively. Nor did he rightly gauge the value of spiritual as contrasted with physical blows, until the day when he himself struck the greatest on the Charleston scaffold.

But if John Brown failed rightly to gauge the movement of the Abolitionists, few of them failed to appreciate him when they met him. Instinctively they knew him as one who grasped the very pith and kernel of the evil which they fought. They asked no proofs or credentials; they asked John Brown. So it was with Gerrit Smith. He saw Brown and believed in him. He entertained him at his house. He heard his detailed plans for striking slavery a heart blow. He gave him in all over a thousand dollars, and bade him Godspeed! Yet when the blow was struck, he was filled with immeasurable consternation. He equivocated and even denied knowledge of Brown's plans. To be sure, he, his family, his fortune were in the shadow of danger — but where was John Brown? So with Dr. Howe, whose memory was painfully poor on the witness stand and who fluttered from enthusiastic support of Brown to a weak wavering when once he had tasted the famous Southern hospitality. He found slavery, to his own intense surprise, human: not ideally and horribly devilish, but only humanly bad. Was a bad human institution to be attacked *vi et armis?* Or was it not rather to be with persuasive argument in the soft shade of a Carolina veranda? Dr. Howe inclined to the latter thought, after his Cuban visit, and he was exceedingly annoyed and scared after the raid. He fled precipitately to Canada. Of the Boston committee only Stearns stood up and out in the public glare and said unequivocally, then and there: "I believe John Brown to be the representative man of this century, as Washington was of the last — the Harper's Ferry affair, and the capacity shown by the Italiens for self-government, the great events of this age. One will free Europe and the other America."*

The attitude of the black man toward John Brown is typified by Frederick Douglass and Shields Green. Said Douglass: "On the evening when the news came that John Brown had taken and was then holding the town of Harper's Ferry, it so happened that I was speaking to a large audience in National Hall, Philadelphia. The announcement came upon us with the startling effect of an earthquake. It was something to make the boldest hold his breath."**

Wise and Buchanan started immediately on Douglass's track and he fled to Canada and eventually to England. Why did not Douglass join John Brown? Because, first, he was of an entirely different cast of temperament and mind; and because, secondly, he knew, as only a Negro slave can know, the tremendous might and organization of the slave power. Brown's plan never in the slightest degree appealed to Douglass's reason. That the Underground Railroad methods could be enlarged and systematized, Douglass believed, but any further plan he did not think possible. Only national force could dislodge national slavery. As it was with Douglass, so it was practically with the Negro race. They believed in John Brown but not in his plan. He touched their warm loving hearts but not their hard heads. The Canadian Negroes, for instance, were men who knew what slavery meant. They had suffered its degradation, its repression and its still more fatal license. They knew the slave system. They had been slaves. They had risked life to help loved ones to escape its far-reaching tentacles. They had reached a land of freedom and had begun to taste the joy of being human. Their little homes were clustering about — they had their churches, lodges, social gatherings, and news-

---

* Report: Reports of Senate Committees, 36th Congress, 1st Session, No. 278; Testimony of George L. Stearns, pp. 241–242.

** Douglass, *Life and Times of Frederick Douglass* (1892), p. 376.

paper. Then came the call. They loved the old man and cherished him, helped and forwarded his work in a thousand little ways. But the call? Were they asked to sacrifice themselves to free their fellow-slaves? Were they not quite ready? No — to do that they stood ever ready. But here they were asked to sacrifice themselves for the sake of possibly freeing a few slaves and certainly arousing the nation. They saw what John Brown did not fully realize until the last: the tremendous meaning of sacrifice even though his enterprise failed and they were sure it would fail. Yet in truth it need not have failed. History and military science prove its essential soundness. But the Negro knew little of history and military science. He did know slavery and the slave power, and they loomed large and invincible in his fertile imagination. He could not conceive their overthrow by anything short of the direct voice of God. That a supreme sacrifice of human beings on the altar of Moloch might hasten the day of emancipation was possible, but were they called to give their lives to this forlorn hope? Most of them said no, as most of their fellows, black and white, ever answer to the "voice, without reply." They said it reluctantly, slowly, even hesitatingly, but they said it even as their leader Douglass said it. And why not, they argued? Was not their whole life already a sacrifice? Were they called by any right of God or man to give more than they already had given? What more did they owe the world? Did not the world owe them an unpayable amount?

Then, too, the sacrifice demanded of black men in this raid was far more than that demanded of whites. In 1859 it was a crime for a free black man even to set foot on Virginia soil, and it was slavery or death for a fugitive to return. If worse came to worst, the Negro stood the least chance of escape and the least consideration on capture. Yet despite all this and despite the terrible training of slavery in cowardice, submission and fatality; the systematic elimination, by death and cruelty, of strength and self-respect and bravery, there were in Canada and in the United States scores of Negroes ready for the sacrifice. But the necessary secrecy, vagueness and intangibility of the summons, the repeated changes of date, the difficulty of communication and the poverty of black men, all made effective coöperation exceedingly difficult.

Even as it was, fifteen or twenty Negroes had enlisted and would probably have been present had they had the time. Five, probably six, actually came in time, and thirty or forty slaves actively helped. Considering the mass of Negroes in the land and the character of the leader, this was an insignificant number. But what it lacked in number it made up in characters like Shields Green. He was a poor, unlettered fugitive, ignorant by the law of the land, stricken in life and homely in body. He sat and listened as Douglass and Brown argued amid the boulders of that old Chambersburg quarry. Some things he understood, some he did not. But one thing he did understand and that was the soul of John Brown, so he said, "I guess I'll go with the old man." Again in the sickening fury of that fatal Monday, a white man and a black man found themselves standing with freedom before them. The white man was John Brown's truest companion and the black man was Shields Green. "I told him to come," said the white man afterward, "that we could do nothing more," but he simply said, "I must go down to the old man." And he went down to John Brown and to death.

If this was the attitude of the slave, what was that of the master? It was when John Brown faced the indignant, self-satisfied and arrogant slave power of the South, flanked by its Northern Vallandighams, that the mighty paradox and burning farce of the situation revealed itself. Picture the situation: An old and blood-bespattered man, half-dead from the wounds inflicted but a few hours before; a man lying in the cold and dirt, without sleep for fifty-five nerve-wrecking hours, without food for nearly as long, with the dead bodies of two sons almost before his eyes, the piled corpses of his seven slain comrades near and afar, a wife and a bereaved family listening in vain, and a Lost Cause, the dream of a lifetime, lying dead in his heart. Around him was a group of bitter, inquisitive Southern aristocrats and their satellites, headed by one of the foremost leaders of subsequent secession.

"Who sent you — who sent you?" these inquisitors insisted.

"No man sent me — I acknowledge no master in human form!"

"What was your object in coming?"

"We came to free the slaves."

"How do you justify your acts?"

"You are guilty of a great wrong against God and humanity and it would be perfectly right for any one to interfere with you so far as to free those you wilfully and wickedly hold in bondage. I think I did right; and that others will do right who interfere with you at any time and at all times. I hold that the Golden Rule, 'Do unto others as ye would that others should do unto you,' applies to all who would help others to gain their liberty."

"But don't you believe in the Bible?"

"Certainly, I do."

"Do you consider this a religious movement?"

"It is in my opinion the greatest service man can render to God."

"Do you consider yourself an instrument in the hands of Providence?"

"I do."

"Upon what principles do you justify your acts?"

"Upon the Golden Rule. I pity the poor in bondage that have none to help them. That is why I am here; not to gratify any personal animosity, revenge, or vindictive spirit. It is my sympathy with the oppressed and the wronged, that are as good as you and as precious in the sight of God."

"Certainly. But why take the slaves against their will?"

"I never did." . . .

"Who are your advisers in this movement?"

"I have numerous sympathizers throughout the entire North. . . . I want you to understand that I respect the rights of the poorest and the weakest of colored people, oppressed by the slave system, just as much as I do those of the most wealthy and powerful. That is the idea that has moved me, and that alone. We expected no reward except satisfaction of endeavoring to do for those in distress and greatly oppressed as we would be done by. The cry of distress of the oppressed is my reason, and the only thing that prompted me to come here."

"Why did you do it secretly?"

"Because I thought that necessary to success; no other reason. . . . I agree with Mr. Smith that moral suasion is hopeless. I don't think the people of the slave states will ever consider the subject of slavery in its true light till some other argument is resorted to than moral suasion."

"Did you expect a general rising of the slaves in case of your success?"

"No, sir; nor did I wish it. I expected to gather them up from time to time, and set them free."

"Did you expect to hold possession here till then?"

"You overrate your strength in supposing I could have been taken if I had not allowed it. I was too tardy after commencing the open attack — in delaying my movements through Monday night, and up to the time I was attacked by the government troops."

"Where did you get arms?"

"I bought them."

"In what state?"

"That I will not state. I have nothing to say, only that I claim to be here in carrying out a measure I believe perfectly justifiable, and not to act the part of an incendiary or ruffian, but to aid those suffering great wrong. I wish to say, furthermore, that you had better — all you people at the South — prepare yourselves for a settlement of this question, that must come up for settlement sooner than you are prepared for it. The sooner you are prepared the better.

You may dispose of me very easily, — I am nearly disposed of now, but this question is still to be settled, — this Negro question, I mean; the end of that is not yet."

"Brown, suppose you had every nigger in the United States, what would you do with them?"

"Set them free."

"Your intention was to carry them off and free them?"

"Not at all."

"To set them free would sacrifice the life of every man in this community."

"I do not think so."

"I know it; I think you are fanatical."

"And I think you are fanatical. Whom the gods would destroy they first make mad, and you are mad."

"Was it your only object to free the Negroes?"

"Absolutely our only object." . . .

"You are a robber," cried some voice in the crowd.

"You slaveholders are robbers," retorted Brown.

But Governor Wise interrupted: "Mr. Brown, the silver of your hair is reddened by the blood of crime, and you should eschew these hard words and think upon eternity. You are suffering from wounds, perhaps fatal; and should you escape death from these causes, you must submit to a trial which may involve death. Your confessions justify the presumption that you will be found guilty; and even now you are committing a felony under the laws of Virginia, by uttering sentiments like these. It is better you should turn your attention to your eternal future than be dealing in denunciations which can only injure you."

John Brown replied: "Governor, I have from all appearances not more than fifteen or twenty years the start of you in the journey to that eternity of which you kindly warn me; and whether my time here shall be fifteen months, or fifteen days, or fifteen hours, I am equally prepared to go. There is an eternity behind and an eternity before; and this little speck in the centre, however long, is but comparatively a minute. The difference between your tenure and mine is trifling, and I therefore tell you to be prepared. I am prepared. You have a heavy responsibility, and it behooves you to prepare more than it does me."*

Thus from the day John Brown was captured to the day he died, and after, it was the South and slavery that was on trial — not John Brown. Indeed, the dilemma into which John Brown's raid threw the state of Virginia was perfect. If his foray was the work of a handful of fanatics, led by a lunatic and repudiated by the slaves to a man, then the proper procedure would have been to ignore the incident, quietly punish the worst offenders and either pardon the misguided leader, or send him to an asylum. If, on the other hand, Virginia faced a conspiracy that threatened her social existence, aroused dangerous unrest in her slave population, and was full of portent for the future, then extraordinary precaution, swift and extreme punishment, and bitter complaint were only natural. But both these situations could not be true — both horns of the dilemma could not be logically seized. Yet this was precisely what the South and Virginia sought. While insisting that the raid was too hopelessly and ridiculously small to accomplish anything, and saying, with Andrew Hunter, that "not a single one of the slaves" joined John Brown "except by coercion," the state nevertheless spent $250,000 to punish the invaders, stationed from one to three thousand soldiers in the vicinity and threw the nation into turmoil. When the inconsistency of this action struck various minds, the attempt was made to exaggerate the danger of the invading white men. The presiding judge at the trial wrote, as late as 1889, that the number in Brown's party was proven by witnesses to have been seventy-five to one hundred and he "expected large reinforcements"; while Andrew Hunter, the state's attorney, saw nation-wide conspiracies.

What, then, was the truth about the matter? It was as Frederick Douglass said twenty-two years later on the very

* Correspondence of the New York *Herald*, Sanborn, pp. 562–571.

spot: "If John Brown did not end the war that ended slavery, he did, at least, begin the war that ended slavery. If we look over the dates, places, and men for which this honor is claimed, we shall find that not Carolina, but Virginia, not Fort Sumter, but Harper's Ferry and the arsenal, not Major Anderson, but John Brown began the war that ended American slavery, and made this a free republic. Until this blow was struck, the prospect for freedom was dim, shadowy, and uncertain. The irrepressible conflict was one of words, votes, and compromises. When John Brown stretched forth his arm the sky was cleared, — the armed hosts of freedom stood face to face over the chasm of a broken Union, and the clash of arms was at hand."*

The paths by which John Brown's raid precipitated civil war were these: In the first place, he aroused the Negroes of Virginia. How far the knowledge of his plan had penetrated is of course only to be conjectured. Evidently few knew that the foray would take place on October 17th. But when the movement had once made a successful start, there is no doubt that Osborne Anderson knew whereof he spoke, when he said that slaves were ready to coöperate. His words were proven by the 200,000 black soldiers in the Civil War. That something was wrong was shown, too, by five incendiary fires in a single week after the raid. Hunter sought to attribute these to "Northern emissaries," but this charge was unproven and extremely improbable. The only other possible perpetrators were slaves and free Negroes. That Virginians believed this is shown by Hinton's declaration that the loss in 1859 by the sale of Virginia slaves alone was $ 10,000,000.** A lady who visited John Brown said, "It was hard for me to forget the presence of the jailer (I had that morning seen his advertisement of 'fifty Negroes for sale')."*** It is im-

* Frederick Douglass in a speech at Storer College at Harper's Ferry, May, 1882.

** Hinton, pp. 325–326.

*** Mrs. Spring in Redpath, p. 377.

possible to prove the extent of this clearing-out of suspected slaves but the census reports indicate something of it. The Negro population of Maryland and Virginia increased a little over four per cent. between 1850 and 1860. But in the three counties bordering on Harper's Ferry — Loudoun and Jefferson in Virginia and Washington in Maryland, the 17,647 slaves of 1850 had shrunk to 15,996 in 1860, a decrease of nearly ten per cent. This means a disappearance of 2,400 slaves and is very significant.

Secondly, long before John Brown appeared at Harper's Ferry, Southern leaders like Mason, the author of the Fugitive Slave Bill, and chairman of the Harper's Ferry investigating committee; Jefferson Davis, who was a member of this committee; Wise, Hunter and other Virginians, had set their faces toward secession as the only method of protecting slavery. Into the mouths of these men John Brown put a tremendous argument and a fearful warning. The argument they used, the warning they suppressed and hushed. The argument was: This is Abolitionism; this is the North. This is the kind of treatment which the South and its cherished institution can expect unless it resorts to extreme measures. Proceeding along these lines, they emphasized and enlarged the raid so far as its white participants and Northern sympathizers were concerned. Governor Wise, on November 25th, issued a burning manifesto for the ears of the South and the eyes of President Buchanan, and the majority report of the Senate Committee closed with ominous words. On the other hand, the warning of John Brown's raid — the danger of Negro insurrection, was but whispered.

Third, and this was the path that led to Civil War and far beyond: The raid aroused and directed the conscience of the nation. Strange it was to watch its work. Some, impulsive, eager to justify themselves, rushed into print. To Garrison, the non-resistant, the sword of Gideon was abhorrent; Beecher thundered against John Brown and Seward bitterly traduced him. Then came an ominous silence in the land while his voice, in his own defense, was heard over the whole country. A great surging throb of sympathy arose and swept the world. That John Brown was legally a lawbreaker and a murderer all men knew. But wider and wider circles were beginning dimly and more clearly to recognize that his lawlessness was in obedience to the highest call of self-sacrifice for the welfare of his fellow men. They began to ask themselves, What is this cause that can inspire such devotion? The reiteration of the simple statement of "the brother in bonds" could not help but attract attention. The beauty of the conception despite its possible unearthliness and impracticability attracted poet and philosopher and common man.

To be sure, the nation had long been thinking over the problem of the black man, but never before had its attention been held by such deep dramatic and personal interest as in the forty days from mid-October to December, 1859. This arresting of national attention was due to Virginia and to John Brown: — to Virginia by reason of its exaggerated plaint; to John Brown whose strength, simplicity and acumen made his trial, incarceration and execution the most powerful Abolition argument yet offered. The very processes by which Virginia used John Brown to "fire the Southern heart" were used by John Brown to fire the Northern conscience. Andrew Hunter, the prosecuting state's attorney, of right demanded that the trial should be short and the punishment swift and in this John Brown fully agreed. He had no desire to escape the consequences of his act or to clog the wheels of Virginia justice. After a certain moral bewilderment there in the old engine-house at his failure on the brink of success, the true significance of his mission of sacrifice slowly rose before him. In the face of proposals to rescue him he said at first thoughtfully: "I do not know that I ought to encourage any attempt to save my life. I am not sure that it would not be better for me to die at this time. I am not incapable of error, and I may be wrong; but I think that perhaps my object would be nearer fulfilment if I should die. I must give it some thought."* And more and more this conviction seized and thrilled him, and he began to say decisively: "I think I cannot now better serve the cause I love so much than to die for it; and in my death I may do more than in my life."**

And again: "I can trust God with both the time and the manner of my death, believing, as I now do, that for me at this time to seal my testimony for God and humanity with my blood will do vastly more toward advancing the cause I have earnestly endeavored to promote, than all I have done in my life before." And then finally came that last great hymn of utter sacrifice: "I feel astonished that one so vile and unworthy as I am would even be suffered to have a place anyhow or anywhere amongst the very least of all who when they came to die (as all must) were permitted to pay the debt of nature in defense of the right and of God's eternal and immutable truth."***

The trial was a difficult experience. Virginia attempted to hold scales of even justice between mob violence and the world-wide sympathy of all good men. To defend its domestic institutions, it must try a man for murder when that very man, sitting as self-appointed judge of those very institutions, had convicted them before a jury of mankind. To defend the good name of the state, Virginia had to restrain the violent blood vengeance of men whose kin had been killed in the raid, and who had sworn that no prisoner should escape the extreme penalty. The trial was legally fair but pressed to a conclusion in unseemly haste, and in obedience to a threatening public opinion and a great hovering dread. Only against this unfair haste did John Brown protest, for he wanted the world to understand why he had done the deed. On the other hand, Hunter not only feared the local mob but the slowly arising sentiment for this white-

* Newspaper report in Redpath, p. 376.
** Mrs. Spring in Redpath, p. 377.
*** Letter to his sister, 1859, in Sanborn, pp. 607–609.

haired crusader. He therefore pushed the proceedings legally, but with almost brutal pertinacity. The prisoner was arraigned while wounded and in bed; the lawyers, hurriedly chosen, were given scant time for consultation or preparation. John Brown was formally committed to jail at Charlestown, the county seat, on October 20th, had a preliminary examination October 25th, and was indicted by the grand jury October 26th, for "conspiracy with slaves for the purpose of insurrection; with treason against the commonwealth of Virginia; and with murder in the first degree."

Thursday, October 27th, his trial was begun. A jury was impaneled without challenge and Brown's lawyers, ignoring his outline of defense, brought in the plea of insanity. The old man arose from his couch and said: "I look upon it as a miserable artifice and pretext of those who ought to take a different course in regard to me, if they took any at all, and I view it with contempt more than otherwise. ... I am perfectly unconscious of insanity, and I reject, so far as I am capable, any attempts to interfere in my behalf on that score."*

On Friday a Massachusetts lawyer arrived to help in the trial and also privately to suggest methods of escape. John Brown quietly refused to contemplate any such attempt, but was glad to accept the aid of this lawyer and two others, who were sent by John A. Andrew and his friends. The judge curtly refused these men any time to prepare their case, but in spite of this it ran over until Monday when the jury retired. Late Monday afternoon they returned. Redpath says:

"At this moment the crowd filled all the space from the couch inside the bar, around the prisoner, beyond the railing in the body of the court, out through the wide hall, and beyond the doors. There stood the anxious but perfectly silent and attentive populace, stretching head and neck to witness the closing scene of old Brown's trial."

* Remarks by John Brown in Redpath, p. 309.

The clerk of the court read the indictment and asked: "Gentlemen of the jury, what say you? Is the prisoner at the bar, John Brown, guilty or not guilty?"

"Guilty," answered the foreman.

"Guilty of treason, and conspiring and advising with slaves and others to rebel, and murder in the first degree?"

"Yes."

Redpath continues: "Not the slightest sound was heard in this vast crowd as this verdict was thus returned and read. Not the slightest expression of elation or triumph was uttered from the hundreds present, who, a moment before, outside the court, joined in heaping threats and imprecations on his head; nor was this strange silence interrupted during the whole of the time occupied by the forms of the court. Old Brown himself said not even a word, but, as on any previous day, turned to adjust his pallet, and then composedly stretched himself upon it."*

The following Wednesday John Brown was sentenced. Moving with painful steps and pale face, he took his seat under the gaslight in the great square room and remained motionless. The judge read his decision on the points of exception and the clerk asked: "Have you anything to say why sentence of death should not be passed upon you?" Then rising and leaning forward, John Brown made that last great speech, in a voice at once gentle and firm:

"I have, may it please the court, a few words to say.

"In the first place, I deny everything but what I have all along admitted, — the design on my part to free the slaves. I intended certainly to have made a clean thing of that matter, as I did last winter, when I went into Missouri and there took slaves without the snapping of a gun on either side, moved them through the country and finally left them in Canada. I designed to have done the same thing again, on a larger scale. That was all I intended. I never did intend murder, or treason, or the destruction of property,

* Newspaper report quoted by Redpath, p. 337.

or to excite or incite slaves to rebellion, or to make insurrection.

"I have another objection; and that is, it is unjust that I should suffer such a penalty. Had I interfered in the manner which I admit, and which I admit has been fairly proved (for I admire the truthfulness and candor of the greater portion of the witnesses who have testified in this case), — had I so interfered in behalf of the rich, the powerful, the intelligent, the so-called great, or in behalf of any of their friends, — either father, mother, brother, sister, wife, or children, or any of that class, — and suffered and sacrificed what I have in this interference, it would have been all right; and every man in this court would have deemed it an act worthy of reward rather than punishment.

"This court acknowledges, as I suppose, the validity of the law of God. I see a book kissed here which I suppose to be the Bible, or at least the New Testament. That teaches me that all things whatsoever I would that men should do to me, I should do even so to them. It teaches me, further, to 'remember them that are in bonds, as bound with them.' I endeavored to act up to that instruction. I say, I am yet too young to understand that God is any respecter of persons. I believe that to have interfered as I have done — as I have always freely admitted I have done — in behalf of His despised poor, was not wrong, but right. Now, if it is deemed necessary that I should forfeit my life for the furtherance of the ends of justice, and mingle my blood further with the blood of my children and with the blood of millions in this slave country whose rights are disregarded by wicked, cruel, and unjust enactments, — I submit; so let it be done! Let me say one word further.

"I feel entirely satisfied with the treatment I have received on my trial. Considering all the circumstances, it has been more generous than I expected. But I feel no consciousness of guilt. I have stated from the first what was my intention, and what was not. I never had any design against the life of any person, nor any disposition to commit treason, or excite slaves to rebel, or make any general insurrection. I never encouraged any man to do so, but always discouraged any idea of that kind.

"Let me say, also, a word in regard to the statements made by some of those connected with me. I hear it has been stated by some of them that I have induced them to join me. But the contrary is true. I do not say this to injure them, but as regretting their weakness. There is not one of them but that joined me of his own accord, and the greater part at their own expense. A number of them I never saw, and never had a word of conversation with, till the day they came to me; and that was for the purpose I have stated.

"Now I have done."*

The day of his dying, December 2d, dawned glorious; twenty-four hours before he had kissed his wife good-bye, and on this morning he visited his doomed companions — Shields Green and Copeland first; then the wavering Cook and Coppoc and the unmovable Stevens. At last he turned toward the place of his hanging. Since early morning three thousand soldiers had been marching and counter-marching around the scaffold, which had been erected a half mile from Charlestown, encircling it for fifteen miles; a hush sat on the hearts of men. John Brown rode out into the morning. "This is a beautiful land," he said. It was beautiful. Wide, glistening, rolling fields flickered in the sunlight. Beyond, the Shenandoah went rolling northward, and still afar rose the mighty masses of the Blue Ridge, where Nat Turner had fought and died, where Gabriel had looked for refuge and where John Brown had builded his awful dream. Some say he kissed a Negro child as he passed, but Andrew Hunter vehemently denies it. "No Negro could get access to him," he says, and he is probably right; and yet all about him as he hung there knelt the funeral guard he prayed for when he said:

"My love to all who love their neighbors. I have asked

* Redpath, pp. 340–342.

272

to be spared from having any weak or hypocritical prayers made over me when I am publicly murdered, and that my only religious attendants be poor little dirty, ragged, bare-headed, and barefooted slave boys and girls, led by some gray-headed slave mother. Farewell! Farewell!"*

* Letter to Mrs. George L. Stearns, 1859, in Sanborn, pp. 610–611.

273

XIII

The Legacy of John Brown

"Ho, every one that thirsteth, come ye to the waters, and he that hath no money; come ye, buy, and eat; yea, come, buy wine and milk without money and without price."

"I, John Brown, am quite certain that the crimes of this guilty land will never be purged away but with blood. I had, as I now think vainly, flattered myself that without very much bloodshed it might be done."

These were the last written words of John Brown, set down the day he died — the culminating of that wonderful message of his forty days in prison, which all in all made the mightiest Abolition document that America has known. Uttered in chains and solemnity, spoken in the very shadow of death, its dramatic intensity after that wild and puzzling raid, its deep earnestness as embodied in the character of the man, did more to shake the foundations of slavery than any single thing that ever happened in America. Of himself he speaks simply and with satisfaction: "I should be sixty years old were I to live to May 9, 1860. I have enjoyed much of life as it is, and have been remarkably prosperous, having early learned to regard the welfare and prosperity of others as my own. I have never, since I can remember, required a great amount of sleep; so that I conclude that I have already enjoyed full an average number of working hours with those who reach their threescore years and ten. I have not yet been driven to the use of glasses, but can see to read and write quite comfortably. But more than that, I have generally enjoyed remarkably good health. I might go on to recount unnumbered and unmerited blessings, among which would be some very severe afflictions and those the most needed blessings of all. And now, when I think how easily I might be left to spoil all I have done or suffered in the cause of freedom, I hardly dare wish another voyage even if I had the opportunity."*

After a surging, trouble-tossed voyage he is at last at peace in body and mind. He asserts that he is and has been in his right mind: "I may be very insane; and I am so, if insane at all. But if that be so, insanity is like a very pleasant dream to me. I am not in the least degree conscious of my ravings, of my fears, or of any terrible visions whatever; but fancy myself entirely composed, and that my sleep, in particular, is as sweet as that of a healthy, joyous little infant. I pray God that He will grant me a continuance of the same calm but delightful dream, until I come to know of those realities which eyes have not seen and which ears have not heard. I have scarce realized that I am in prison or in irons at all. I certainly think I was never more cheerful in my life."**

To his family he hands down the legacy of his faith and works: "I beseech you all to live in habitual contentment with moderate circumstances and gains of worldly store, and earnestly to teach this to your children and children's children after you, by example as well as precept." And again: "Be sure to remember and follow my advice, and my example too, so far as it has been consistent with the holy religion of Jesus Christ, in which I remain a most firm and humble believer. Never forget the poor, nor think anything you bestow on them to be lost to you, even though they may be black as Ebedmelech, the Ethiopian eunuch, who cared for Jeremiah in the pit of the dungeon; or as black as the one to whom Philip preached Christ. Be sure to entertain strangers, for thereby some have ... Remember them that are in bonds as bound with them."***

Of his own merit and desert he is modest but firm: "The great bulk of mankind estimate each other's actions and

* Letter to his cousin, 1859, in Sanborn, pp. 594–595.
** Letter to D. R. Tilden in Sanborn, pp. 609–610.
*** Letters to his family, 1859, in Sanborn, pp. 579–580, 613–615.

motives by the measure of success or otherwise that attends them through life. By that rule, I have been one of the worst and one of the best of men. I do not claim to have been one of the latter, and I leave it to an impartial tribunal to decide whether the world has been the worse or the better for my living and dying in it."*

He has no sense of shame for his action: "I feel no consciousness of guilt in that matter, nor even mortification on account of my imprisonment and irons; I feel perfectly sure that very soon no member of my family will feel any possible disposition to blush on my account."**

"I do not feel conscious of guilt in taking up arms; and had it been in behalf of the rich and powerful, the intelligent, the great (as men count greatness), or those who form enactments to suit themselves and corrupt others, or some of their friends, that I interfered, suffered, sacrificed, and fell, it would have been doing very well. But enough of this. These light afflictions, which endure for a moment, shall but work for me a far more exceeding and eternal weight of glory."***

With desperate faith he clings to his belief in the providence of an all-wise God: "Under all these terrible calamities, I feel quite cheerful in the assurance that God reigns and will overrule all for His glory and the best possible good."****

True is it that the night is dark and his faith at first wavers, yet it rises ever again triumphant: "As I believe most firmly that God reigns, I cannot believe that anything I have done, suffered, or may yet suffer, will be lost to the cause of God or of humanity. And before I began my work at Harper's Ferry, I felt assured that in the worst event it would certainly pay. I often expressed that belief; and I can now

* Letter to D. R. Tilden in Sanborn, pp. 609–610.
** Letter to his family, 1859, in Sanborn, pp. 579–580.
*** Letter to a friend, 1859, in Sanborn, pp. 582–583.
**** Letter to his family, 1859, in Sanborn, pp. 579–580.

see no possible cause to alter my mind. I am not as yet, in the main, at all disappointed. I have been a good deal disappointed as it regards myself in not keeping up to my own plans; but I now feel entirely reconciled to that, even, — for God's plan was infinitely better, no doubt, or I should have kept to my own."*

He is, after all, the servant and instrument of the Almighty: "If you do not believe I had a murderous intention (while I know I had not), why grieve so terribly on my account? The scaffold has but few terrors for me. God has often covered my head in the day of battle, and granted me many times deliverances that were almost so miraculous that I can scarce realize their truth; and now, when it seems quite certain that He intends to use me in a different way, shall I not most cheerfully go?"**

"I have often passed under the rod of Him whom I call my Father, — and certainly no son ever needed it oftener; and yet I have enjoyed much of life, as I was enabled to discover the secret of this somewhat early. It has been in making the prosperity and happiness of others my own; so that really I have had a great deal of prosperity. I am very prosperous still; and looking forward to a time when 'peace on earth and good-will to men' shall everywhere prevail, I have no murmuring thoughts or envious feelings to fret my mind. I'll praise my Maker with my breath."***

"Success is in general the standard of all merit. I have passed my time quite cheerfully; still trusting that neither my life nor my death will prove a total loss. As regards both, however, I am liable to mistake. It affords me some satisfaction to feel conscious of having at least tried to better the condition of those who are always on the under-hill side, and am in hopes of being able to meet the consequences without a murmur. I am endeavoring to get ready for

* Letter to H. L. Vaill, 1859, in Sanborn, pp. 589–591.
** Letter to Rev. Dr. Humphrey, 1859, in Sanborn, pp. 603–605.
*** Letter to H. L. Vaill, 1859, in Sanborn, pp. 590–591.

another field of action, where no defeat befalls the truly brave. That 'God reigns,' and most wisely, and controls all events, might, it would seem, reconcile those who believe it to much that appears to be very disastrous. I am one who has tried to believe that, and still keep trying."*

"I cannot remember a night so dark as to have hindered the coming day, nor a storm so furious or dreadful as to prevent the return of warm sunshine and a cloudless sky."**

More and more his eyes pierce the gloom and see the vast plan for which God has used him and the glory of his sacrifice:

"'He shall begin to deliver Israel out of the hands of the Philistines.' This was said of a poor erring servant many years ago; and for many years I have felt a strong impression that God had given me powers and faculties, unworthy as I was, that He intended to use for a similar purpose. This most unmerited honor He has seen fit to bestow; and whether, like the same poor frail man to whom I allude, my death may not be of vastly more value than my life is, I think quite beyond all human foresight."***

"I think I feel as happy as Paul did when he lay in prison. He knew if they killed him, it would greatly advance the cause of Christ; that was the reason he rejoiced so. On that same ground 'I do rejoice, yea, and will rejoice.' Let them hang me; I forgive them, and may God forgive them, for they know not what they do. I have no regret for the transaction for which I am condemned. I went against the laws of men, it is true, but 'whether it be right to obey God or men, judge ye.' "****

"When and in what form death may come is but of small moment. I feel just as content to die for God's eternal truth

* Letter to Miss Stearns, Sanborn, p. 607.
** Postscript of letter to his family, 1859, in Sanborn, pp. 585–587.
*** Letter to Rev. Dr. Humphrey, 1859, in Sanborn, pp. 603–605.
**** Letter to Mr. McFarland, 1859, in Sanborn, pp. 598–599.

and for suffering humanity on the scaffold as in any other way; and I do not say this from disposition to 'brave it out.' No; I would readily own my wrong were I in the least convinced of it. I have now been confined over a month, with a good opportunity to look the whole thing as 'fair in the face' as I am capable of doing; and I feel it most grateful that I am counted in the least possible degree worthy to suffer for the truth."*

"I can trust God with both the time and the manner of my death, believing, as I now do, that for me at this time to seal my testimony for God and humanity with my blood will do vastly more toward advancing the cause I have earnestly endeavored to promote, than all I have done in my life before."**

"My whole life before had not afforded me one-half the opportunity to plead for the right. In this, also, I find much to reconcile me to both my present condition and my immediate prospect."***

Against slavery his face is set like flint: "There are no ministers of Christ here. These ministers who profess to be Christian, and hold slaves or advocate slavery, I cannot abide them. My knees will not bend in prayer with them, while their hands are stained with the blood of souls."**** He said to one Southern clergyman: "I will thank you to leave me alone; your prayers would be an abomination to God." To another he said, "I would not insult God by bowing down in prayer with any one who had the blood of the slave on his skirts."

And to a third who argued in favor of slavery as "a Christian institution," John Brown replied impatiently: "My dear sir, you know nothing about Christianity; you will have to learn its A, B, C; I find you quite ignorant of what

* Letter to his younger children, 1859, in Sanborn, pp. 596–597.
** Letter to his wife and children in Sanborn, pp. 585–587.
*** Letter to D. R. Tilden in Sanborn, pp. 609–610.
**** Letter to Mr. McFarland, 1859, in Sanborn, pp. 598–599.

the word Christianity means. .. I respect you as a gentle-man, of course; but it is as a heathen gentleman."*

To his children he wrote: "Be determined to know by experience, as soon as may be, whether Bible instruction is of divine origin or not. Be sure to owe no man anything, but to love one another. John Rogers wrote his children, 'Abhor that arrant whore of Rome.' John Brown writes to his children to abhor, with undying hatred also, that sum of all villanies, — slavery."**

And finally he rejoiced: "Men cannot imprison, or chain, or hang the soul. I go joyfully in behalf of millions that 'have no rights' that this great and glorious, this Christian republic 'is bound to respect.' Strange change in morals, po-litical as well as Christian, since 1776."***

"No formal will can be of use," he wrote on his dooms-day, "when my expressed wishes are made known to my dutiful and beloved family."****

This was the man. His family is the world. What legacy did he leave? It was soon seen that his voice was a call to the great final battle with slavery.

In the spring of 1861 the Boston Light Infantry was sent to Fort Warren in Boston harbor to drill. A quartette was formed among the soldiers to sing patriotic songs and for them was contrived the verses,

"John Brown's body lies a-mouldering in the grave,
His soul is marching on," etc.

This was set to the music of an old camp-meeting tune — possibly of Negro origin — called, "Say, Brother, Will You Meet Us?" The regiment learned it and first sang it publicly when it came up from Fort Warren and marched past the scene where Crispus Attucks fell. Gilmore's Band

* Redpath, pp. 382–383.
** Last letter to his family, 1859, in Sanborn, pp. 614–615.
*** Letter to F. B. Musgrave, 1859, in Sanborn, p. 593.
**** Report: Reports of Senate Committees, 36th Congress, 1st Session, No. 278; Testimony of Joshua R. Giddings, pp. 147–156.

learned and played it and thus "the song of John Brown was started on its eternal way!"

Was John Brown simply an episode, or was he an eternal truth? And if a truth, how speaks that truth to-day? John Brown loved his neighbor as himself. He could not endure therefore to see his neighbor, poor, unfortunate or oppressed. This natural sympathy was strengthened by a saturation in Hebrew religion which stressed the personal responsibility of every human soul to a just God. To this religion of equality and sympathy with misfortune, was added the strong influence of the social doctrines of the French Revolution with its emphasis on freedom and power in political life. And on all this was built John Brown's own inchoate but growing belief in a more just and a more equal distribution of property. From this he concluded, — and acted on that conclusion — that all men are created free and equal and that the cost of liberty is less than the price of repression.

Up to the time of John Brown's death this doctrine was a growing, conquering, social thing. Since then there has come a change and many would rightly find reason for that change in the coincidence that the year in which John Brown suffered martyrdom was the year that first published the *Origin of Species*. Since that day tremendous scientific and economic advance has been accompanied by distinct signs of moral retrogression in social philosophy. Strong arguments have been made for the fostering of war, the utility of human degradation and disease, and the inevitable and known inferiority of certain classes and races of men. While such arguments have not stopped the efforts of the advocates of peace, the workers for social uplift and the believers in human brotherhood, they have, it must be confessed, made their voices falter and tinged their arguments with apology.

Why is this? It is because the splendid scientific work of Darwin, Weissman, Galton and others has been widely interpreted as meaning that there is essential and inevitable inequality among men and races of men, which no philanthropy can or ought to eliminate; that civilization is a struggle for existence whereby the weaker nations and individuals will gradually succumb, and the strong will inherit the earth. With this interpretation has gone the silent assumption that the white European stock represents the strong surviving peoples, and that the swarthy, yellow and black peoples are the ones rightly doomed to eventual extinction.

One can easily see what influence such a doctrine would have on the race problem in America. It meant moral revolution in the attitude of the nation. Those that stepped into the pathway marked by men like John Brown faltered and large numbers turned back. They said: He was a good man — even great, but he has no message for us to-day — he was a "belated Covenanter," an anachronism in the age of Darwin, one who gave his life to lift not the unlifted but the unliftable. We have consequently the present reaction — a reaction which says in effect, Keep these black people in their places, and do not attempt to treat a Negro simply as a white man with a black face; to do this would mean the moral deterioration of the race and the nation — a fate against which a divine racial prejudice is successfully fighting. This is the attitude of the larger portion of our thinking people.

It is not, however, an attitude that has brought mental rest or social peace. On the contrary, it is to-day involving a degree of moral strain and political and social anomaly that gives the wisest pause. The chief difficulty has been that the natural place in which by scientific law the black race in America should stay, cannot easily be determined. To be sure, the freedmen did not, as the philanthropists of the sixties apparently expected, step in forty years from slavery to nineteenth century civilization. Neither, on the other hand, did they, as the ex-masters confidently predicted, retrograde and die. Contrary to both these views, they chose a third and apparently quite unawaited way. From the great, sluggish, almost imperceptibly moving mass, they sent off larger and larger numbers of faithful workmen and artisans, some merchants and professional men, and even men of educational ability and discernment. They developed no world geniuses, no millionaires, no great captains of industry, no artists of the first rank; but they did in forty years get rid of the greater part of their total illiteracy, accumulate a half-billion dollars of property in small homesteads, and gain now and then respectful attention in the world's ears and eyes. It has been argued that this progress of the black man in America is due to the exceptional men among them and does not measure the ability of the mass. Such an admission is, however, fatal to the whole argument. If the doomed races of men are going to develop exceptions to the rule of inferiority, then no rule, scientific or moral, should or can proscribe the race as such.

To meet this difficulty in racial philosophy, a step has been taken in America fraught with the gravest social consequences to the world, and threatening not simply the political but the moral integrity of the nation: that step is denying in the case of black men the validity of those evidences of culture, ability, and decency which are accepted unquestionably in the case of other people; and by vague assertions, unprovable assumptions, unjust emphasis, and now and then by deliberate untruth, aiming to secure not only the continued proscription of all these people, but, by caste distinction, to shut in the faces of their rising classes many of the paths to further advance.

When a social policy, based on a supposed scientific sanction, leads to such a moral anomaly, it is time to examine rather carefully the logical foundations of the argument. And as soon as we do this many things are clear: First, assuming the truth of the unproved dictum that there are stocks of human beings whose elimination the best welfare of the world demands, it is certainly questionable if these stocks include the majority of mankind; and it is indefensible and monstrous to pretend that we know to-day with any reasonable assurance which these stocks are. We can point to degenerate individuals and families here and there among all races, but there is not the slightest warrant for assuming that there does not lie among the Chinese and Hindus, the African Bantus and American Indians as lofty possibilities of human culture as any European race has ever exhibited. It is, to be sure, puzzling to know why the Soudan should linger a thousand years in culture behind the valley of the Seine, but it is no more puzzling than the fact that the valley of the Thames was miserably backward as compared with the banks of the Tiber. Climate, human contact, facilities of communication and what we call accident, have played a great part in the rise of culture among nations: to ignore these and assert dogmatically that the present distribution of culture is a fair index of the distribution of human ability and desert, is to make an assertion for which there is not the slightest scientific warrant.

What the age of Darwin has done is to add to the eighteenth century idea of individual worth the complementary idea of physical immortality. And this, far from annulling or contracting the idea of human freedom, rather emphasizes its necessity and eternal possibility — the boundlessness and endlessness of human achievement. Freedom has come to mean not individual caprice or aberration, but social self-realization in an endless chain of selves; and freedom for such development is not the denial but the central assertion of the evolutionary theory. So, too, the doctrine of human equality passes through the fire of scientific inquiry, not obliterated but transfigured: not equality of present attainment but equality of opportunity, for unbounded future attainment is the rightful demand of mankind.

What now does the present hegemony of the white races threaten? It threatens by means of brute force a survival of some of the worst stocks of mankind. It attempts to people the best parts of the earth and put in absolute authority over the rest, not usually (and indeed not mainly) the culture of Europe but its greed and degradation — not only some representatives of the best stocks of the West End of London, upper New York and the Champs Elysées, but also, in as large if not larger numbers, the worst stocks of Whitechapel, the East Side and Montmartre; and it essays to make the slums of white society in all cases and under all circumstances the superior of any colored group, no matter what its ability or culture. To be sure, this outrageous program of wholesale human degeneration is not outspoken yet, save in the backward civilizations of the Southern United States, South Africa and Australia. But its enunciation is listened to with respect and tolerance in England, Germany, and the Northern states by those very persons who accuse philanthropy with seeking to degrade holy white blood by an infiltration of colored strains. And the average citizen is voting ships and guns to carry out this program.

This movement gathered force and strength during the latter half of the nineteenth century and reached its culmination when France, Germany, England and Russia began the partition of China and the East. With the sudden self-assertion of Japan, its wildest dreams collapsed, but it is still today a living, virile, potent force and motive, the most subtle and dangerous enemy of world peace and the dream of human brotherhood. It has a whole vocabulary of its own: the strong races, superior peoples, race preservation, the struggle for survival and a variety of terms meaning the right of white men of any kind to beat blacks into submission, make them surrender their wealth and the use of their women and submit to dictation without murmur, for the sake of being swept off the fairest portions of the earth or held there in perpetual serfdom or guardianship. Ignoring the fact that the era of physical struggle for survival has passed away among human beings, and that there is plenty of room accessible on earth for all, this theory makes the possession of Krupp guns the main criterion of mental stamina and moral fitness.

Even armed with this morality of the club, and every advantage of modern culture, the white races have been unable to possess the earth. Many signs of degeneracy have appeared among them: their birth-rate is falling, their average ability is not increasing, their physical stamina is impaired, and their social condition is not reassuring. Lacking the physical ability to take possession of the world, they are to-day fencing in America, Australia, and South Africa and declaring that no dark race shall occupy or develop the land which they themselves are unable to use. And all this on the plea that their stock is threatened with deterioration from without, when in reality its most dangerous threat is deterioration from within.

We are, in fact, to-day repeating in our intercourse between races all the former evils of class distinction within the nation: personal hatred and abuse, mutual injustice, unequal taxation and rigid caste. Individual nations outgrew these fatal things by breaking down the horizontal barriers between classes. We are bringing them back by seeking to erect vertical barriers between races. Men were told that abolition of compulsory class distinction meant leveling down, degradation, disappearance of culture and genius and the triumph of the mob. As a matter of fact, it has been the salvation of European civilization. Some deterioration and leveling there was but it was more than balanced by the discovery of new reservoirs of ability and strength. So to-day we are told that free racial contact — or "social equality" as Southern *patois* has it — means contamination of blood and lowering of ability and culture. It need mean nothing of the sort. Abolition of class distinction did not mean universal intermarriage of stocks, but rather the survival of the fittest by peaceful, personal and social selection — a selection all the more effective because free democracy and equality of opportunity allow the best to rise to their rightful place. The same is true in racial contact. Vertical race distinctions are even more emphatic hindrances to human evolution than horizontal class distinctions, and their tearing away involves fewer chances of degradation and greater opportunities of human betterment than in case of class lines. On the other hand, persistence in racial distinction spells disaster sooner or later. The earth is growing smaller and more accessible. Race contact will become in the future increasingly inevitable not only in America, Asia, and Africa but even in Europe. The color line will mean not simply a return to the absurdities of class as exhibited in the sixteenth and seventeenth centuries, but even to the caste of ancient days. This, however, the Japanese, the Chinese, the East Indians and the Negroes are going to resent in just such proportion as they gain the power; and they are gaining the power, and they cannot be kept from gaining more power. The price of repression will then be hypocrisy and slavery and blood.

This is the situation to-day. Has John Brown no message — no legacy, then, to the twentieth century? He has and it is this great word: the cost of liberty is less than the price of repression. The price of repressing the world's darker races is shown in a moral retrogression and an economic waste unparalelled since the age of the African slave-trade. What would be the cost of liberty? what would be the cost of giving the great stocks of mankind every reasonable help and incentive to self-development — opening the avenues of opportunity freely, spreading knowledge, suppressing war and cheating, and treating men and women as equals the world over whenever and wherever they attain equality? It would cost something. It would cost something in pride and prejudice, for eventually many a white man would be blacking black men's boots; but this cost we may ignore — its greatest cost would be the new problems of racial intercourse and intermarriage which would come to the front. Freedom and equal opportunity in this respect would inevitably bring some intermarriage of whites and yellows and browns and blacks. This might be a good thing and it might not be. We do not know. Our belief on the matter may be strong and even frantic, but it has no adequate scientific foundation. If such marriages are proven inadvisable, how could they be stopped? Easily. We associate with cats and cows, but we do not fear intermarriage with them, even though they be given all freedom of development. So, too, intelligent human beings can be trained to breed intelligently without the degradation of such of their fellows as they may not wish to breed with. In the Southern United States, on the contrary, it is assumed that unwise marriages can be stopped only by the degradation of the blacks — the classing of all darker women with prostitutes, the loading of a whole race with every badge of public isolation, degradation and contempt, and by burning offenders at the stake. Is this civilization? No. The civilized method of preventing ill-advised marriage lies in the training of mankind in the ethics of sex and child-bearing. We cannot ensure the survival of the best blood by the public murder and degradation of unworthy suitors, but we can substitute a civilized human selection of husbands and wives which shall ensure the survival of the fittest. Not the methods of the jungle, not even the careless choices of the drawing-room, but the thoughtful selection of the schools and laboratory is the ideal of future marriage. This will cost something in ingenuity, self-control and toleration, but it will cost less than forcible repression.

Not only is the cost of repression to-day large — it is a continually increasing cost: the procuring of coolie labor, the ruling of India, the exploitation of Africa, the problem of the unemployed, and the curbing of the corporations, are a tremendous drain on modern society with no near end in sight. The cost is not merely in wealth but in social progress and spiritual strength, and it tends ever to explosion, murder, and war. All these things but increase the difficulty of beginning a régime of freedom in human growth and development — they raise the cost of liberty. Not only that but the very explosions, like the Russo-Japanese War, which bring partial freedom, tend in the complacent current philosophy to prove the wisdom of repression. "Blood will tell," men say. "The fit will survive; stop up the tea-kettle and eventually the steam will burst the iron," and therefore only the steam that bursts is worth the generating; only organized murder proves the fitness of a people for liberty. This is a fearful and dangerous doctrine. It encourages wrong leadership and perverted ideals at the very time when loftiest and most unselfish striving is called for — as witness Japan after her emancipation, or America after the Civil War. Conversely, it leads the shallow and unthinking to brand as demagogue and radical every group leader who in the day of slavery and struggle cries out for freedom.

For such reasons it is that the memory of John Brown stands to-day as a mighty warning to his country. He saw, he felt in his soul the wrong and danger of that most daring and insolent system of human repression known as American slavery. He knew that in 1700 it would have cost something to overthrow slavery and establish liberty; and that by reason of cowardice and blindness the cost in 1800 was vastly larger but still not unpayable. He felt that by 1900 no human hand could pluck the vampire from the body of the land without doing the nation to death. He said, in 1859, "Now is the accepted time." Now is the day to strike for a free nation. It will cost something — even blood and suffering, but it will not cost as much as waiting. And he was right. Repression bred repression — serfdom bred slavery until in 1861 the South was farther from freedom than in 1800.

The edict of 1863 was the first step in emancipation and its cost in blood and treasure was staggering. But that was not all — it was only a first step. There were other bills to pay of material reconstruction, social regeneration, mental training and moral uplift. These the nation started to meet in the Fifteenth Amendment, the Freedman's Bureau, the crusade of school-teachers and the Civil Rights Bill. But the effort was great and the determination of the South to pay no single cent or deed for past error save by force, led in the revolution of 1876 to the triumph of reaction. Reaction meant and means a policy of state, society and individual, whereby no American of Negro blood shall ever come into the full freedom of modern culture. In the carrying out of this program by certain groups and sections, no pains have been spared — no expenditure of money, ingenuity, physical or moral strength. The building of barriers around these black men has been pushed with an energy so desperate and unflagging that it has seriously checked the great outpouring of benevolence and sympathy that greeted the freedman in 1863. It has come so swathed and gowned in graciousness as to disarm philanthropy and chill enthusiasm. It has used double-tongued argument with deadly effect. Has the Negro advanced? Beware his further strides. Has the Negro retrograded? It is his fate, why seek to help him? Thus has the spirit of repression gained attention, complacent acquiescence, and even coöperation. To be sure, there still stand staunch souls who cannot yet believe the doctrine of human repression, and who pour out their wealth for Negro training and freedom in the face of the common cry. But the majority of Americans seem to have forgotten the foundation principles of their government and the recklessly destructive effect of the blows meant to bind and tether their fellows. We have come to see a day here in America when one citizen can deprive another of his vote at his discretion; can restrict the education of his neighbors' children as he sees fit; can with impunity load his neighbor with public insult on the king's highway; can deprive him of his property without due process of law; can deny him the right of trial by his peers, or of any trial whatsoever if he can get a large enough group of men to join him; can refuse to protect or safeguard the integrity of the family of some men whom he dislikes; finally, can not only close the door of opportunity in commercial and social lines in a fully competent neighbor's face, but can actually count on the national and state governments to help and make effective this discrimination.

Such a state of affairs is not simply disgraceful; it is deeply and increasingly dangerous. Not only does the whole nation feel already the loosening of joints which these vicious blows on human liberty have caused — lynching, lawlessness, lying and stealing, bribery and divorce — but it can look for darker deeds to come.

And this not merely because of the positive harm of this upbuilding of barriers, but above all because within these bursting barriers are men — human forces which no human hand can hold. It is human force and aspiration and endeavor which are moving there amid the creaking of timbers and writhing of souls. It is human force that has already done in a generation the work of many centuries. It has saved over a half-billion dollars in property, bought and paid for landed estate half the size of all England, and put homes thereon as good and as pure as the homes of any corresponding economic class the world around; it has crowded eager children through a wretched and half-furnished school system until from an illiteracy of seventy per cent., two-thirds of the living adults can read and write. These proscribed millions have 50,000 professional men, 200,000 men in trade and transportation, 275,000 artisans and mechanics, 1,250,000 servants and 2,000,000 farmers working with the nation to earn its daily bread. These farmers raise yearly on their own and hired farms over 4,000,000 bales of cotton, 25,000,000 pounds of rice, 10,000,000 bushels of potatoes, 90,000,000 pounds of tobacco and 100,000,000 bushels of corn, besides that for which they labor on the farms of others. They have given America music, inspired art and literature, made its bread, dug its ditches, fought its battles, and suffered in its misfortunes. The great mass of these men is becoming daily more thoroughly organized, more deeply self-critical, more conscious of its power. Threatened though it has been naturally, as a proletariat, with degeneration and disease, it is to-day reducing its death-rate and beginning organized rescue of its delinquents and defectives. The mass can still to-day be called ignorant, poor and but moderately efficient, but it is daily growing better trained, richer and more intelligent. And as it grows it is sensing more and more the vantage-ground which it holds as a defender of the right of the freedom of human development for black men in the midst of a centre of modern culture. It sees its brothers in yellow, black and brown held physically at arms' length from civilization lest they become civilized and less liable to conquest and exploitation. It sees the world-wide effort to build an aristocracy of races and nations on a foundation of darker half-enslaved and tributary peoples. It knows that the last great battle of the West is to vindicate the right of any man of any nation, race, or color to share in the world's goods and thoughts and efforts to the extent of his effort and ability.

Thus to-day the Negro American faces his destiny and doggedly strives to realize it. He has his tempters and temptations. There are ever those about him whispering: "You are nobody; why strive to be somebody? The odds are overwhelming against you — wealth, tradition, learning and guns. Be reasonable. Accept the dole of charity and the cant of missionaries and sink contentedly to your place as humble servants and helpers of the white world." If this has not been effective, threats have been used: "If you continue to complain, we will withdraw all aid, boycott your labor, cease to help support your schools and let you die and disappear from the land in ignorance, crime and disease." Still the black man has pushed on, has continued to protest, has refused to die out and disappear, and to-day stands as physically the most virile element in America, intellectually among the most promising, and morally the most tremendous and insistent of the social problems of the New World. Not even the silence of his friends, or of those who ought to be the friends of struggling humanity, has silenced him. Not even the wealth of modern Golconda has induced him to believe that life without liberty is worth living.

On the other side heart-searching is in order. It is not well with this land of ours: poverty is certainly not growing less, wealth is being wantonly wasted, business honesty is far too rare, family integrity is threatened, bribery is poisoning our public life, theft is honeycombing our private business, and voting is largely unintelligent. Not that these evils are unopposed. There are brave men and women striving for social betterment, for the curbing of the vicious power of wealth, for the uplift of women and the downfall of thieves. But their battle is hard, and how much harder because of the race problem — because of the calloused conscience of caste, the peonage of black labor hands, the insulting of black women, and the stealing of black votes? How far are business dishonesty and civic degradation in America the direct result of racial prejudice?

Well do I know that many persons defend their treatment of undeveloped peoples on the highest grounds. They say, as Jefferson Davis intimated, that liberty is for the full-grown; not for children. It was during Senator Mason's inquisition after the hanging of John Brown, whereby the Southern leader hoped to entrap the Abolitionists. Joshua R. Giddings, keen, impetuous and fiery, was on the rack. Senator Davis, pale, sallow and imperturbable, with all the aristocratic poise and dignity built on the unpaid toil of two centuries of slaves, said:

"Did you, in inculcating, by popular lectures, the doctrine of a law higher than that of the social compact, make your application exclusively to Negro slaves, or did you also include minors, convicts, and lunatics, who might be restrained of their liberty by the laws of the land?"

Mr. Giddings smiled. "Permit me," he said, ". . . with all due deference, to suggest, so that I may understand you, do you intend to inquire whether those lectures would indicate whether your slaves of the slave states had a right at all times to their liberty?"

"I will put the question in that form if you like it," answered Davis, and then Giddings flashed:

"My lectures, in all instances, would indicate the right of every human soul in the enjoyment of reason, while he is charged with no crime or offense, to maintain his life, his liberty, the pursuit of his own happiness; that this has reference to the enslaved of all the states as much as it had reference to our own people while enslaved by the Algerines in Africa."

But Mr. Davis suavely pressed his point: "Then the next question is, whether the same right was asserted for minors and apprentices, being men in good reason, yet restrained of their liberty by the laws of the land."

Giddings replied: "I will answer at once that the proposition or comparison is conflicting with the dictates of truth. The minor is, from the law of nature, under the restraints of parental affection for the purposes of nurture, of education, of preparing him to secure and maintain the very rights to which I refer."*

This debate is not yet closed. It was not closed by the Civil War. Men still maintain that East Indians and Africans and others ought to be under the restraint and benevolent tutelage of stronger and wiser nations for their own benefit. Well and good. Is the tutelage really benevolent? Then it is training in liberty. Is it training in slavery? Then it is not benevolent. Liberty trains for liberty. Responsibility is the first step in responsibility.

Even the restraints imposed in the training of men and children are restraints that will in the end make greater freedom possible. Is the benevolent expansion of to-day of such a character? Is England trying to see how soon and how effectively the Indians can be trained for self-government or is she willing to exploit them just so long as they can be cajoled or quieted into submission? Is Germany trying to train her Africans to modern citizenship or to modern "work without complaint?" Is the South trying to make the Negroes responsible, self-reliant freemen of a republic, or the dumb driven cattle of a great industrial machine?

No sooner is the question put this way than the defenders of modern caste retire behind a more defensible breastwork. They say: "Yes, we exploit nations for our own advantage purposely — even at times brutally. But only in that way can the high efficiency of the modern industrial process be maintained, and in the long run it benefits the oppressed even more than the oppressor." This doctrine is as widespread as it is false and mischievous. It is true that the bribe of greed will artificially hasten economic development, but

---

* Report: Reports of Senate Committees, 36th Congress, 1st Session, No. 278; Testimony of Joshua R. Giddings, pp. 147–156.

it does so at fearful cost, as America itself can testify. We have here a wonderful industrial machine, but a machine quickly rather than carefully built, formed of forcing rather than of growth, involving sinful and unnecessary expense. Better smaller production and more equitable distribution; better fewer miles of railway and more honor, truth, and liberty; better fewer millionaires and more contentment. So it is the world over, where force and fraud and graft have extorted rich reward from writhing millions. Moreover, it is historically unprovable that the advance of undeveloped peoples has been helped by wholesale exploitation at the hands of their richer, stronger, and more unscrupulous neighbors. This idea is a legend of the long exploded doctrine of inevitable economic harmonies in all business life. True it is that adversity and difficulties make for character, but the real and inevitable difficulties of life are numerous enough for genuine development without the aid of artificial hindrances. The inherent and natural difficulties of raising a people from ignorant unmoral slavishness to self-reliant modern manhood are great enough for purposes of character-building without the aid of murder, theft, caste, and degradation. Not because of but in spite of these latter hindrances has the Negro-American pressed forward.

This, then, is the truth: the cost of liberty is less than the price of repression, even though that cost be blood. Freedom of development and equality of opportunity is the demand of Darwinism and this calls for the abolition of hard and fast lines between races, just as it called for the breaking down of barriers between classes. Only in this way can the best in humanity be discovered and conserved, and only thus can mankind live in peace and progress. The present attempt to force all whites above all darker peoples is a sure method of human degeneration. The cost of liberty is thus a decreasing cost, while the cost of repression ever tends to increase to the danger point of war and revolution. Revolution is not a test of capacity; it is always a loss and a lowering of ideals.

But if it is a true revolution it repays all losses and results in the uplift of the human race. One could wish that John Brown could see today the results of the great revolution in Russia; that he could see the new world of Socialism and Communism expanding until it already comprises the majority of mankind; until it has conquered the problem of poverty, made vast inroads on the problem of ignorance and even begun to put to flight the problem of avoidable disease. It has abolished unemployment and is approaching the great day when all men will do for the world what they are best suited to do and will receive in return from the world not all that they want but everything that each man needs.

The greatest source of human rejoicing today is the phenomenal rise of the people of Russia. From an ignorant, despised, suppressed peasantry they have in less than a century become in many respects the leading nation of the world. They have abolished poverty and from the masses have risen an extraordinary number of gifted men. Their system of education surpasses that of any other part of the world and their scientific contribution during the Twentieth Century is among the wonders of mankind.

To this must be added the resurrection of China. This largest nation in the world is rushing forward with unexampled speed and efficiency. Despite the effort of the United States to dismember it, lie about it, and keep it out of the United Nations, it is becoming one of the greatest modern nations.

These are the dates whose events conditioned John Brown and his acts. Beginning with the Battle of Plassy in 1757 the loot of India began to pour into England. In 1769 the steam engine was invented and in 1793, the cotton gin. Between 1784 and 1804 the Sugar Empire in the West Indies began to disintegrate and former slaves and free Negroes controlled Haiti. For this reason and because of the revolt of the British conscience against the cruelties of the trade, in 1808 the British made the African slave trade illegal and other *nations including the United States slowly followed. In 1820 the Cotton Kingdom in the United States began to rise, reaching its zenith in 1860. The cotton crop increased from a half million bales in 1822 to five million bales in 1860. All this meant a world change in the production and distribution of goods. Capital increased immensely in the hands of private owners and their subsequent control of labor in industry became almost complete.*

The French Revolution had demanded freedom for the individual — the liberty to do as he pleased for what he considered his own good and the consequent good of mankind. But in the Nineteenth Century this freedom rapidly became license for private owners of capital to control industry and income and thus rule mankind. In the first half of the Nineteenth Century, in 1848, Karl Marx and Frederick Engels called attention to this state of affairs in their Communist Manifesto *which later Marx further developed in his great work on capital.*

In the United States where John Brown lived the demand for "freedom" was still paramount and could be widely realized because land was free and there was an abundance of labor. John Brown never read the Communist Manifesto *and knew little of the rise of Socialism. But he did realize that a suppressed and exploited part of the laboring class in America — the Negroes — had been deprived by capitalists and land monopolists of the freedom to earn a living and to direct their lives which was vital in John Brown's mind to a human being. He espoused therefore the freedom of the slave knowing well that freedom alone was not the settlement of the Negro problem; that this must be followed by education, the right to vote, and treatment as human beings. But all this he assumed was inherent in the American system and would follow the freedom of the slaves. Then in the year that he was crucified came Darwin's* Origin of Species *and gradually a changed attitude of science toward human beings. At the same time many assumed that the doctrine of race superiority was a logical deduction from the* doctrine of evolution, but Karl Marx would easily prove the contrary. The Industrial Revolution had taken place in the Nineteenth Century which increased the amount of capital in private hands and this coupled with an extraordinary technical advance and new widely desired materials like sugar and cotton made great increase of wealth under private control possible. It was this itch for larger private capital in Britain and France together with the sugar monopoly in the West Indies and the Cotton Kingdom in the United States that made West Europe and North America seek scientific justification for despising the mass of mankind and refusing to admit them to the new democracy. Those who desired large incomes through ownership of capital used Darwin's doctrine to excuse the growing reduction of the majority of the world's laborers to the cheap use of their toil and land for the increasing profit of capitalism. The result was colonial imperialism built on the new technique of Western industry, fed by free land and raw materials in Asia and Africa and especially capped by the cheapest of labor.

The state impelled by the capitalists seized control of colonies using the labor in Asia and Africa and the islands of the seas instead of transporting it to America. By the use of this capital in far-off colonies the absentee landlord was replaced by the absentee investor so that the owners of capital knew less and less how their capital was used and were rewarded for this ignorance by increase of profit. This is characteristic of the capitalist system in this day. Owners do not know and gradually begin not to care how their capital is used so long as their income is assured and increases. The Western world consciously or unconsciously depends for its civilization, comfort and luxury on the low wage of colonial labor and the seizure of colonial land and materials. As a result of this we have war to force new divisions in the ownership of colonies and war between colonies and imperial powers.

All this John Brown did not know and could not foresee, but nevertheless he left a clear legacy: First, the right of the *enslaved to repel oppression. Then beyond this a new attitude toward human beings and belief in the abilities and character of the great mass of mankind. Even then as Lenin has shown must come a plan of life and work which will ensure the best interests of the masses and a discipline and dictation which shall through education and force compel the workers to follow and activate these plans. Out of this will arise a new interpretation of the word* freedom. *There must be left a wide individualism and yet no individual must be allowed to infringe upon another's freedom. In other words, the future world will not be free in the sense that anyone can do what he pleases, but freedom in the larger sense of having his acts work for the best interests of the peoples of the world.*

All this John Brown did not know and yet his life's work was in consonance with it. He believed in the abilities and worth of the souls of black folk. He believed in the gifts that they would be able to furnish America and he regarded them as equals to all Americans of any color. He believed that men should labor for what they earned and should not get their income by chance or inheritance. He believed in the freedom of the land and its fruits to be distributed in accord with the labor which was put upon it. Thus he was a pioneer in the fight for human equality and in the uplift of the masses of men.

There can be no doubt that the progress of the emancipated slave in the United States since 1863 has been phenomenal. He has touched every phase of American development. He has furnished subjects for American writers and thinkers and himself contributed to American art, music, and literature. He has given the nation invaluable labor and service, has taken notable part in the advance of science and discovery and without his own work, American industry could never have reached the heights which it has. The American Department of State in its desperate effort to fight Socialism and Communism has sought to emphasize Negro progress and has paid out considerable sums of money to bribe Negroes and induce them to travel and praise America in various parts of the world. Despite this, however, it is perfectly clear that while Negro progress has been great, it has not been nearly as rapid as it might have been had the Negro received decent treatment. He has been deliberately paid a lower wage than whites doing the same work or than immigrants from abroad. He has been denied preferment and promotion in industry; kept out of scientific laboratories; discriminated against in scholarships and often actually beaten to submission to superior force and impudent assumption. If American Negroes had been given the chance that the Russian peasant has had since 1917 his contribution to the uplift of the world might easily have been startling. The repression and discrimination which he has met has held back the progress of the United States and the world and is a thing of which this country must always be ashamed.

In murder and unjust punishment America has made a disgraceful record against the Negro race. Between 1882 and 1900, the whites lynched without trial four thousand Negroes besides killing more than ten thousand by mobs. When public opinion stopped lynching, injustice in the courts succeeded. A Negro had only to be arrested, to be found guilty and convicted in most Southern courts and many Northern. Three times as many Negroes in proportion to population go to prison as whites. Among children twice as many Negroes are arrested as delinquent. Half the prisoners serving life sentences and half those executed in the nation are Negroes who form but a tenth of our population. There is certainly crime among Negroes but it does not exceed that of the whites in anything like this proportion. The chief crime of Negro prisoners is the color of their skin. Not all America has approved or encouraged this injustice. Many have helped and defended the Negro, but the majority have permitted injustice without protest.

John Brown taught us that the cheapest price to pay for liberty is its cost to-day. The building of barriers against the advance of Negro-Americans hinders but in the end cannot altogether stop their progress. The excuse of benevolent tutelage cannot be urged, for that tutelage is not benevolent that does not prepare for free responsible manhood. Nor can the efficiency of greed as an economic developer be proven — it may hasten development but it does so at the expense of solidity of structure, smoothness of motion, and real efficiency. Nor does selfish exploitation help the undeveloped; rather it hinders and weakens them.

It is now a *full century* since this white-haired old man lay weltering in the blood which he spilled for broken and despised humanity. Let the nation which he loved and the South to which he spoke, reverently listen again to-day to those words, as prophetic now as then:

"You had better — all you people of the South — prepare yourselves for a settlement of this question. It must come up for settlement sooner than you are prepared for it, and the sooner you commence that preparation, the better for you. You may dispose of me very easily — I am nearly disposed of now; but this question is still to be settled — this Negro question, I mean. The end of that is not yet."

Bibliography

For the general reader the following works are indispensable:

Sanborn, Franklin Benjamin. The Life and Letters of John Brown, Liberator of Kansas, and Martyr of Virginia. 1885. (The most complete collection of John Brown letters.)

Hinton, Richard Josiah. John Brown and His Men, with some account of the roads they traveled to reach Harper's Ferry. 1894. (Valuable for its treatment of Kansas and its lives of Brown's companions.)

Redpath, James. Public Life of Captain John Brown, with autobiography of his childhood and youth. (The best contemporary account.)

Connelley, William Elsey. John Brown. 1900. (Valuable for Kansas life of Brown.)

To the above may be added the shorter estimate by H. E. von Holst, 1899, and some may like Chamberlain's pert essay (Beacon Biographies, 1889).

Students must add to these the following books and articles which contain many of the original sources of our knowledge:

Anderson, Osborne P. A Voice from Harper's Ferry. A narrative of events at Harper's Ferry; with incidents prior and subsequent to its capture by John Brown and his men. 1861. (The best account of the raid by a participant.)

Manuscript Diary of John Brown in the Boston Public Library. (2 volumes) 1838-1844, 1855-1859.

Garrison, Wendell Phillips. The Preludes of Harper's Ferry. In the *Andover Review*, December, 1890, and January, 1891.

Josephus, Jr. (Joseph Barry). The Brown Raid. In his annals of Harper's Ferry, 1872. (Excellent local account.)

United States Congressional Reports. Report of the select committee of the Senate appointed to inquire into John Brown's invasion and the seizure of the public property at Harper's Ferry. Thirty-sixth Congress, first session. Senate Reports of Committees.

Transactions of the Kansas State Historical Society, together with addresses, etc., Volumes I–IX. (Contains many personal narratives.)

Calendar of Virginia State papers, Volume XI, pp. 269-349. (A large
amount of the Brown data copied from the papers found in his
carpetbag at Harper's Ferry.)

Virginia Senate Journal and Documents for the session of 1859-60:
Report of the joint committee of the Senate and House of
Delegates, appointed to consider the Harper's Ferry affair by
Alexander H. Stuart, the chairman of the committee.

Virginia, Journal of House of Delegates of Virginia, 1859-60, containing messages of the governor, the trial and publication of
John Brown's papers.

Featherstonhaugh, Thomas. Bibliography of John Brown, Part I.
Publications of the Southern History Association, Volume I,
pp. 196-202.

‒ John Brown's Men; the lives of those killed at Harper's Ferry, with
a supplementary bibliography of John Brown. In Southern
History Association publications. Volume 3, pp. 281-306. (The
best bibliography.)

Douglass, Frederick. John Brown, an address at the fourteenth anniversary of Storer College, 1881.

‒ Life and Times of. 1892.

Redpath, James. Echoes of Harper's Ferry. 1860.

Hunter, Andrew. John Brown's Raid. In Southern History Association publications. Volume I, pp. 165-195. 1897. (The story of
the prosecuting attorney.)

Higginson, Thomas Wentworth. A Visit to John Brown's-Household
in 1859. (In "Contemporaries," 1899.)

Wright, Harry A. John Brown in Springfield. New England Magazine, pp. 272-281.

Webb, Richard D., Editor. The Life and Letters of Captain John
Brown, who was executed at Charlestown, Va., December 2,
1859, for an armed attack upon American slavery; with notices
of some of his confederates. 1861.

Boteler, Alexander L. Recollections of the John Brown Raid. Century.
July, 1883. Comment by F. B. Sanborn.

Daingerfield, John E. P. John Brown at Harper's Ferry. Century.
June, 1885, pp. 265-267. (The story of an engine-house prisoner.)

Voorhees, Daniel W. Argument delivered at Charlestown, Va.,
November 8, 1859, upon the trial of John E. Cook. Richmond,
Va., 1861.

Hamilton, James Cleland. John Brown in Canada. Illustrated. Republished from *Canadian Magazine*, December, 1894.

The purely controversial literature raging around John Brown is endless. Those interested might read:

Utter, David N. John Brown of Osawatomie. *North American Review*, November, 1883.

Nicolay, John G. and Hay, John. Abraham Lincoln, a history. 1890. (Volume 2 contains history of John Brown and Harper's Ferry Raid.)

Robinson, Charles. The Kansas Conflict. 1892.

Brown, George Washington, M. D. False claims of Kansas historians truthfully corrected. Principally a refutation of the claim that the rescue of Kansas from slavery was due to John Brown. Rockford, Ill. The author. 1902.

— Reminiscences of Old John Brown. Thrilling instances of border life in Kansas. With appendix by Eli Thayer. Rockford, Ill. 1880. Printed by Eli Smith.

Wright, Marcus Joseph. Trial of John Brown. Its impartiality and decorum vindicated. Southern History Society Papers, Vol. XVI, pp. 357–363.

Spring, L. W. Kansas. 1885.

Williams, G. W. History of Negro Race in America. 1883. Two volumes. (For John Brown, see volume 2, pp. 213–227.)

Thayer, Eli. The Kansas Crusade. 1889.

Hugo, Victor. John Brown. 1861.

Wise, Barton H. The Life of Henry S. Wise. 1899.

Index